# BEGINNING UN

## Thinking, resea
## writing for success

# ONE WEEK LOAN

ALLEN & UNWIN

First published in 1999 by
Allen & Unwin
9 Atchison Street, St Leonards NSW 1590
Australia
Phone: (61 2) 8425 0100
Fax:    (61 2) 9906 2218
E-mail: frontdesk@allen-unwin.com.au
Web:    http://www.allen-unwin.com.au

National Library of Australia
Cataloguing-in-Publication entry:

Wallace, Andrew, 1945– .
    Beginning university: thinking, researching and writing for success.

    Bibliography.
    Includes index.
    ISBN 1 86448 889 1.

    1. Study skills—Australian. 2. Universities and colleges—Australia.
    I. Schirato, Anthony. II. Bright, Philippa. III. Title.

371.30281

Illustrations by David Egan
Set in 11/13 pt Garamond by DOCUPRO, Sydney
Printed by South Wind Productions, Singapore

10 9 8 7 6 5 4 3 2

# Contents

# Introduction: how this book can help you

This book is intended to make university study more enjoyable, successful and beneficial.

When you enrol in a university course, you are very much 'on your own'. Even when staff realise that you may need help with some of the basics, they can often find no time in a crowded semester to provide it. We offer you a lot of practical advice. However, this is not a simple 'how to' guide to study skills. Our aim is to help you in more fundamental ways. We explain what makes universities the way they are and why you may need to rethink some of your assumptions about learning. We draw attention to the reasons why students respond to some situations in unproductive ways. Ultimately, the only person who can ensure your success is you yourself. What will make all the difference is the extent to which you reflect thoughtfully on what you do.

The book makes a particular point of explaining why certain kinds of tasks and abilities are expected of you. When students realise the relevance of their learning to life after uni, they are more purposeful and enthusiastic, less passive and fatalistic.

If students tend not to make connections between the different subjects they study, it is often because universities do not do as much as they could to help students appreciate the fundamental intellectual principles and practices underlying all academic work. We introduce you to reasoned argument and exposition (in Part II), as these are basic to all your reading, class discussions and assignments. You will find many connections between the topics of the different chapters.

Regard this book as a long conversation with some university teachers who have seen many first-year students—year after year—make the same

kinds of mistakes, or display the same misguided attitudes. It's the most useful general advice we can think of giving you. However, you have to make active use of it. Work your way patiently through the examples; do the activities; and when engaged on a particular assignment task, look again at relevant chapters. Try out some of the strategies we suggest. This will sometimes require a deliberate commitment on your part to learning how to learn, as other demands on your time will seem more urgent. Yet a small investment of time can help to make you a much more effective student. Learning to allocate time for what is important—not just what is urgent—is one of the most important skills that you can acquire at university, even though it is not on the curriculum.

# part 1

# BACKGROUND

## chapter 1

# Communication in context

Imagine that you are a 25-year-old just arrived in a foreign country, where you will live and work for the next few years. You have been left in a small, run-down hotel where nothing works, you don't know anybody, you cannot work out the money, it's raining, and you know next to nothing about where you are going to be spending the next three years of your life. You're not used to the weather, the insects, noises, smells, shops, food. Nothing is quite what you expected. Things will get better—eventually—but meantime you will have to learn to adjust if you are to make a success of your time here.

When students first enter a university, it doesn't really matter whether they are 17-year-olds fresh out of school or 40-year-olds with plenty of work experience—they are moving into a field of activity they do not know much about. Universities are different from schools and most workplaces: they have their own rules, regulations, cultures, activities, expectations and values.

First-year university students know that going to university is a challenging experience, but their ideas about the challenges they will face are not always accurate. They are likely to worry too much about some kinds of potential problems, and not enough about others. This book aims to help. (Naturally, we cannot help with all the problems a first-year student might experience. We don't, for instance, offer any advice about which course or subjects to enrol in, how to find accommodation or how to live on a limited budget.)

## COMMUNICATION IS THE KEY

This text deals with university study primarily in terms of *communication*. Most of what you do as a student involves communication. You will spend a lot of time reading and listening to lectures. In assignments you will have to communicate by writing or (in the case of oral presentations) speaking. Discussion with staff and other students will probably be an important part of your learning. You cannot succeed at university without effective communication skills.

By communication skills we do not mean merely being clear and precise when talking to people, dressing well, smiling, or writing neatly. It involves being able to find and understand information, to deal with ideas, make decisions, learn and adapt in unfamiliar situations, and organise work. A university graduate should be a good communicator—but not in the same way that a salesperson or television newsreader is a good communicator. A university graduate is someone who can participate effectively in an exchange of ideas, and good communication in this sense means being able to think effectively. Skill in critical thinking (or reasoning) and the procedures of exposition (explaining and analysing things) are central to academic communication of all kinds.

You will have to develop high-level communication skills to succeed at university. These are some of the most important assets you will take with you into the workforce. The skills you pick up—in critical thinking, researching, analysing, putting together an argument, speaking to a group, planning, time management, writing a report, editing, using communication technology—are precisely what employers want of graduates.

Graduates are worth employing not just because they *possess* certain facts but because they know how to deal with information and people. They have learned a specialised vocabulary (such as that used by accountants or social scientists), and learned how to use other tools and procedures. They are thus able to make sense of facts, discover new facts, look at facts in new ways. The real benefit of university education often has more to do with mastering the *process* of dealing in knowledge than with the specific *content* of what is taught. It is important to be aware that the communication skills you use and develop at university have a relevance beyond your years of formal study. These skills are transferable to your future job. Your university studies are much more relevant and beneficial than you may realise. Although we have been using the word 'skills', the term *literacies* is another way of expressing what we mean.

## THE IMPORTANCE OF CULTURAL CONTEXT

There is another reason why it is useful to approach university education in terms of communication. Modern communication theory provides insight into the way human beings behave and interact because it takes account of the cultural contexts that influence what people think and do. While psychology contributes a lot to our understanding of learning—by helping us understand how memory works, for example—psychology tends to concentrate on the human individual in isolation. The fact that life is very different in Estonia, Japan, Bolivia and Australia, and that life in the 20th century is radically different, in most countries, from that in the 19th, is due to the different cultures that exist in each place and time—not to the attributes of individuals. Knowing about a person's personality or intelligence doesn't tell us much about how they interact with the culture in which they find themselves.

To return to our example of arriving in a foreign country, many of your problems would involve communication. You might not know the local language, for instance. But language itself would be only one difficulty. All kinds of local attitudes, values, customs and conventions would be equally unfamiliar. Is it impolite to sit on a table? Will people be offended by a lot of eye contact or a lack of eye contact? Is bargaining normal when you buy something? As well as conventions relating to interpersonal communication, you would need to know something about the laws of the country—including which laws no-one took seriously ('You're not allowed to park under trees, so everybody does it') and which were taken very seriously ('Illegal drug possession means 20 years in jail'). You would need to know what sources of information there were in the country, and which ones were reliable. To communicate effectively in this foreign country, you would need to learn something about its culture.

In the first place, though, you need to realise that cultural awareness is what matters. If you are completely insensitive to the differences in the new country's culture you will not get very far. It is no good blaming the locals for laziness, stupidity or ignorance when they behave in ways that are perfectly normal and appropriate in their culture. Nor would it be useful to blame yourself: it is not that you lack certain inner qualities; what you lack is knowledge of the 'rules of the game' that apply in this part of the world. It probably will not matter that you don't already know a lot about the new country when you arrive, as long as you are prepared to begin 'reading it'—that is, picking up its rules and conventions, learning how it works, and adapting your own actions accordingly.

Communication is not the same everywhere and in all circumstances. Communication is affected by cultural context—in fact, it is inseparable from its context. To be an effective communicator, you have to be able to analyse the context in which you are operating.

## UNIVERSITIES AS A CULTURAL CONTEXT

Of course there are cultural differences *within* countries as well as between them. We can speak of any society as having many different **cultural fields**. Students coming into the university field (and leaving the fields of business, government or secondary education) have to become familiar with different rules, values, expectations and conventions. Moving to a new cultural field is in many ways like moving to another country. You encounter new:

- institutions (in a university, this would include the library, student administration, the international office, the student union);
- rules (you have to enrol by a certain date; if you fail several subjects you might be excluded; fines are imposed for overdue library books);
- titles (professor, doctor, vice-chancellor, student counsellor);
- conventions (you are supposed to talk in tutorials but remain quiet and pay attention in lectures; there are certain ways to go about getting an extension for your assessment);
- genres (lectures, tutorials, practical classes, workshops, reports, essays, oral presentations);
- discourses (sociology does not use the same 'language' as journalism, or electronics the same language as biology); and
- activities (going to classes, student parties).

While you will be able to rely on *some* of your present skills and habits, you will have to pick up many new perspectives and adapt to new practices. Some of the new requirements will be made clear, but there are unspoken assumptions and conventions you will have to pick up on your own.

In the list above we mention discourses and *genres*. **Discourse** refers to the types of language that are used in a field or subfield. Sometimes the use of language in a field is very formal. For instance, in a courtroom, judges and lawyers use legal discourse (made up of words such as plaintiff, defendant, *habeas corpus*) rather than ordinary, everyday language. Other discourses are less formal but still specialised (the sport of cricket has square leg, googly, wrong-un, and if a batter is caught, the fielding team will all scream 'Howzat?' rather than 'Please give him out').

The university has its own discourses, some of which are to be found across the field (terms such as monograph, hypothesis, bibliography, tutor), while others are more specific to disciplines or subject areas (e.g. in psychology, words such as cognition, introversion and regression). Discourses are characteristic ways of using language which tend to be associated with different values, attitudes and social purposes. In chapter 2 we discuss the values associated with academic discourse.

Every field is characterised by certain communication **genres**—kinds or types of communication. Films have a number of genres (the musical, the western, science fiction, horror), which are different from one another in terms of story, audiences and audience expectations, and discourses. Universities have their own genres—the lecture and tutorial being examples of teaching genres. There are also various assessment genres: essay writing, oral presentations, case studies, experiment write-ups, and exams (which have their own subgenres, such as multiple choice, take-home and long essay).

In order to communicate effectively in any field of activity, it is important to be familiar with, and understand the requirements of, discourses and genres. This is particularly the case at university, where so many of the genres are directly or indirectly related to your success. It will take time to master all the discourses and genres involved in your course and to feel comfortable with them. The main thing is to appreciate that you do have to adapt to different requirements. If you are reading or writing in a history subject, you have to use a discourse that is different from the discourse of a tourism or management subject. If you are writing a report, you must conform to the conventions of that genre, not to those of the essay or exam answer.

## CULTURAL LITERACY

Communication theorists use the term **cultural literacy** to describe the ability to operate effectively in a particular cultural field. Being 'literate' originally meant being able to read and write. Now we describe people as literate in a particular cultural context if they have the knowledge, insight, experience and skills that allow them to function well in that context. Strangers in a foreign country learn how and where to obtain information and make sense of it, how to make their needs known, how to achieve what they want. They become literate in that particular context. University students have the job of acquiring 'tertiary literacy'. This includes knowledge of relevant discourses and genres, which in turn depends on understanding the nature of the academic enterprise, knowing how to respond to requirements, and so on. The term 'literacy' is more useful than the narrower term 'communication skill'.

Not only can the general skills in dealing with ideas and communicating that you develop at university be transferred to your job after graduation, but once you understand that any field has its own rules, values, genres and discourses, and that different audiences don't have the same literacies and expectations, you can use this knowledge to guide your activities. For instance, engineering students have to absorb a lot of technical information. They also need to learn that the genres and discourses of the field of engineering are very different from the fields that most of their future clients work in—such as bureaucracies, trade unions, businesses, public utilities and local councils. Engineering courses now usually include subjects which help students appreciate that the logics and values of the field of engineering are different from those of, say, environmental groups. The students develop insight which helps them to communicate with clients, protesters, union officials or business rivals. They realise they have to become familiar with other people's fields, priorities, expectations, discourses and genres, particularly if what has to be communicated is complex and highly technical.

All graduates, not just engineers, need to realise that contexts—and thus the kind of communication appropriate to them—vary a great deal. But you will become a graduate who is alert to context only if you practise analysing your context as an undergraduate. This means you must acquire the habit of thinking about the processes of learning you are involved in, and not just plod unthinkingly from one task to another.

## LEARNING TO ADAPT

It would be useful, if you were moving overseas, to have a guide who showed you around, explained things to you, provided you with information, and could be consulted when you had to make a decision. In a sense this book has been set up to do just that—in your university life. We cannot provide detailed advice on the particular subjects in which you are enrolled: this is a general guide. In any case, we think the best way to help you is to encourage you to learn to help yourself. Even if it were possible to provide specific advice on every problem you might encounter, that would only make you dependent on the book. So while we provide suggestions about strategies you will find useful, we do not offer simple solutions or formulas. Instead, we want to get you into the habit of *thinking*.

An important thing to think about is the *purpose* of what you do. Because they are anxious, or in a mad panic to get an assignment finished, or distracted by thoughts of more exciting things, students often ignore purpose. They forget that a paragraph they are writing should serve some purpose in relation to the set topic of the assignment. They lose sight of the purpose of the assignment itself. If forced to think about it, they would probably say that the assignment (together with other pieces of assessment) serves the purpose of determining whether they deserve to pass the subject. And that is true, but it's not the full story. The assignment also has the purpose of providing an opportunity to research, read, analyse, sift and sort ideas, and improve writing skills. Its ultimate value is that it helps students develop those skills that will be taken into the world beyond university. The more a student recognises that the assignment has that kind of purpose—and is not just an unpleasant task—the less likely it is that he or she will leave things to the last minute (which also means getting a lower mark).

It is understandable that you might put off beginning work. (Writing an assignment—even an enjoyable one—falls into the category of 'work'.) And even if you *are* interested in the topic, the fact remains that the assignment will have to be graded. You might be immobilised by fear of a poor mark. Or perhaps you're unsure about how to interpret the assignment topic but don't feel you can ask the tutor about it. Or you might be overwhelmed with work from other subjects.

The best advice to give someone who has to do some writing might be to think about purpose. Or to start work early and break the overall task up into stages. Students faced with the task of producing an assignment in the next fortnight often do not realise that what they most need is advice about fundamental strategies. Instead, they may think they merely need to be told where to put the commas. This book does not have the purpose of filling in the gaps in your knowledge of English grammar and punctuation. Its purpose is to encourage you to assess the learning tasks and activities you are presented with and respond to them with appropriate strategies—even if these are not strategies you have used before.

> ### Some common misconceptions
>
> There are a number of wrong ideas that people carry with them into their university life. Here are some of the most obvious ones.
>
> - *Those who succeed at university are 'bright', those who fail are 'dumb'.* This isn't the case. Persistence and the ability to adapt and organise yourself are more important than being 'brainy'.
> - *University is hard but pretty much the same as school.* Yes and no. You have a lot of work to do. You also have much more freedom. Some students who have done very well at school do poorly in the less structured environment of university.
> - *At university you finally start learning job skills.* Yes, but compared to trade courses, for example, university courses tend to be theoretical rather than practical—even with vocational courses like dentistry or social work. Some of your subjects will not seem directly and obviously relevant to particular jobs. But university education gives you the kinds of skills and literacies that will help you no matter what area you work in.

## GETTING INFORMATION AND HELP

Like the visitor to a strange new country, your first need is to find things out. It is up to you to inform yourself: the staff do not take responsibility for making sure you know what you need to know, as they probably did at your school. Below are a few examples of sources of information.

The *university handbook* will list services, offerings, and rules and regulations. It may look both boring and complex, but it contains information that is important, such as what subjects you can do and in which semesters, the prerequisites, as well as rules about plagiarism, penalties for misconduct, appeals mechanisms, and so on. The handbook informs you of your rights.

Faculties and departments also put out *general documents* (style guides, referencing requirements, procedures for handing in assignments or seeking extensions). Knowing how and when to ask for an extension could save you from failing a subject, while getting advice from the course adviser should ensure that you enrol in subjects that are right for you.

Individual subjects usually have *outlines* with details such as due dates for assignments, the topics covered each week, and required reading. This is vital to enable you to plan ahead and obtain library books, which are often scarce.

Services and divisions in the university (student health, counselling, equity office, student administration, student union) will put out *brochures or leaflets* outlining what services they provide, and how to contact them. Student unions in particular are valuable, not only in academic matters (what your rights are, how to handle disputes with academic staff, appeals mechanisms) but for financial advice and student loans, entertainment and cultural activities and clubs, and part-time work opportunities.

We have put most of the emphasis, in these examples, on getting advice or information on the academic side of things (supposedly why you are at university—to pass your subjects, and get a degree). However, part of being literate with regard to university life is understanding that the happier, healthier and less stressed you are, the greater the likelihood of succeeding in your studies. If you are not healthy, or have financial worries or relationship problems, you are not going to be devoting sufficient time to your studies, or thinking clearly when you do have time.

## CONCLUSION

In this chapter we have pointed out that communication is a central part of university study. Being skilled in communication means, among other things, being able to deal with and communicate ideas. The abilities and insight you develop as a communicator in academic contexts will make you useful as an employee. Communication is not simple and straightforward; it depends on a range of factors we can describe with the word 'context'. Developing academic literacy requires you to relate the different kinds of communicating that go on at university to their

context—both the general context of the university environment and the more specific context of individual subjects and tasks. In the following chapters we go into more detail about the culture of university, look at the kinds of literacies you will need to pick up, and give you advice on acquiring them. While this is a practical guidebook, to help you adapt to the 'foreign country' that is university, our main aim is to help you to help yourself.

## chapter 2

# All about universities

We suggest in chapter 1 that going to university is like going to live in a foreign country, because universities are very different from schools, businesses and other institutions where you might have worked. We point out that universities are different because they have their own discourses, genres (tutorials, lectures, end-of-term parties), values (critical thinking, scholarship), expectations (you should be able to use a library, write coherently) and institutions (departments, schools and faculties, student union). We also suggest that going to university, like living in a foreign country, involves a long and difficult learning process. If you want to survive (and get out in good shape, having achieved everything you wanted), you must learn how things are done, and adapt your thinking and behaviour.

All this involves becoming literate with regard to universities and the way they operate. We can start by giving you a brief history of universities—where they came from, how they changed, what they are like today, and what they expect from students.

## UNIVERSITIES IN HISTORY

Most texts suggest that the first equivalent of a university was Plato's Academy, which was founded in the 4th century BC in Athens and lasted for about 800 years until it was closed down by the Roman Emperor Justinian. This is a Eurocentric version: there is evidence, for instance, that India and China had 'academies' of higher learning similar to Plato's Academy as early as 1500 BC.

Plato's Academy had little in common with what we understand by a university today: students learned philosophy, mathematics and science, but the main function of the Academy was to train students to be statesmen—in other words, it was supposed to help students to recognise truth, and to become wise rulers.

Universities have been operating continuously in the West for the past eight centuries, much longer than almost any other kind of institution. Although they have changed in many ways, universities value this long history, and some of their customs—such as the mediaeval cap and gown worn at graduation ceremonies—reflect pride in this tradition. Like other old institutions, universities have been conservative and reluctant to change. They take pride in what makes them special and different; and they are concerned to maintain their reputation as centres of excellence in scholarship.

In the Middle Ages universities were established as institutions to train young men for careers in law and the Church. Higher learning was in Latin, the language of ancient Rome. By the time the Roman Empire collapsed in the 5th century AD, it had adopted the Christian religion. Christianity preserved some of its culture, especially intellectual, legal and administrative aspects, in Western Europe. For many centuries Western European society was rural and backward compared with the urban sophistication of the classical world—or with Islamic civilisation.

The countries of Europe in the Middle Ages were different from one another, but wherever you went there was the same religion and learned culture. People were prepared to travel a long way to attend a renowned university: Cambridge in England, Paris in France or Padua in Italy. From their beginnings, universities were made up of people from different national and cultural backgrounds, like universities today. They are more international in outlook and practice than most institutions.

Although the first universities had the primary purpose of preparing young men for their vocations in the 'outside world', universities were not required to concern themselves much with what went on in the realm of politics and business. Until recently, there was little attempt made to take into account the practical needs of the graduate. University teachers studied closely and compared the existing texts in each of the branches of learning (i.e. they practised scholarship) and refined or extended some of the ideas in them. The pursuit of *knowledge for its own sake*, whether or not it had some practical use, was highly valued. The idea of getting knowledge for its own sake remains an important part of the distinctions drawn between universities and other kinds of educational institutions (e.g. technical colleges).

> The mediaeval university was a closed community. Students slept in dormitories, and students and teachers ate together. Many United States universities, and the older British ones, have maintained this tradition by insisting that undergraduates live on campus for at least one year of their course. Mixing with and getting to know other members of the university is seen by many as an important part of the 'university experience'. In Japan it is accepted that an important function of university education is to make friends and acquaintances who will be useful in later life.

While the Church may have kept the universities alive, by the time of the Renaissance, Europe had become more prosperous, confident and outward-looking. Over the next few centuries intellectual inquiry in the West moved away from traditional areas like theology. In the 18th century, new scientific discoveries (e.g. those of Isaac Newton) produced great confidence that all the laws of nature would eventually be discovered and that human progress, based on scientific reason, would continue indefinitely.

## UNIVERSITIES TODAY

In the 20th century universities have become important and successful institutions in society. Perhaps the main reason is that universities— although they were rather sleepy places a couple of centuries ago—have been able to organise the production of knowledge with great success. Because they are seen as contributing to the good of society generally, governments and businesses support universities financially. Knowledge is organised into disciplines, and nowadays most of these have their 'home' in universities. Professions and trades which once had no connection with universities (e.g. nursing, accountancy, surveying) now have university degree courses. This is partly explained by a desire for prestige. More importantly, the knowledge in these fields is now extensive and complex enough to justify their status as university disciplines in which systematic research is conducted and in which students undertake degree courses.

Universities have been able to make their significant contribution to modern society not *despite* what they were but *because* of what they were. Their role as powerhouses of knowledge production is quite recent. Most of the technological advances that we sum up with the term 'the industrial revolution' (the steam engine, mechanised factories, steel bridges, better navigation instruments) did not emerge from universities (in many cases the inventors were not even university graduates). Even 100 years ago no-one could have predicted that universities would become such an important driving force for change and development in the modern world. They did so because some features of the university, such as the idea of knowledge for its own sake and the willingness to keep asking questions rather than being satisfied with old answers, turned out to be useful. Because scholars are interested in knowledge for its own sake—whether or not it leads to anything useful—all kinds of scientific (and other) breakthroughs have been made. Perhaps more valuable than anything else has been the role of universities in organising knowledge into academic disciplines. These disciplines allow useful connections to be made (e.g. engineering can be related back to physics and chemistry, education to psychology, medicine to biology).

 In the 20th century universities have undergone important changes, particularly in the past 30 years or so:

- Universities have gone from being exclusive (once most students were well-off men) to including many kinds of students (there are now more women than men in Australian universities, as well as students from lower socioeconomic groups and from overseas).
- Although the reasons students go to university have not changed much (the main reason still being to help them get a good job), the areas of study (disciplines) available to them have changed a great deal. A new range of subjects, in areas such as the human sciences (psychology, sociology) and the humanities (literature, geography, history) have become widely available.
- In the past 15 years Australian universities have begun to teach vocational courses which formerly were found only, or mainly, in institutions such as colleges of advanced education or institutes of technology. These include business, nursing, school teaching, tourism and hospitality, journalism and computing. Similar trends have occurred in many other countries.

The explosion of knowledge in the past 200 years was gradually followed by an increase in the number of universities, not just in Europe but around the world. Universities in non-European countries were often founded by colonial powers (the first Indian university came about during British rule in 1857). Interestingly, the universities founded by colonial governments in Asia and Africa often became a breeding ground for the leaders of independence and national movements (many of the leaders of Sun Yat-Sen's Nationalist party were graduates of China's first university, the University of Peking).

Although universities in the 20th century are very different places from Plato's Academy or the mediaeval universities, modern university culture is based on certain core values and interests not so very different from the values and interests of the earlier universities. These include:

- an interest in knowledge for its own sake;
- reason;
- exhaustive inquiry;
- specialised knowledge;
- an interest in origins or first principles;
- disputation;
- openness;
- scepticism;
- concern for truth;
- honesty;
- respect for intellectual property;
- collegiality;
- autonomy;
- critique;
- tolerance.

These principles, which we explain in detail below, are meant to guide academic staff in their teaching and research—whether they are giving a lecture, taking a tutorial, marking an assignment, conducting experiments or writing a book. Students, who in a sense are apprentice academics, are also expected to follow these principles, and they help to give universities their distinctiveness—that is, to mark them as a separate cultural field.

These are some of the differences of cultural context that make going to university like going to a foreign country. There are many different

languages, ideas, customs, values and traditions that you need to learn
before you can feel at home.

## ACADEMIC DISCOURSE AND CULTURE

We now provide you with a short guide to some of the features of
academic discourse.

### Knowledge for knowledge's sake

In universities knowledge is valued for its own sake: it does not need to
have any obvious practical value or use. For instance, asking and answering questions like 'When did the universe begin?' or 'What happened
to the dinosaurs?' won't help you to build a bridge but is still considered
important.

### Reason

Academic work, ideas and thinking are supposed to be based on reason.
Using reason means limiting knowledge to those things that can be
observed, tested or explained through logical arguments (which is different
from working things out through reading chickens' entrails or the shape of
a person's head, or watching the stars). Intuition, guesses, hunches and faith
are sometimes useful in helping people to work things out, but academic
work requires evidence or rational arguments.

If you were evaluating a new diet as part of an assessment in a health
studies subject, for instance, you couldn't dismiss it as a mere fad or
useless. You would have to provide arguments or evidence, and perhaps
quote precedents or authorities that supported your position.

### Exhaustive inquiry

Professional academics and researchers want to know *everything* about
whatever they have chosen to study. If they are studying whales, they
want to know all about whales—not just what might be useful for
economic or conservation reasons. They like to be aware of everything
that other scholars have had to say on a subject. New students are
sometimes demoralised by the huge lists of recommended reading lecturers make available. You may rightly feel it would be impossible to
read them all in the time available. The lecturer probably doesn't expect
you to, but is displaying characteristic academic thoroughness.

## Specialised knowledge

Scholars have to specialise. Nowadays they can absorb all the details of what is already known, and add to it, only by keeping to one area of a discipline—or at most to a few limited areas. What makes life difficult for students is that the ideas, discourses and approaches that are accepted in one discipline are sometimes not accepted in another. Freudian theories still have some currency in literary studies, film studies and gender studies, but not in modern mainstream psychology courses.

## An interest in origins or first principles

In academic discourse there is a tendency to analyse things down to their most basic ideas or trace them back to their beginnings. What you are reading at the moment is reasonably typical. In explaining the nature of modern universities we have looked back at their history, in order to make sense of what is happening now. Before nursing became something taught in universities, trainee nurses would be instructed from the outset in how to carry out practical tasks. Now first-year nursing students at university are required to write essays analysing the concept of health.

## Disputation

In disputation, two opposed opinions or theories are tested against one another to see which holds up better, or whether they can be brought together in some way to produce an improvement on both of them. You will be expected to do this in a lot of your assessment tasks, especially essays and reports. You should realise that you can put forward a point of view which differs from your tutor's, as long as it is supported with good reasons. The tutor will not resent this but welcome it, as it shows that you are beginning to learn to think for yourself.

## Openness

Everything is open to challenge. You must have a full understanding of what others believe so you can either agree with it or dispute it. There must be opportunities for different points of view to be put forward. Ideas must circulate freely. In order to challenge a position, though, you need to put forward evidence and rational arguments about why it should be rejected. Your tutor will probably encourage you to debate issues in class. 'That's a load of rubbish' is not an acceptable response.

## Scepticism

There must be a willingness to think about and evaluate new ideas and theories rather than merely to take them on trust. Within university culture it is regarded as better to continue in uncertainty—to accept that we do not yet have an answer—than to accept dubious ideas just because it is comforting to have something to believe, or because others believe them.

## Concern for truth

Scholars must be critical of their own ideas and theories. They must be cautious about making statements until they have reasonably good evidence to support them. At university you should not expect to write the way journalists sometimes do, where it doesn't matter what the facts are as long as you produce a good story. This does not work in university—not even in journalism subjects.

## Honesty

Scholars must be willing to accept and take into account some new piece of evidence even if it disproves their theory. You must not fake evidence. You must also acknowledge that some other scholar deserves the credit for having made a discovery or having been first to advance some idea. Even if you are arguing for one position, you should still mention arguments and evidence that support the other side. This gives you, and your arguments, much greater credibility.

## Respect for intellectual property

As we have seen, ideas must move freely in a university, and be available to people both inside and outside the university rather than hidden or sold for personal gain. In the business world a good idea can often be exchanged for a financial reward. In academic life people profit from a new idea or insight only by having their reputation enhanced (which might help their career), or they may get a small amount of money from publishing their findings in books. If ideas are published without acknowledging their source, and if copyright is violated, the true originator of the idea goes unrewarded. Academic discourse always involves documentation (citation of sources, bibliographies), which gives credit to the person who first made the discovery or came up with the idea.

Plagiarism—the use of work without acknowledgement—is regarded as a serious violation of university rules.

## Collegiality

Universities are supposed to operate on democratic principles, and staff are supposed to treat each other fairly and reasonably. The same applies to the relations between staff and students, and among students. If someone is giving an oral presentation, for instance, you should not criticise or attack that person just for fun: your comments are supposed to be fair and helpful.

## Autonomy

Academic work should not be carried out to help or promote any interest group, such as a government or business enterprise. Outside organisations should not dictate what universities can teach.

## Critique

Although this does not always apply to academic work, there is supposed to be a willingness to draw attention to ideas and practices in society that are unproductive, unjust, illegitimate and harmful. Academics—although in some senses detached from the world—should be prepared to comment on what is wrong with the world from the perspective of their discipline—that is, to engage in critique.

## Tolerance

Compared with many other institutions, universities are supposed to display an openness to and a tolerance of difference and cultural diversity. If you do not comply with this, you might find that people won't tolerate you.

## Military discourse and culture

We can perhaps understand academic discourse better if we compare it with other discourses and cultures. Many young people around the world find themselves in armies rather than universities. Armies don't value knowledge for its own sake. They exhibit a practical approach to knowledge: it is worth having if it can get you something, like a better bomb or tank; otherwise it is an unnecessary and distracting complication. Except in the higher ranks, army personnel are supposed to do what they are told and not cultivate original ideas, which might challenge the official line and lead to unpredictable behaviour. Soldiers are more useful when they behave predictably. Thinking is discouraged. A soldier is supposed to say 'Yes, sir!' and obey immediately.

Nor is 'openness' valued. Information is kept secret: unless it is essential that you know, you are not told. Military organisations are authoritarian, and loyalty to the group is highly valued. In universities you are supposed to be loyal to ideas and principles and the truth, whether or not others agree. Military culture does not welcome difference—it just eliminates it.

Armies, then, are very different from universities, though both are proud of their long traditions. In recent times military organisations have realised the benefits of rational analysis and inquiry: if you want to shoot people, or blow up other countries, it makes sense to think about it and work out how to do it properly. University education is now provided for many officers. In the 20th century, many aspects of traditional military culture have not worked very well. The military did a great job of producing bravery and blind obedience, but after thousands of soldiers lost their lives charging machine guns their leaders began to realise that relying on traditional practices was not good enough. Academic ideas of critical inquiry and analysis and testing were applied to military situations.

## Commercial/business discourses and culture

Commerce, business and industry comprise another cultural field which we can contrast with universities. As in the military, knowledge has use value: if certain knowledge can contribute in some way to making a profit, then it is worthwhile; otherwise it is useless and is ignored. A company will research and improve products where there is a market—whether or not these products contribute to the good of society. Criticism of its values does not much bother the world of business. A business corporation may keep the results of research secret so that it will be the one to benefit financially.

Because they have to respond to market forces which can change quickly, businesses have to be flexible and adaptable. Universities tend to be more rigid and traditional. As with the military, business and industry now realise that academic learning and ideas have a lot to offer them. For instance, companies use the methods of the social sciences (sociology, psychology) to try to predict the behaviour of potential customers. Again, although commercial discourse and culture is different from university culture, these days businesses want their staff to be university-educated. People good at critical thinking and analysis do well in business, provided they can adapt to that cultural environment.

## WHAT UNIVERSITY DOES FOR YOU

Universities are meant to produce qualified people for the job market. They do this partly by providing students with a body of knowledge relevant to some field. Whether students are training as vets, journalists, social workers, chemists, engineers or accountants, there are certain things they need to know if they are to do their job properly. A vet needs to know about animal anatomy and diseases, a print journalist needs to be able to put a newspaper together, a mechanical engineer needs to know how to build a bridge (so it won't fall down).

Universities are supposed to give their students something more than mere qualifications. They are meant also to:

- prepare people for leadership in society;
- teach them important principles, such as an interest in truth and knowledge;
- orient them towards lifelong learning;
- teach them to think critically and imaginatively.

There is no contradiction between training 'for the job' and these other important general skills (what we have called literacies). Not all courses prepare students for a specific career (e.g. primary school teaching or dentistry). But even in those that do, the general skills—the fundamental literacies—are part of what prepares the student for the job.

Universities help people find professional employment both because they then have a piece of paper (which says they graduated in a certain course) and because that piece of paper stands for something. In a sense it testifies that, in finishing a university course, this person learned to relate to others responsibly (and thus has leadership potential), to meet deadlines, to pursue truth and knowledge, and to think critically and imaginatively. Employers give jobs to university graduates because they expect that those qualities are 'part of the package' of a university

education. In other words, people who go to university are supposed to be different from other people, not just because they know more but because they are more imaginative, thoughtful and alert—they are supposed to be thinkers.

## CONCLUSION

In this chapter we have introduced you to some of the more important points about what universities are, the discourses they use, and the features that make them valuable but different from other cultural fields. In chapter 3 we look at teaching and learning practices in universities.

# Learning at university level

Many students go through university without giving much thought to just what they are doing there, and why. They alternate between taking it fairly easy and getting into a desperate panic to complete assessment tasks on time. They are satisfied to survive each assessment obstacle and it does not occur to them that there might be better ways of doing what they do, or that they may not be making the most of the years they have put aside to prepare for a career.

## LEARNING TO LEARN

Students need to become more aware of:

- what they are really learning when they do academic work; and
- their strategies for learning and producing work.

A student writing an essay on Australian taxation policy in the 1990s is not just learning about the particular details of this policy. He or she is gaining an understanding of economic and political structures and theories. Twenty years from now the government may have a radically different policy, but what the student learns today about those structures and theories will still be relevant.

In writing the essay, the student had a chance to develop skills in researching and writing which could be applied in a future occupation, for instance in writing a report for his or her organisation. Skills can be much better developed when you take time to think about them as distinct from the content of the essay. Students seldom do this because they are usually too worried about content.

Contrast this attitude with the way professional sportspeople carefully analyse the various aspects of their performance after a contest. They are highly self-aware—they do not simply trust to instinct and explain away success or failure by resorting to superstition. They may make comments like 'I was lucky' or 'It just wasn't my day' to the media, but to themselves or their coach they say 'Why did [or didn't] that work—and what should I do next time?'. The most important factor in being successful at sport is to understand why things happen, because then you can reproduce the techniques and approaches that brought the success, or eliminate the technical problems that caused the failure. If a professional throws a bad pass or misses an open goal it is usually because his or her technique was bad—and the coach will be quick to point this out. (This book is your professional coaching manual: it aims to make you more self-aware in all your present and future university study. It encourages you to think about the techniques and strategies you use in your university work and about how these will be relevant to your future career.)

Part of the process of becoming more aware as a university learner is to think about the disciplines you are studying. To do well in, say, economics or tourism studies you have to know what kind of knowledge the discipline produces, why it is produced, and how it is different from other disciplines. You also need to be aware how much the knowledge and skills you are acquiring in your different subjects have in common. You may be learning to use statistical evidence, to work with others to solve a problem, and to access databases. We call these **generic skills**: they are needed to get through your academic subjects, and each of your subjects develops them further. When you leave university they become the skills and understanding that make you worth hiring. In the workplace, the content to which you apply these skills may be different but the intellectual processes will be much the same. The more you are aware of these generic skills as something distinct from the content of each subject, the more you will see them as important to your future—not just as something attached to your next assignment task. They are one of the main reasons you are at university in the first place.

## CULTURAL CONTEXTS AND LEARNING

We know that communication is always influenced by its cultural context, and that the form communication takes is likely to change if the situation changes. As we move from one cultural context to another, different kinds of communication become more appropriate. The person writing a letter to his or her mother, the student writing an assignment, and the employee writing a recommendation that the company expand its product range, are operating in different cultural contexts. Among many other differences that apply, there is a different relationship between writer and reader in each case. The mother, the tutor who will grade the assignment and the managing director of the company may have some things in common (they may all be treated with respect, for instance), but a different kind of communication will be required. You need to know the kind of cultural context you are operating within as a university student—something about its characteristics and purposes, and how you relate to it, if you are to communicate successfully in such an environment—that is, if you want to learn and produce good work.

Communication is a complex thing. There is no single ideal way of writing a letter to your mother, or of producing any other kind of writing. What we can do is help you to *contextualise* your learning more effectively. Even within the cultural field of education, there are different contexts. Imagine someone sitting in a classroom. There are rows of desks and chairs and someone out the front drawing diagrams on the whiteboard. Yet this could be:

- a high school;
- a technical college or polytechnic (e.g. a trade course, like plumbing);
- a university;
- a training session being conducted by a large organisation for some of its employees (e.g. to explain how a new computer system will require new work procedures).

There will, of course, be many similarities in each case. But it will help us to understand university if we contrast it with the three other learning situations.

At school, learners feel they have no choice about being there. Parents or the government, or both, make them attend. The company employees may have little choice, but they are being paid for their time and may feel that they are valued workers. In the other cases, students are probably there as a result of their own free choice. This in itself does not mean their motivation will be strong. It could be that their morale is high because they now feel they are making their own decisions in life. On the other hand, there are advantages in having other people decide for you. A student who isn't sure he/she made the right decision about enrolling in a course may not feel fully committed.

The main purpose of school is to develop the individual in a general way for later life. Pupils are taught selected aspects of certain academic disciplines in a carefully structured and usually 'watered-down' way. The main emphasis is on moulding the individual for entry into adult society and the workforce. Senior high school admittedly places more emphasis on academic development, yet the central concern is still with the maturing individual. In universities, as they have evolved historically, there is a sense in which the academic discipline is central: certain scholars have gathered at a place (e.g. Macquarie University) to pursue knowledge in a discipline (e.g. chemistry). These scholars are willing to share their knowledge with others (students). The students are regarded as adults with their own reasons for wanting such knowledge, and as fully responsible for their own success or failure.

At university, unlike school, students are expected to 'master' one or more disciplines—that is, acquire a solid grasp of the main principles of the discipline, become familiar with its terminology, and so on. Unlike high school graduates, university graduates have expertise in a discipline that most people do not have.

Of course many students and their families do see university as an experience to further their general intellectual and social development, quite apart from the specific qualifications they are acquiring. And universities do recognise and cater for this in various ways. However, at the level of the individual lecturer teaching a subject, the priority is with the subject itself. Universities are characterised by a refusal to compromise: there are limits on how far the subject can be adjusted to the student (as might happen at school). Students must adjust to the subject and meet certain standards. University staff see themselves as having responsibilities to their disciplines.

University is more specialised than school, but in one sense many university courses are less narrowly focused than those in technical colleges. A university course in, say, business prepares students for a wide range of possible jobs, not just one. Many university graduates eventually work in fields other than the one they qualified for (e.g. engineers can become administrators). In contrast, technical/trade courses teach people to do one kind of job (e.g. plumbing or hairdressing). The company training course provides even more specific, directly applicable knowledge. The technical college students and the employees have the advantage of knowing exactly why they are learning something: they can visualise how, when and where they will put it to use on the job. University students often do not have this advantage.

A school teacher has knowledge of one or more disciplines, and also has special qualifications in teaching. He or she knows how to introduce material to students in a way that helps them to learn it. The technical college instructor and the company trainer have been trained in instructional techniques or have been hired because of their ability to teach. University staff are not required to have teaching qualifications. A university professor who is a leading authority in a field will have high status even if he/she is a poor teacher. Of course, many university staff are competent and inspiring teachers (and some high school teachers are not). But historically universities have not given teaching much attention (although this is beginning to change); it has been assumed that any staff member who is qualified in a discipline can teach in that discipline. At school the institution, in various ways, accepts some responsibility for whether or not students are learning. For instance, the high school teacher will take the time to make sure students understand requirements. School students are reminded about things; their progress is monitored so that any problems they are having can be detected early. In contrast, universities view learning as the student's responsibility.

One more difference. For high school students, time spent in class takes up most of the total learning time, and the same goes for employees being trained at work. But for most university students the hours spent in face-to-face teaching sessions takes up only a small proportion of the total time that must be spent in learning. What's more, their learning time outside class is unstructured. School students have more direction about what to do at home or in the library, and more frequent assignments. The biggest problem facing first-year university students is the problem of organising themselves to use their unstructured, unsupervised time effectively. An inability to handle their freedom is a more common cause of failure than a lack of mental ability.

Each different context (school, university, technical college, work) has its own particular set of conditions: economic circumstances, relationship of individual to institution, interpersonal relationships, constraints and opportunities. The important thing about these differences is that they influence the way learners respond to their situation: that is, they affect behaviour. For example, it's a good thing for learners to ask questions. But learners in our four different situations are not equally likely to ask questions.

---

### Likelihood of asking questions

- The *employees* in the training session would be most likely to ask questions. They know that it is important for them to understand the principles now because they will soon need them on the job; they will look silly if they don't know. They are also likely to be mature and self-confident.
- The *high school students* would be the least likely to ask questions, unless the teacher specifically encourages this. They are used to being passive. They don't feel much obligation to take responsibility for the gaps in their learning; they expect the institution to 'feed' them.
- The *university and technical college students* will be somewhere in between. They may not yet have shaken off high school attitudes. They may feel they can find out later, when they begin studying for their exams. Or they may feel embarrassed about displaying ignorance in front of others. Because the material is theoretical, it may even be a bit harder for university students to work out what to ask than it is for the employees.

---

The student who walks into the teaching room assuming it will be the same as the educational experience he or she is used to, makes a serious mistake. Learning outcomes are affected by how people respond to the learning situation they are in, not just by such factors as intelligence. Contextual factors (e.g. worry about what other students will think of you) can interfere with good learning for even the brightest students.

## KNOWLEDGE

When we talk about acquiring knowledge, we do not mean merely absorbing information. Think of something you know quite a lot about—it might be football, movie stars, martial arts, motorcycles, Chinese cooking, astronomy or cosmetics. You do not merely have a lot of information on this subject. If someone were forced to learn all the facts that you know about the subject—if they were forced to memorise recipes or the results of football matches—it still would not amount to the knowledge you have. To have knowledge is to understand how the thousands of individual facts fit together. It means being able to tell whether some new fact is significant or trivial. Once the person had learned the information ('Pak Doo Ik scored the goal for North Korea that knocked Italy out of the 1966 World Cup') they would soon forget it—unless they had become interested in the subject. But knowing a lot of facts would not in itself be enough to make them interested. You remember a lot about the subject (possibly more than you realise) because you have a reason to remember it—it is made meaningful by your interest and your appreciation of how one fact relates to some larger pattern of significance.

Once you have knowledge (or literacy, to use a term introduced in chapter 1) in a particular area, it becomes easier to learn about similar or related things. The person with knowledge (theoretical or practical) of Chinese cooking will find he/she can easily learn about Bulgarian cooking.

Think about how you came to have knowledge of your pet subject. Maybe you picked it up in a classroom, with rows of desks and chairs, and someone at the front talking and pointing to things on a whiteboard. But there are other places in which learning goes on. Quite probably you learned a lot before you realised that you were learning anything, simply because you had interest and pleasure in the thing. When you became aware of having a particular interest, you might have begun to find out more on the subject in a systematic way. Being interested and motivated makes a huge difference.

You may know a lot about Kung Fu or frogs or Bulgarian cooking, but it is likely to be informal knowledge. The formal knowledge in universities is organised in and by academic disciplines (e.g. botany, history, accounting, fine arts, mathematics). Sometimes we meet people who know a great deal about a subject, even though they have never studied it at university: for instance, they might be interested in gardening and have a related extensive knowledge of botany. A police officer or a legal secretary may know a great deal about law because it is relevant to their job. Compared to graduates, however, such people may have a lopsided kind of understanding. They may know a huge amount of detail (specimens of plants, sections and subsections of various Acts of Parliament) without knowing much about the bigger picture or principles. The gardener may know nothing about the evolution of plants; the policeman may know little about the constitutional basis of the law.

Having good knowledge of a discipline does involve knowing a lot of facts. An example of a fact is that polar bears are white. More important is knowing how to make sense of facts by relating them to other relevant facts: for example, that polar bears hunt other animals in a snow-covered environment. This means understanding principles that can be derived from the facts (e.g. the principle of camouflage, which can be found everywhere in nature). It means understanding the main theories that have been put forward in the discipline (the theory of evolution) and having some awareness of whether these theories are well established and widely accepted or laughed at.

Usually knowledge of a discipline includes some familiarity with its history—that is, a knowledge of how it has developed over recent centuries or decades. It will include some understanding of the way the discipline relates to other, 'neighbouring' disciplines. There are links, for example, between chemistry and biology, maths and computing, cultural studies and sociology. An important part of knowledge, though, is an awareness of where the boundaries of the discipline have been drawn. Stan the gardener's amateur enthusiasm for plants may extend to an interest in their use as remedies. He might claim that a tea brewed from the leaves of a particular plant can cure baldness. He regards this as part of his knowledge of plants. The person with a formal education in botany would refuse to go so far (at least while speaking as a botanist). The botanist would be interested in the biological characteristics of the plants, but would leave it up to the pharmacist or medical expert to determine whether or not the plant was able to cure a human ailment. Knowledge of a discipline includes knowing what it does not investigate or try to explain. And, just as important as anything else, knowledge of a discipline means understanding how research is conducted in the discipline, how new knowledge is generated.

Discipline knowledge includes knowing how to *do* things—that is, it includes skills. Here, again, we should distinguish between a simple, precise skill and more generalised capabilities. An old-time barber who can give a standard haircut using a basin and wool shears is not the same as a more highly trained hairdresser who can invent new hairstyles. A short-order cook who can make hamburgers is not the same as a chef who can create new and original dishes. A person with a deep understanding of the principles will know how to apply skills—when to break the rules or vary the standard routine, and when to call in someone with more specialised skills.

## FUNCTIONING AS A LEARNER

So far we have seen that knowledge of an academic discipline is a complex thing—also that universities largely leave responsibility for learning to the student. You are clearly facing a real challenge. But, while university staff will regard the responsibility for learning as ultimately resting with you, they will do a range of things to help you learn, more than you may realise if your idea of teaching is someone talking to the class.

In the first place, staff have selected and structured the most important or useful aspects of knowledge in a discipline. They work out which concepts are best to begin with. Lectures or study guide chapters take you through the concepts systematically—although much more is covered each week than was the case at school. Material is condensed or simplified, and connections are pointed out. You will be directed towards what is essential to read and probably given suggestions about other things it would be good to read if you get time.

Another important function of staff is to promote discussion. Talking and debating with other people (or even listening to ideas being debated) can contribute much to learning, especially learning in the sense of developing a deeper understanding as opposed to acquiring hard facts. Think of university teachers as people who set up conditions that enable you to learn, not as people who instruct you directly by telling you things.

Staff also help you learn by devising exercises and setting and marking assessment tasks. Assessment determines whether you deserve to move on to the next stage of your degree, but that is not its only purpose. It provides an opportunity for you to check on your progress. It helps you improve, if you make use of the feedback on assignments. However, assessment does not measure everything. If you adjust your learning effort solely to deal with assessment tasks you are treating your university education too narrowly, and not getting as much benefit from it as you could.

On the other hand, you do have to be practical and ensure that you succeed in the set assessment tasks. Make sure that you understand all the rules and requirements—both general university ones and those of individual subjects. Keep referring to the subject profile in each subject. Be clear about due dates for assignments, and set yourself interim deadlines for each phase of the work by working backwards from these dates. You also need to know where to go for help of various kinds. Seek help promptly if you need it.

## Teaching genres

In high school there may have been a single undifferentiated teaching genre, the lesson. At university there are several: they include the lecture, the tutorial, and the practical or laboratory session.

## Lectures

**Lectures** involve one-way delivery of material. They may provide information not available in textbooks and other study materials. More often they reinforce, explain or summarise such material. Used well, lectures can stimulate interest in a subject and are good for students who absorb concepts better by listening than reading.

> Some advantages of the lecture mode are:
>
> - One staff member can reach many students simultaneously.
> - A lecturer can demonstrate the stages of solving a problem (e.g. in maths).
> - Attention can be drawn to particularly important concepts or requirements.
>
> Some disadvantages are:
>
> - Students have limited opportunities to discuss or ask questions.
> - Lectures tend to encourage passivity: students expect to be fed with information.
> - They are usually an inefficient way of transmitting information.

## Tutorials

**Tutorials** are not as predictable as lectures: they take different forms and are more 'open-ended'. Normally they are interactive and involve smaller groups. Tutorials allow for student participation. They are meant to switch on the parts of the brain required for thinking and talking, as well as the listening part.

Tutorials help students review and consolidate knowledge gained from lectures and reading by talking about it. You should not go into a tutorial having no idea what it will be about. The talking may involve:

- responding to questions asked by the tutor;
- informal discussion;
- talking with other students in subgroups;
- more structured kinds of oral communication, such as debates or seminar presentations.

When tutors ask questions in class it is usually to promote thought and discussion. It is *not* to test students or to expose their ignorance publicly (although it is useful to the tutor to find out whether students are unclear about the concepts). A student who finds questions intimidating may keep quiet rather than take the risk of saying what might be the wrong thing. This is a classic case of misreading the cultural context. The tutor is not there to judge. If the student has misunderstood the material it is better that the tutor finds that out sooner rather than later. When other students in the group have similar misconceptions, and the tutor finds out what needs further explanation, everyone benefits.

Students themselves are responsible, at least in part, for ensuring that a tutorial is a useful learning session. If students have nothing relevant to say (i.e. they haven't done the necessary reading) the tutorial will revert to a mini-lecture. Those students who regard learning as a passive activity will just sit back and listen. They may busily scribble down every word that is said, ignoring the fact that it is simply a repetition of the lecture they have already attended—or should have attended. These students are cheating themselves, because decades of research prove that active participatory sessions are the most useful kind of learning experience. (This is not to deny that asking the tutor to go over certain difficult concepts is sometimes a good use of tutorial time.)

 Some advantages of the tutorial mode are:

- Students can ask questions and perhaps even help set the agenda.
- People tend to understand and remember what they have talked about.
- Students get to know other students.

Some disadvantages are:

- They may not work well if students come unprepared.
- Discussions sometimes get off the topic. It may be difficult to 'get through' all the content scheduled for that week.
- They will not work well unless *both* tutor and students believe in the value of discussion and activities.

The important thing in tutorials, as always, is to *think*. If you are thinking, you will find yourself contributing to the discussion from time to time in some appropriate way. Some people talk readily and freely; others say less but are more careful and considered in what they say.

Groups benefit from having both kinds of members—the first to get things going; the second to keep things on track.

## Practical or laboratory sessions

Practical activities, such as lab sessions, are usually presided over by a demonstrator who takes you through the steps of the experiment or task, checks that things are going well and answers questions. For science subjects, lab sessions introduce you to the practices, technologies and conventions of scientific disciplines and you learn how to collect, organise and record data. They often involve working within a group or team, reflecting work practices in relevant industries. Although lab sessions are supposed to replicate the conditions, activities, procedures and results of scientific work, they are generally fairly artificial situations—everything is set up, there isn't much space or time, and you have to work towards a 'pre-arranged' result. But the point is that you are introduced, in a general way, to the field of science and its 'ways of doing things'.

 The main advantages of lab sessions are:

- They allow you to relate theory to practice.
- You gain experience in scientific procedures and practices.
- There is an opportunity to talk to demonstrators on a one-to-one basis, and to learn to work within a team.

The disadvantages are:

- They can be artificial—you often know the result before you start.
- There may be frustrating limitations in time, space and equipment.
- There may be no opportunity to 'think about things'—you just have to get through the set task.

## ATTITUDES AND APPROACHES TO LEARNING

Research shows that students in a particular subject can be divided into two basic types: those with the **surface** approach, and those with the **deep** approach.

A student adopting the surface approach typically:

- emphasises memorisation (rote learning of facts) rather than understanding;
- fails to make connections between the separate facts and ideas;
- fails to see the overall picture or underlying themes; fails to see how the material relates to other fields of knowledge;
- has no personal involvement with the material; sees the learning task as something imposed from outside, and the sooner it is over with, the better.

Surface learning usually turns out to be non-learning in the long run. Three weeks after cramming for the exam the student has forgotten it all or cannot apply it in other situations.

The deep approach student:

- aims to understand the material;
- is alert to the links that can (or should) be made between the separate parts;
- appreciates the meaningfulness of the material and its implications for other fields;
- is interested in the material and finds learning satisfying even though it is challenging (or *because* it is challenging).

Think back to the subject you know a lot about (e.g. astronomy or Bulgarian cooking). You took a deep approach to learning that subject:

- You had your own real reasons for learning—you found the subject interesting for its own sake.
- You made meaningful connections between different aspects of the subject, and between that subject and other things in your life or in the world.

There is no gene for deep learning. We are all sometimes deep learners and sometimes surface learners, depending on our response to the context. It would be unrealistic to expect everything you have to study to be fascinating and worth learning for its own sake, but try to get as interested as you can. Activate your curiosity. Ask the tutor or other students what interests them about the discipline (or some aspect of it). Ask yourself questions about the discipline. Why does it exist? What human needs or questions does it satisfy or answer? Where did it come from? How do the parts of it relate to each other? In what other fields could someone apply the thinking skills developed in this kind of academic work?

We suggest that you try to think in the same way as researchers in the discipline think. As you move through uni, you will acquire more understanding, insight and techniques than many other people. The problem is that at first you are most conscious of how little you know about all there is to be known. This in itself is a kind of enlightenment.

In a sense university staff and students are on different 'wavelengths'. Students can become impatient with subjects that don't seem relevant to the job they have in mind. Younger students are also impatient to get answers to the great questions of life. Why am I the way I am? Are my parents right about *anything?* Does God exist? How can I get Mandy to go out with me? University staff, on the other hand, have got jobs and have given up expecting to get answers to the Big Questions. They are excited by the answers their discipline provides to more modest questions, by the logic with which concepts fit together in the field, by the elegance of the theories.

You too, as you progress through your course, will enjoy becoming conversant with the disciplines in which you have chosen to specialise. Any academic field is a testament to the human capacity to find solutions, generate rules, capitalise on the past and construct complex systems. Of course, the notion that intellectual activity can be deeply satisfying is not well publicised in our culture. For all the glamorous starlets it has put into tight college sweaters, Hollywood has a bad track record at depicting the excitement of using the mind. Some university staff will have the knack of infecting you with their enthusiasm for the subjects they teach, but you cannot leave everything up to them.

## Being strategic

We do not want to oversimplify anything here. It is unrealistic to divide all learning activity into two neat categories. Sometimes it is appropriate to be a surface learner. If in a particular subject all you need to do to pass a test is learn things parrot-fashion, then it may make sense to do so. Always being a deep learner may use up too much time and interfere with the completion of tasks. It is good to be interested in a subject for its own sake, but there is the difference we pointed out above between informal and formal knowledge. A university student studying astronomy cannot just follow his or her own interests in the stars—it is necessary to cover the ground specified by the university in order to acquire formal knowledge of the discipline. Successful students are often said to have a **strategic approach**—they alternate between surface and deep learning to suit the occasion.

## Dependent *vs* independent

There are other ways of looking at student learning styles and attitudes. We can distinguish between students who respond as if they were still at school (or in some other environment where instruction is provided in a highly structured manner) and students who realise that they must take the initiative and do their own learning. We can call the first kind **dependent learners** and the second **independent learners**. Students are fairly dependent for most of their school careers. At university they need to become independent.

---

 Dependent learners:

- need the institution (school or university) to set the agenda;
- want to be told what to do;
- want rewards and punishment;
- assume that they are learning just because they are sitting in class;
- blame the system (or a particular teacher) if they perform poorly;
- expect that help will come to them.

Independent learners:

- do not need so much structure;
- take responsibility for their own learning;
- give constructive feedback on how things could be improved;
- know that if help is needed they will have to seek it themselves;
- have confidence they can learn, even if the subject seems hard at first.

---

## Unaware *vs* aware learning

**Aware students** take time to reflect on their own learning attitudes and strategies. They plan their work. If something is going badly or well, they try to figure out why. If a learning technique has worked for them they will use it again in a similar situation. They try new methods. **Unaware students** may work hard but do not *think* about what they are doing, or why.

There is considerable overlap between the categories of surface, dependent and unaware. Because a student expects to be operating in a surface way, he or she lets (or wants) the institution to set the agenda and is thus dependent. And people used to being told what to do and having things structured for them tend to behave as surface learners.

Students who do well at university tend to be deep, independent and aware learners. Students who do less well tend to be surface, dependent and unaware in their approach.

Clearly, academic work ought to involve deep learning, because the aim is to understand, to make meaningful connections, and to deal in principles rather than facts and formulas. Certain things work against this. One is the fact that universities have historically taken teaching and learning issues for granted. That is, they have not seen the need to modify traditional practices to suit the particular needs of students. This is changing: for instance, study skills support is available, and there are books like this one. However, it will continue to be the student's responsibility to motivate him- or herself, to get organised, to develop useful strategies, to do a lot of work which is not supervised or promptly assessed.

Furthermore, because knowledge is expanding in every discipline, academics feel obliged to cover a lot of material in a semester. The sheer amount of material students are exposed to in some subjects may stop them from taking a deep approach. But students may have reasons of their own for tending to be surface learners:

- They have brought surface habits with them from school (where they may have been rewarded for surface learning).
- They may feel a particular subject is not relevant to their needs, and find it difficult to become interested in that subject.
- They may not allow themselves enough time for study.
- They may not understand assessment requirements and wrongly assume that a surface approach is appropriate.
- Anxiety always causes regression to earlier ways of coping. If students were mostly surface learners at school (as is quite likely) and have begun to worry about falling behind, this in itself will reinforce surface tendencies.

Surface learning tends to be associated with dependent attitudes. Dependent learners have difficulty seeing their learning as something separate from the institution they happen to be enrolled in. They like to be told exactly what to do and when (they don't care about why). They may feel it is important to attend class—but that *being* there is all that matters, not staying awake and thinking. A lot of students are dependent to begin with, but learn to be more independent.

Universities tend to encourage dependency. On the surface they are a bit like other big institutions—schools, hospitals, prisons, airport terminals—where human beings are subjected to schedules and regulations. The fact that every student in the subject 'Advanced Estonian Aquaculture' is supposed to attend a class at 2 pm on Wednesday results from an attempt to bring students into contact with a teacher and fellow students in an organised and cost-efficient way. It doesn't necessarily have much to do with wanting to learn and learning. If you had a young sister who wanted you to help her learn to play chess or the bagpipes, your response would not be to give her a rigid schedule; to do so would rob her of much of her instinct for deep learning. Now although university study *does* have to be bureaucratically organised, and assessed, this doesn't mean that the institution has to take over altogether. Unfortunately, some students begin to adapt their learning behaviour to the institution's structures. As soon as the tutorial is over, for instance, learning in that subject finishes for them. They let the assignment deadline determine when they begin thinking about the task, but because they have left their effort until close to the deadline they hardly have time to think.

The student who is more independent sees the class as something that can help his or her learning, and tries to make the most of it. Learning doesn't necessarily finish when the class does. This student may continue discussing ideas over coffee with fellow students later in the afternoon, and think about the concepts on the bus home. It may be at these times that certain things make sense. You cannot expect everything to be understood in the lecture or tutorial. Dependent students are deprived of this sort of opportunity for learning because they have 'switched off'. Their learning is related to outward structures and short-term goals rather than inner interests and long-term goals. Research shows that motivation and time spent 'on task' are crucial to success.

---

 *Motivation*

You won't learn anything you don't want to learn. Having a long-term goal helps (e.g. 'I am going to become a chartered accountant'). But you must have more immediate, specific goals too ('I am going to learn to do the maths required in this subject'). If you can acquire these short-term goals it will not matter that the long term is a bit hazy.

*Time on task*

This is a really important one. Is that a surprise? The Australian swimming champion Kieran Perkins has said that you can be the world's best at anything if you do it for six hours a day for years on end. Well, maybe. Certainly anyone who achieves anything worthwhile—as a sportsperson, rock musician, student, tightrope walker, entrepreneur—spends a lot of time doing it or practising for it. They won't necessarily admit this—they don't want to appear obsessive. Other students who do well are probably spending more time on their work than they pretend. Even if they're not, the fact they get away with it doesn't mean that you can.

---

## CONCLUSION

In this chapter we have looked at how universities differ from other teaching and learning contexts. We have seen that university involves acquiring formal knowedge in organised disciplines rather than the informal knowledge picked up by enthusiastic amateurs. Yet enthusiasm is something you should try to develop—it helps you become a deep learner. This in turn makes it more likely that you will be an independent and aware learner. That wraps up the background. In chapter 4 we get to work.

### Activities

1. Think of a *specific* occasion on which you operated as a deep learner. (It might have been recently, or it might have been years ago.) Write down a few points about why you were a deep learner in that context.

2. Repeat the exercise, this time thinking of a specific occasion on which you were a surface learner.

# part II

# THE BASICS

## chapter 4

# Critical thinking

To be successful at university you do not only need to learn the content (or subject matter) of your chosen disciplines: You also have to develop general skills or literacies. One of the most important of these is the ability to think critically.

In some ways the whole point of going to university is to learn to think. Now everybody thinks—not just university graduates. But you can actually *learn* to think, or at least learn to be a better thinker. One way to help you change the way you think is to expose you to different ideas. We may have used the same approach to thinking all our lives, but seeing how other people do things, and how other people think, can be very rewarding and productive.

People usually think and act in terms of how other people think and act—that is, they follow the lead of others because they cannot think things through for themselves. But it doesn't have to be like that.

There is a book by a Chinese philosopher, Sun Tzu, called *The Art of War*, probably written in the 5th or 4th century BC, which is virtually a handbook for 'thinking differently'. Although the book is devoted to the arts of war, it demonstrates how important creative and imaginative thinking is to success. For Sun Tzu, every situation and circumstance was different. Before taking action, there had to be analysis (of information, opponents' strengths and weaknesses, climate, terrain, past experiences). Analysing all these things would allow options to be generated. Action was based on thinking and intelligence, and was therefore likely to be different from what was expected, or the way things had usually been done.

At university, as you read books and articles and listen to lectures, you will be exposed to many examples of people responding to the modern world in the manner of Sun Tzu: not taking things for granted, not repeating what everyone else has always said; instead, assessing issues objectively and working out better explanations or finding new solutions. But the fact that productive thinking processes underlie the material they study is often not brought to students' attention. Lecturers are under pressure to get through a range of topics in a subject. They want to teach students some new theory that has been put forward but tend not to point out how a good piece of thinking went into producing the new theory. Time pressure also means that there are not so many exercises and activities allowing students to practise thinking skills (e.g. by weighing theory X against theory Y) as would be ideal. Students can get the impression that they are at university to learn a series of facts.

Whether you realise it or not, the knowledge in the academic subjects you are studying has been derived from processes of thinking critically. You are not learning the end products of other people's reasoning merely so that you can reproduce them. By examining the arguments that other people have put forward, you are learning how to be a reasoner yourself. Good thinking is at the heart of the academic enterprise. Thinking is also crucial in the sense that your own study effort has to be thoughtful and directed. As we keep pointing out, you need to think about your own learning strategies and activities. Effective learners reflect on what they are doing and why. When there is a lot of material to cover and too little time, students are tempted to function on 'automatic pilot', in superficial, unproductive ways (surface learning).

The term **critical thinking** in a broad sense can include all of the following:

- *Creative thinking.* This is sometimes called 'lateral thinking', and means being alert to new perspectives and possibilities rather than staying within familiar, routine patterns. Brainstorming techniques are a way of getting into this mode.
- *Analysing.* To analyse is to inspect something (a book, a plan, a situation) closely in order to determine what it consists of, or what it means or implies. (Analysis and related procedures such as classification are discussed in chapter 6.)
- *Problem-solving.* This means systematically considering possible solutions to a problem and choosing the best of them. Some books on critical thinking have special chapters or sections on problem-solving.

University subjects that involve a lot of problem-solving will provide further details on suitable methods and approaches.

- *Reasoning.* This is what most authors mean when they use the term 'critical thinking', and it is the aspect we concentrate on here. To reason is to think in a sensible and connected manner. More precisely, it means to work out from what you already know to be the case that some other thing is true.
- *Evaluating.* This means examining the arguments, explanations, ideas or solutions that others have put forward to determine whether they are useful, reliable and well reasoned.

You already practise these kinds of thinking from time to time. But in everyday life you are likely to do so in a casual, unsystematic way in which thinking is mixed with intuitions, guesswork, suppositions and feelings. The term 'critical' suggests a more rigorous intellectual process in which you test your own thinking and that of others to see if it is logical and convincing. You make sure that the thinking meets certain objective standards. For this reason, many authors would prefer not to regard creative thinking (which should be free and spontaneous, and can be intuitive) as a variety of critical thinking.

Critical thinking means trying to determine what is true, even if this forces you to confront ideas that are uncomfortable or unwelcome. It means being prepared to examine your own assumptions, as well as those of others, and question whether they are reasonable. However, the term 'critical' does not imply negativity or fault-finding. If you critically evaluate something, you test it for reasonableness; only if it fails to measure up does it need to be condemned.

## LANGUAGE AND CULTURE

Critical thinking requires awareness of the role of language and culture in producing knowledge. What we believe to be true about the world is shaped and constrained by language. You already know that you should be a bit suspicious when a politician says something which begins 'All freedom-loving Australians believe that . . . .'. Here the words 'freedom-loving' are **emotive** or **loaded words**; they are a manipulative tactic rather than a precise description of some actuality.

A less obvious example of the same thing is a word like 'civilisation'. This is a useful word to have in certain contexts, but it can be deeply misleading. 'We are bringing civilisation to the continent of Africa' is something the British would have claimed in the 19th century. At least until recent times, most people (certainly most British people!) would have accepted the word at face value in that sentence about Africa. Good critical thinkers must look at language closely.

The word 'civilisation', as used by the British in the 1800s (and it had come into their language only within the previous century), meant different things in different contexts (as is often the way with words). When using the word in connection with Africa, they would not have spelled out which shade of meaning they had in mind (e.g. civilisation meaning refinement, or complex social organisation, or big cities and advanced technology). To have done so would have required them to explain just which aspects of British social organisation, for instance, were more 'complex' than the elaborate, highly evolved social interrelationships and practices of African tribal groups. They would have had to explain what made big cities so desirable and how they were going to help Africans build big cities (which of course they had no intention of doing).

The word operated as a kind of code word, meaning 'we are superior to them'. Superiority justified their colonial domination of Africa. It is no coincidence that the term 'civilisation' came into the English language at a time in history when Europeans were beginning to expand all over the globe. The problem is that a word like civilisation is used as if it referred to a discrete, objective reality—obvious to anyone who observed the world accurately—when it is just a way of invoking the supposed superiority of certain cultural preferences and practices.

In any cultural field, knowledge and behaviour tend to be organised in ways appropriate to some dominant paradigm. A **paradigm** is a model of how things work, or how they should be done or thought about. Until a few centuries ago, the notion that the sun orbits the Earth was a dominant scientific paradigm that influenced how people thought about a whole range of other things. Here is another example. Even when patients are incurably ill or injured and suffering, Australian hospitals make every effort to keep them alive as long as possible, even if this goes against their wishes and their family's, and is very costly to the family and/or the taxpayer. Preserving life in all circumstances is part of the ethos of Western medical science, though the origins of this outlook are religious and cultural rather than scientific. This may or may not be a desirable way to do things, but clearly it is only one way in which human societies have responded—or could respond—to the problem. In other words, other paradigms are conceivable. Most people, however, tend to stay within paradigms that are never questioned, and perhaps are not even noticed. The critical thinker tries not to take for granted—or regard as an unalterable part of nature—ideas and assumptions that have emerged within particular cultural contexts.

In every field certain truths are accepted as 'commonsense', or as the wisdom of the elders, or as too 'obvious' to question. In tennis, for example, it has long been accepted that there is an advantage in being first to serve in a set. Sports commentators rely on a stock of such **truisms**. (They are called **myths** when it is accepted that they may not be true.) According to a news report, a recent statistical investigation of thousands of Wimbledon matches has proven many such beliefs about tennis to be false. The player who is first to serve is *not* more likely to win the set, at least in professional tennis. The critical thinker is sceptical—always ready to ask whether we really know that something is so, and always willing to take compelling new evidence into account.

## REASONING

In **reasoning** you arrive at new knowledge not by seeing or hearing something new, but by making use of what you have already got. Sometimes the new knowledge involves making a relatively simple prediction that something will happen, or realising something can or should be done. But suppose you wanted to draw some conclusion about the Chinese economy five years from now. Could you be so certain that you had made the correct inference from the facts available? Well, there are certain rules and guidelines that help us to make inferences—or to warn us that it is impossible, in the circumstances, to make an inference we can be confident about. These rules and guidelines have been generated within the body of knowledge called **logic**. If critical thinking involves proceeding in a systematic way that can be tested against a standard, logic gives us that method and standard.

In academic contexts we need to be more aware of reasoning processes than most people are. Leaving it to intuition is not enough. Learning some elementary logic will sharpen your ability to reason well, and give you some terms with which to analyse and evaluate reasoning processes. In academic contexts, reasoning processes are embodied in **arguments**. Whatever has led them to some new idea or theory (which could have involved some guesswork and lucky breaks as well as strict reasoning), academic and scientific researchers communicate their findings to others by producing reasoned arguments (published in books and journals or delivered orally at conferences).

> Suppose you see that someone is repairing a broken electrical appliance which is still plugged into the power supply. You predict that sooner or later the person will get a nasty shock, so you warn them or turn off the power. Sometimes reasoning involves working back from some observed outcome to explain what caused it. A person is lying dead on the floor clutching a screwdriver and a broken appliance plugged into the socket. You conclude that electrocution was the cause of death.
>
> This kind of reasoning is not too difficult for anyone with an elementary knowledge of electricity. Even if your conclusion was wrong (if the power supply for the whole building had been disconnected, or if it was later shown that the person had died of cyanide poisoning), your inference was perfectly reasonable in the circumstances. But what if the circumstances are more complicated?

## UNDERSTANDING ARGUMENT

At university, as in other areas of life, you are often called on to argue: that is to say, you may have to convince your lecturer, boss or partner that a particular claim is true or false, or that a course of action is justified. Maybe you are writing a research paper in which you wish to establish that:

• Most juvenile crime is caused by some breakdown in normal family life.

Or that:

• Price is the most important factor for tourists in choosing a hotel.

In a business context, you might write a report in which you recommend that:

• The company needs to move into new markets if it is to remain viable.

In each case the claim you are making is a proposition. You cannot merely assert that any one of these things is true. If someone asked how you knew that was true, it would be no use telling them that you just had a hunch. You would have to give reasons for claiming the proposition to be true. Rather than making such an assertion, a researcher might say:

- More than 85% of young offenders interviewed in a large-scale survey had experienced some breakdown in normal family life.
- Therefore we can conclude that most juvenile crime is caused by some breakdown in normal family life.

We call the proposition we want to establish as true 'the conclusion', and the other relevant proposition(s) 'the premises'. An argument consists of premise(s) and a conclusion, and a notion that one leads to the other. Put more simply, an argument consists of one or more reasons (premises) used in support of a claim. Some textbooks on introductory logic use the term 'claim' for the conclusion and 'reason' for the premise.

In some arguments there are two premises:

- All residents were exposed to the toxic fumes.
- Mr Jackson was a resident.

And then there is the conclusion which can be inferred from these premises, namely that:

- Therefore Mr Jackson was exposed to the toxic fumes.

Not all arguments, though, are so simple. Before we go any further, we need to distinguish argument in this sense from the more extended kind of argument that might be needed to convince someone that something is true. We know that the conclusion about Mr Jackson is true if we can be certain that both premises are true. We may be absolutely certain that, yes, he is a resident (second premise). But are we certain that the first premise ('All residents were exposed to the toxic fumes') is true? We will have to prove that before we can expect our conclusion to be accepted.

Sometimes a chain of short, logical arguments will have to be put forward to prove a point. The conclusion of one argument becomes the premise in a further argument. In the argument about juvenile crime, a researcher might need to provide further arguments to show that the survey was reliable, and produce arguments to disprove alternative explanations (e.g. by offering evidence that the proportions of offenders who were unemployed or uneducated or addicted were much lower, in order to show that these were not the causes).

The word argument, then, is sometimes used to refer to a specific set of premises and conclusions, and sometimes to refer to more extended pieces of writing or speaking—what we will call an 'extended argument'. An extended argument about crime might set out to show that crime can be reduced by:

- reducing certain causal factors (e.g. by easing strain on families);
- identifying potential offenders at an early age;
- establishing preventive programs for potential offenders;
- strengthening police powers;
- educating the public in security measures.

These different aspects of the extended argument are called issues. (We discuss extended argument in chapter 5.)

As well as making a distinction between simple and extended arguments, we need to distinguish argument from another sense in which the word is used. When we use the term 'argument' we are not referring to a quarrel, but the idea of two sides which are not in agreement is a useful one, as arguments often arise in this kind of situation. But even if there is no other person ready to disagree, you should see your own ideas as propositions that need to be proven, and not accepted at face value. The idea of a debate is useful because there are always two sides: a proposition may be true but it may turn out to be false. There is always a potential counterargument. In other words, doubt is always present when argument is going on: if there can be no doubt, argument is not needed.

## The nature of the proposition

Arguments are about propositions. A **proposition** is something that can be shown to be true or false. It cannot be a mere expression of personal taste, such as 'Melbourne is nicer than Brisbane'; while an individual might feel strongly about this, it is unlikely that anyone could ever be convinced that Melbourne is 'nicer' through rational argument. What is understood by 'nicer' involves subjective feelings. Exclamations like 'Brazil forever!' cannot be argued either. The test is whether you can put in front of the proposition the words 'it is true that' or 'it is not true that'. If you can, then your conclusion is a proposition; if you cannot, then it is not.

Arguments must be worth proving. Something that is already an accepted fact is true by definition. A fact may need to be tested, but it does not need to be argued about. It is pointless for two people to begin disputing whether or not Sydney had its hottest November on record in 1997. The matter can be settled by consulting the records.

Arguments should be single. You can argue only one thing at a time. 'Eating chicken kebabs causes juvenile crime and indigestion' is not suitable, because the evidence may support one of these claims but not the other. The two claims need to be separately investigated and argued before being combined in this way.

Arguments might need to be qualified. As it is often impossible to prove that something is always and everywhere the case, it may be necessary to restrict (qualify) the proposition with a word like 'most' or 'some' ('Eating chicken kebabs causes indigestion in most people').

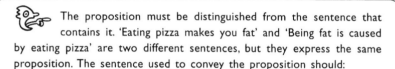

The proposition must be distinguished from the sentence that contains it. 'Eating pizza makes you fat' and 'Being fat is caused by eating pizza' are two different sentences, but they express the same proposition. The sentence used to convey the proposition should:

- be a statement rather than a question;
- be clear rather than ambiguous;
- contain as little unnecessary material as possible: in other words, it should express the proposition. Other information should be conveyed in other sentences;
- use straightforward language that can be easily understood by most audiences. Avoid words that are imprecise and/or value-laden (like 'civilisation' in our earlier example).

## Premises

What makes an acceptable premise? There are three main kinds: assertion, axioms, and evidence.

Mere **assertion**, such as unsupported opinion (e.g. the view that the movie *Titanic* was a brilliant film, or that the government should introduce a new tax system), does not make an acceptable premise. It is not good enough simply to ask someone to take your word for it.

**Axioms**, however, can be used. Axioms are propositions that are self-evident. It is axiomatic that tomorrow will come, that parallel lines never meet, that junk food does not constitute a balanced diet. Some propositions that are not strictly axioms are so widely accepted that they can be treated as axioms, at least in particular contexts.

**Evidence** can take a number of forms. One is authoritative opinion—what some acknowledged expert considers to be the case: this type of evidence is often used in legal cases. There are also facts that can be verified by experiment, as well as non-scientific facts (such as having handed in an assignment) that can be verified by an eyewitness. Finally, there are statistics: these are simply facts expressed as numbers. They are particularly useful in showing relationships between things (e.g. between smoking and cancer).

However, there are different degrees of reliability in propositions that involve evidence. Authorities, no matter how famous, are sometimes mistaken, just as eyewitnesses do not always see what they think they see. (This is why we often get vastly different accounts of an event such as an accident.) The value of statistical evidence also varies.

Another kind of evidence involves analogy. That is, we claim something is true of A because it is true of B, and A is like B. For example, to support our proposition that there is no life on Mars, we might put forward the premise that there is no life on the moon. Analogies are not strong arguments.

## THE CONDITIONS FOR ARGUMENT

We have seen that one condition for argument is the existence of doubt. Otherwise argument is pointless. There are other conditions that should be satisfied before we proceed with argument.

First, there must be **clarification**. In other words, everyone must know exactly what is being argued about. The proposition must be clear. Quite often, in real-life debates, it is not clear at all. Sometimes we have to 'read between the lines' to decide what the arguer wants to prove. Sometimes people launch into arguments without even clarifying for themselves what it is they want to prove. Many letters to the editor of newspapers and calls to talkback radio shows are of this sort.

It may not be enough merely to state the conclusion. It may be necessary to define terms like 'juvenile' or 'crime' or 'breakdown' so that we know whether the argument relates to every kind of offence, even trivial ones, or only to serious crime. It is often useful to define what a term will mean for the present occasion—that is, for the purposes of the argument about to be conducted.

Second, there must be some **common ground**. Argument will proceed more productively if people work out beforehand what they already do agree on. In face-to-face situations this can be accomplished by conversation. In writing it will help if you indicate to your readers the areas where they probably see things the same way you do. There has to be some agreement on the departure point of the argument. Two people may differ on the degree to which the government should intervene in the economy. Views on this have changed considerably in the main Australian political parties during the past couple of decades. But almost everyone believes that some government intervention is appropriate; it is simply a matter of determining what kind and how much. It would probably be a waste of time arguing on this subject with someone who didn't believe that governments should exist in the first place, or with someone who believed that the government should run everything, and who did not accept that there should be any such thing as private property.

Third, there must be **open-mindedness**. Unless each party to the argument (whether fellow debater or reader) is prepared to accept that the other side at least potentially has a better case, there is no point in that person participating in argument at all. If you argue, you trust that the others will allow themselves to be convinced by a good argument. Similarly, you should be ready to change your opinion if you are rationally (not emotionally) convinced that what your opponent says is more likely to be true than what you have been arguing for. Obviously there are contexts in which people argue a case as strongly as they can and do not give ground (or at least not publicly). This occurs with debating competitions, and with lawyers paid to argue on behalf of clients. It remains true that rational argument as a means of determining what is true can work only if there is intellectual honesty. If, for whatever reason, people are committed to a view from which they will not move whatever evidence is put forward, they should make their conviction clear and not pretend to be open to rational argument.

## KINDS OF ARGUMENT

We stated earlier that, in logic, an argument involves:

- one or two premises;
- a conclusion; and
- a claim about the relationship between them.

Most often the claim is one of probability rather than of certainty. That is, we say that if this premise is true the conclusion is probably true. A simple example:

- Most people are right-handed.
- Therefore the next person to enter the room will be right-handed.

We call these types of arguments **inductive arguments**. Here we can establish the probability with a fair degree of accuracy, as the proportion of right-handed people in the population is known. The following is an argument in which the degree of probability is lower:

- Anne has enjoyed all the films starring Keanu Reeves that she has seen.
- Therefore Anne will enjoy the next Keanu Reeves film she sees.

We could say that this argument is inductively weak. Even though the premise is true, the conclusion may well not be true—though it is more likely to be true than false.

Next is an example of an argument that is inductively very strong:

- In all instances observed so far, acid turns litmus paper red.
- Therefore this piece of litmus will turn red if placed in acid.

The fact that an argument is inductively strong, however, does not guarantee that the conclusion will be true. Europeans used to believe that swans were white because all the swans ever seen were white. When they came to Australia they discovered swans that were black.

While books on logic provide rules for determining how good an inductive argument is, merely thinking carefully about what is being claimed will provide some criteria. Consider the argument:

- Almost all the pupils in the class hate the maths teacher.
- Therefore the new girl will hate the maths teacher.

This argument will be strong if:

- There are lots of pupils in the class.
- The new girl is a typical case (e.g. if, like the other pupils, she is a girl from a rural area who wants to be a kindergarten teacher. If the new girl is a mathematical genius from Nigeria, or the teacher's granddaughter, the argument will not be so strong).

In another kind of argument, the claim is that if the premises are true the conclusion must be true: that is, it is a claim of certainty. Here is an example:

- All children are impulsive.
- John is a child.
- Therefore John is impulsive.

It should be clear why this has to be true if the premises are true. If John does in fact belong to the class of things called children, who all have a particular characteristic, then John must have that characteristic too. Note, though, that one or both of the premises could be false and the conclusion could still be true. We call arguments of this kind **deductive arguments.**

## Valid and invalid syllogisms

There is a special name for a deductive argument with two premises and a conclusion. It is called a syllogism. As well as the examples shown, syllogisms can take other forms. The first premise of a syllogism often takes the general form 'If A then B' (if you have ever written a computer program you will immediately recognise this type of language). Another common first premise has the form 'Either A or B'. We should always understand this to mean 'either but not both'.

Not all syllogisms allow a claim of certainty such that if the premises are true the conclusion must be true. It depends on the form. The following is a valid form:

- All the members of the team were upset at losing.        All As are B.
- Mark was a member of the team.                          C is an A.
- Therefore Mark was upset at losing.                      Therefore C is B.

The syllogism below, however, is an invalid form:

- All Australians are good at sport.                       All As are B.
- Ben is good at sport.                                    C is B.
- Therefore Ben is an Australian.                          Therefore C is an A.

Can you see why both premises can be true here but the conclusion false? When a syllogism has an invalid form, the conclusion may be true or it may be false, even if (as in the above cases) both premises are true.

When a syllogism has valid form, the conclusion may be true or false if one premise is false. If both premises are true, the conclusion must be true. When an argument has true premises and valid form it is called a sound argument.

If we put forward a deductive argument which has invalid form or an inductive argument in which the conclusion does not follow from the premise(s), we have committed a **fallacy**. (We have more to say about fallacies in chapter 5.)

## Questioning assumptions

One of the difficulties with arguments is that they often rest on assumptions that are not spelled out by the arguer. The example about the person entering the room being right-handed, for instance, is a reasonable inductive argument only if it is assumed that the next person to enter the room will do so entirely at random. If it is known by the arguer that for some reason Candy, who happens to be right-handed, is on her way and is likely to be the next to enter the room, the conditions for a prediction based on population statistics are not met. Similarly, if we know that the room in question is being used by the Left-Handed Persons' Club, the assumption the argument rests on is violated. This is one reason why clarification and finding common ground at the outset is important. Sometimes assumptions should be included as premises in the argument so that there can be no misunderstanding.

## IDENTIFYING ARGUMENT

When we read academic and other texts, we need to be able to tell whether or not a given passage contains an argument. For example:

> There has been a severe drought in many parts of Australia. Farm income is declining and many family farms are being replaced by big agribusiness enterprises. The government's policy of economic deregulation has led to declining services (such as railways, banks, post offices, hospitals) in rural areas. Most of the benefits of economic deregulation have been enjoyed by city-dwellers.

Is this an argument? No. It certainly contains several propositions that could be argued. And we begin to sense that each of the sentences has a certain connection with the others—that they are all beginning to point in a similar direction. But none of the sentences is in fact identified as the conclusion of a process of reasoning: each is a separate assertion; in the passage as it stands, no sentence is put forward as evidence of anything.

Suppose we add these sentences:

> For these reasons there is widespread despair and resentment in country areas. So the government will lose the support of rural voters at the next election.

Now the four sentences have been used as premises for an intermediate conclusion about despair and resentment. This becomes a premise for the overall conclusion about loss of votes. With the additional sentences the passage is an argument. Note that the presence of argument is signalled by the words 'For these reasons' and 'So'. A careful writer often uses such signpost words. Note, though, that it would still be an argument without these words, even with the additional sentences placed at the beginning rather than the end.

To determine whether a passage of writing is an argument, check whether there is a proposition that is clearly a conclusion in relation to other statements in the passage. One author suggests that you should first look for 'conclusion indicator' words like 'therefore', 'so', 'must', 'should'. If such words do not identify any sentence as the conclusion, then look at each sentence in turn. Ask yourself whether anything in the rest of the passage gives you a reason to believe that what the sentence asserts is true. If not, then that sentence cannot be a conclusion. If none of the sentences qualify as a conclusion, then the passage is not an argument.[1]

## STANDARD FORM

In real-life situations, arguers often fail to reveal their background assumptions. They may not even provide all the premises. Sometimes even the conclusion is implied rather than actually articulated. For instance, the sentence 'Nine out of ten dentists recommend Colgate' states a premise. The unspoken conclusion is that 'you should use Colgate'. We call these informally expressed arguments 'enthymemes'. They often need to be converted to standard form so that we can evaluate them properly. This is the case with the following example, which has a missing premise:

• Steve has decided not to run so Jim will win the race.

The standard form is:

• Either Steve or Jim will win the race.
• Steve has decided not to run.
• Therefore Jim will win the race.

Recasting the argument in standard form allows us to examine the first premise, which was missing. It forces us to think about whether this really is an 'either/or' situation. In the enthymeme the arguer glosses this over.

When we put an argument into standard form we sometimes need to change the words to get rid of colloquial or emotive language. It is also appropriate to have consistency of expression between all the propositions. Writers and speakers often employ some variation in the terms they use. In argument it is best to be as clear and consistent as possible, even if the language is not very colourful.

## CONCLUSION

Academic discourse is not concerned with simply amassing facts (although it certainly does this) but rather with putting forward arguments to show why something should be accepted as true. Argument relies on reasoning—a form of critical thinking in which what we already know (accept as true) allows us to infer that some further thing is true, as long as we operate according to the rules and procedures of logic. Having looked at the fundamentals of argument, we go on in chapter 5 to look at argument in practice.

### Activities

1. In this chapter it is explained that critical thinkers have to be alert to:
   (a) words that are emotive or 'loaded';
   (b) cultural paradigms;
   (c) truisms or myths.
   Look again at our examples and find one additional example of each.

2. Bearing in mind the criteria on pp. 52–3, read through the following list. Do the statements qualify as propositions that could be argued?
   (a) The Australian government should privatise hospitals and do more to help farmers.
   (b) Why should we put up with old computers?
   (c) Australians love to play sport.
   (d) If you don't stop spending money at the casino you won't be able to pay your school fees.
   (e) Australian women hockey players have done better than the men in international competition.
   (f) Because they lost money making reckless loans in the 1980s the banks,

with a few notable exceptions, are now reluctant to lend money to anyone, thus preventing the development of new export industries.

3.  Put the following enthymemes into standard form.
    (a)  Barry, being so articulate and charming, would make an excellent sales-person.
    (b)  Don't buy your daughter a violin. She was hopeless on the piano.
    (c)  Dave is a wrestler. Don't ask him to arrange the flowers.
    (d)  You have entered the Pharaoh's tomb. You will die.
    (e)  You would not expect a watch to suddenly spring into existence without a watchmaker, would you? So why believe that the infinitely more complex universe could just spring into existence?

## Answer to Activity 2

In their present form, none of the statements is strictly acceptable as a proposition that can usefully be argued about.

(a)  This contains two terms ('privatise hospitals', 'help farmers') which must be argued about separately.
(b)  Propositions cannot take the form of questions. Recast as: 'We should not have to put up with old computers.'
(c)  Strictly, this should be qualified, for example: '*Most* Australians love to play sport.'
(d)  The conditional clause ('If you don't stop spending money') indicates that this is a premise in an argument rather than the conclusion.
(e)  This does not need to be argued about. It is a fact that could be confirmed by consulting records.
(f)  This sentence contains a whole argument (actually two arguments) instead of expressing a single proposition. You should first prove the proposition 'the banks are reluctant to lend money to anyone' and then go on to argue that a lack of bank loans is preventing development.

## Answer to Activity 3

(a)  Excellent salespersons are articulate and charming.
     Barry is articulate and charming.
     Therefore Barry would be an excellent salesperson.
(b)  Those who cannot learn to play the piano cannot learn to play the violin.
     Your daughter could not learn to play the piano.
     Therefore your daughter will not learn to play the violin.
(c)  Wrestlers lack skill in arranging flowers.
     Dave is a wrestler.
     Dave lacks skill in arranging flowers.
(d)  Everyone who has entered the Pharaoh's tomb has died.

You have entered the Pharaoh's tomb.
You will die.

(e) Complex mechanisms have to be created by someone.
The universe is a complex mechanism.
The universe had to be created by someone.

Note that (a) has an invalid form. The others have valid forms, though some of them contain dubious premises.

## chapter 5

# Dealing with ideas: argument

We have explained that argument involves providing reasons for establishing whether something is true or not true. In logic, an argument consists of:

- one or more premises (which have already been accepted as true or probably true);
- a conclusion;
- an implicit claim about the degree of probability with which the conclusion follows from the premises—ranging from fair probability to absolute certainty.

In practice we may need a chain of prior arguments to prove that our premises are true. Or it may be that separate arguments have to be conducted relating to different aspects of whatever it is we want to prove. Hence we often encounter 'extended argument'. Here we look at how argument can go wrong and what must be done to ensure good argument. We also return in more detail to the topic of extended argument.

## FALLACIOUS ARGUMENT

There are many ways in which argument can go wrong, through either carelessness or some deliberate attempt to bend the rules. Some fallacies relate to the choice of unsuitable propositions as premises; some violate the rules governing the relationship between premises and conclusion; others involve illegitimate tactics used to mislead or intimidate an opponent.

Fallacies have to do with the claim that the conclusion follows from the premises. Fallacious arguments are so inductively weak as to be untenable or, if they involve deduction, have an invalid form. It is possible to have true premises but a fallacious argument. Some arguments are fallacious because unsuitable premises have been chosen. But essentially a fallacy is a fault in logic; it does not mean that the facts (evidence) are wrong in themselves—it means that they are not being used legitimately.

## Kinds of fallacy

There are four main kinds of fallacy. We provide some examples of each below. For a more complete list, consult a book on elementary logic or reasoning.

### General fallacies

These apply to both inductive and deductive arguments.

*Equivocation.* In this fallacy, a word is used in two different senses as if it had the same meaning each time. For example: 'In a democracy all people are meant to be equal. But clearly people are unequal in talent, energy, physique, etc. Therefore democracy can't work.' This confuses equality of political rights with equality of natural endowment.

*Non-qualification.* This fallacy occurs when you state as absolute, premises that should be qualified or restricted in some way (by a word like 'some' or 'most'). For example: 'Public servants are lazy.'

*'Begging the question'.* This occurs when the conclusion (the proposition to be proven) is already assumed to be true in one of the premises. For example: 'Smith is an honest man. Therefore he was not the thief.'

### Fallacies of induction

These usually involve some form of 'hasty generalisation'. What may be true in a few cases (which may not be typical cases) is claimed to be true in all or most cases. Alternatively, what tends to be characteristic of some group or population is claimed to apply to some specific case (which, again, may not be at all typical). The fallacy of *hasty generalisation* often involves misuse of statistics.

*Illicit appeal to authority.* This means citing expert evidence from someone unqualified to give it or invoking the prestige of someone who believes the proposition instead of proving the proposition, as in: 'Hi, I'm Kylie. I'm a stunning blonde and I always choose Dulux paint so you should too.' The fact that someone has won a Nobel Prize for chemistry does not make them an expert on economics, and vice versa.

*The 'post hoc' fallacy.* This common fallacy is known by its name in Latin (*post hoc, ergo propter hoc*, meaning 'after this, therefore because of this'). It is the belief or claim that because B came after A in time, B was *caused* by A. In earlier times a crop failure or mouse plague or flood which happened to come shortly after an eclipse of the sun would sometimes be explained as being a result of the eclipse.

## Fallacies of deduction

These involve syllogisms which have the wrong form. In chapter 4 we saw the valid form:

* All the members of the team were upset at losing.   All As are B.
* Mark was a member of the team.                      C is A.
* Therefore Mark was upset at losing.                 Therefore C is B.

Both premises are true and the form is valid, so the conclusion *must* be true.

The invalid form looks like this:

* All the members of the team were upset at losing.   All As are B.
* Wendy was upset at losing.                          C is B.
* Therefore Wendy is a member of the team.            Therefore C is A.

Both premises are true (Wendy was upset because the captain of the team is her boyfriend) but the form is invalid. A logician has only to look at the form as shown on the right-hand side, where letters replace the terms in each proposition, to know that the truth of the premises does not guarantee the truth of the conclusion. In syllogisms with this form the conclusion *might* be true but it doesn't have to be true. You don't have to be a logician who knows that this is called the *fallacy of the undistributed middle term* (which for technical reasons we won't go into here). You can recognise that it is fallacious—as long as you take the time to inspect the argument closely. Commonsense shows that the conclusion does not follow from the premises.

Unfortunately this fallacy easily goes undetected, especially if the argument is not set out in standard form. For example: 'The communists have always wanted the government to resign. Wendy was heard to say resignation would be a "good outcome". Wendy must be a communist.' People in countries around the world have been sentenced to death on the basis of this sort of bad reasoning.

The fallacy can be exposed for what it is by substituting other terms in the A, B and C 'slots'. The argument 'Cats like to be stroked. Wendy likes to be stroked. Therefore Wendy is a cat' is refuted by being 'reduced to absurdity'.

## Informal (or diversionary) fallacies

Many of these relate to shabby debating tactics. Others can result from careless or confused thinking.

*Slanting.* This is selecting or overemphasising evidence that is favourable to your proposition. The tobacco companies, for instance, tend to make much of any scientific opinion or survey which throws doubt on a link between smoking and damage to health.

*Red herring.* This is introducing an irrelevant but exciting or provocative issue which in effect changes the subject and diverts attention. (The name comes from the practice of dragging a herring across the trail to distract hounds following a scent.)

*'Agreement of people' fallacy.* This is the fallacious claim that something is true because most people (now or historically) believe it to be true. As in: 'Everyone knows you can't trust a politician', or 'Human societies have always sensed that there is an afterlife'.

*False dichotomy (the 'either/or fallacy').* This is an illegitimate claim that only two alternatives exist. The middle ground between two extremes is ignored. This is the thinking in 'black and white' we are all prone to at times (some more than others). For example: 'You have questioned the doctrine of the First National Reformed Church. That means you are a wicked atheist', or 'I did not get a place at Tokyo University. My life is ruined'.

*'Arguing to the man'.* This is an irrelevant personal attack on an opponent or an attempt to discredit a proposition by claiming that those who hold it are of dubious reputation. The fact that some disliked group (monarchists, republicans, greenies, farmers, capitalists, communists, teenagers, economists) tend to believe something does not in itself make that thing untrue.

**Barry versus Bev**

To look at argument in action, we can examine a verbal debate between two people. There has been a lot of discussion recently about literacy standards (literacy in this context having the narrow meaning of the ability to read and write effectively). Some people argue that standards have fallen due to new teaching methods used in the teaching of reading and writing. This is Barry's general position in the following dialogue.

Read the dialogue carefully, taking the numbered speeches one at a time. In each speech see if you can spot any fallacies or poor argument strategy. Then read our comments.

1. Barry: I tell you, education is in a bad way. None of the five new typists we hired can write correct English.

2. Bev: If you're trying to tell me that literacy standards have declined, then I think you're talking trash. Don't you know that more young people than ever before are gaining admission to university?

3. Barry: What about the rest, though? Personally I blame the teachers. Most of them are misfits. They went into teaching because they missed out on getting into some other course. How can our kids learn when they are being taught by a bunch of misfits?

4. Bev: Well, even if standards of literacy have fallen a bit, I don't see that teachers are necessarily to blame. They don't have any say in what they teach. It's the education department that decides.

5. Barry: Look, Bev, you're on the losing side with this one. A survey in Saturday's paper showed seven out of ten Australians are worried about literacy standards. It's all fun and games in schools these days—special activities and trips to the zoo. Fancy going to the zoo for an English lesson! I bet it puts the animals off.

6. Bev: Yes, well, there are a lot of excursions and extracurricular activities now. But I could show you timetables which prove that on any given day most time is devoted to teaching. Now, to teach is to 'impart knowledge of or skill in'—look it up in the dictionary.

7. Barry: Parents are at fault too. How can kids do their homework when they watch TV for five or six hours a night? Teachers can't compete with that. This is the whole problem. If they taught them properly and gave them an interest in good books they wouldn't want to watch all that rubbish on TV.

8. Bev: You don't know what you're talking about. A survey done at one of our top private schools last year showed that the standard of literacy in 1997 was exactly the same level as in 1972. And last week an American professor said on the Roy and H.G. Nelson Show that he thought Australian education was first-rate.

9.  Barry: You see, it's the same as what happened in the Soviet Union. The so-called experts thought you could collectivise farms. Everything had to change. And within a decade they couldn't feed themselves. We have to do a U-turn on this. Either we go on with more trendy experiments, or we bring back the good old syllabus, and tried-and-true teaching techniques, including the cane.

10. Bev: Why don't you give the schools some credit? Look at the excellent social skills the students pick up these days. You've got to admit that young people are better adjusted and more mature and self-confident these days.

11. Barry: I suspect you really agree with me, my dear. You are just recycling nonsense you have picked up from those trendy teacher friends of yours. Twenty years ago trendy ideas began infiltrating education. You want to know the result? My house has been burgled by youngsters 15 times in the last year. That's the result!

12. Bev: If you're an example of what they turned out in 'the good old days', then thank goodness things have changed!

## Comments on Barry and Bev

As well as committing logical fallacies, both Barry and Bev fail to observe the protocols of good argument. (We have more to say about good argument practice later.)

1.  Barry is vague; he does not clearly indicate the proposition he wishes to prove. Precisely clarifying the matter to be argued is important at the outset of any argument. Then Barry commits the fallacy of *hasty generalisation*, because five new staff is a very small sample.

2.  Bev begins well. She tries to clarify the issue. To say 'you're talking trash', though, does not help to create a calm, rational atmosphere. She slips into the fallacy of trying to settle an issue by proving the wrong thing. While it is true that more are entering university, this is irrelevant, as entrance standards might also be declining.

3.  Barry switches from what he still has to prove (that standards have fallen) to an argument about why it has happened. He also uses a word in two different senses *(fallacy of equivocation)*. At first, 'misfits' seems to mean those who miss out on their first career preference, but in the last sentence it suggests they are incompetents. People can be good at their job even if they once had some other career preference.

4.  Bev's concession here is quite unnecessary. Barry has proven nothing so far. She should point that out, rather than conceding that he might be right.

5. Barry begins with the *agreement of people fallacy*. A majority of Australians might be worried about the issue, but this doesn't prove they are right to be worried. Barry then switches to another issue ('fun and games'). Nowhere does he overtly identify this as an issue. He is still taking it for granted that standards have fallen and is talking about causes. He has not established that standards have fallen.

6. Bev may be right to concede in her first sentence. But she is then guilty of *equivocation*. She uses the word 'teach' in two distinct senses: (a) formal classroom sessions as opposed to extracurricular activities, and (b) the actual imparting of knowledge. The fact that time is being devoted to (a) doesn't mean that pupils are actually acquiring knowledge and skills. Her use of 'teach' in the second sense could also be regarded as *begging the question*. (Note: dictionary definitions are rarely useful in argument.)

7. Barry should not let Bev get away with her fallacy. What he goes on to say involves the *fallacy of circular argument*. He has said that TV makes school learning impossible. Then he says that there should be a particular kind of school learning (learning to appreciate good books). But by his own argument this could not happen because TV makes learning impossible.

8. *Statistical fallacy*. The survey proves nothing: it is a non-typical school and the sample is too small. Bev then makes an *illicit appeal to authority*, at least unless she tells us a lot more about what makes this American an authority on this specific issue.

9. *Fallacy of false analogy*. The two things compared are much too different for the analogy to have any inductive strength. The last sentence involves *false dichotomy*, as the two extremes are not the only possibilities. The terms 'good old' and 'tried-and-true' involve *begging the question*.

10. *'Red herring' fallacy*. Bev tries to steer the debate towards a quite different issue.

11. Barry is resorting to manipulative tactics. Even if Bev *does* privately agree with him, this does not establish the truth of the point at issue (fallacy of *tu quoque*, or 'you too'). Barry then commits the *genetic fallacy*. Bev may have picked up her ideas from friends, but the origin of an opinion has nothing to do with whether it is true or false. The sentence involves the *post hoc fallacy*.

12. This is *'arguing to the man'*—substituting personal abuse for rational argument.

In the dialogue, both Barry and Bev are quick to make insulting personal comments about one another, yet each ignores the defects in the other's reasoning. Neither really attempts to clarify and examine an issue in a reasoned way. Nothing is achieved except mutual hostility.

## PROPER PROCEDURES FOR ARGUMENT

In chapter 4 we mention that certain conditions are necessary before argument can usefully proceed. There must be:

- a condition of doubt (some things do not need to be resolved by argument, while other things cannot be resolved by argument);
- clarification (making clear exactly what proposition is to be proved or disproved);
- common ground between the parties to the argument (what is already agreed and does not need to be argued);
- commitment to rationality (including willingness to be convinced by superior logic or evidence put forward by one's opponent).

Barry and Bev could have made more progress if they had been prepared to spend some time clarifying what they were going to try to decide by argument. In this preliminary stage it can be useful to work out the assumptions that might lie behind an argument, to frame propositions in an appropriate way (getting rid of emotive, ambiguous or superfluous words), and to agree on definitions.

In a written text the writer has to do this preliminary work in his or her introduction. The main thing is to be clear—to leave no doubt about what it is you want to argue for.

You may also need to explain your assumptions, although there is no space to do so at great length. You can assume that your reader shares your assumptions on matters concerning the general context in which your set topic or precise argument is located. For example, in a biology assignment the theory of evolution could probably be taken for granted as something accepted by the reader, but it would be worth explaining less well-established and widely accepted theories.

In written arguments that depend on research, one of the preliminaries may consist of reviewing the history of the question. An argument about how communication between human beings should best be understood, for instance, might note that this general activity (as distinct from specific aspects of it, such as effective public speaking) has been systematically studied for only a century or so. It might go on to mention some of the main theories that have been applied (the American 'process' approach, the semiotic approach) and then locate the argument in the context of some particular theory or current debate.

## The onus of proof

It is often appropriate to clarify where the onus (or 'burden') of proof lies in an argument. You are probably familiar with the idea that in the Western world someone charged with an offence is 'innocent until proven guilty'. In a justice system where this applies everyone is presumed to be innocent, so it is up to the State to prove that they are not innocent. The person charged does not have to prove that he or she is innocent. The **onus of proof** rests with the State, not the accused.

Usually the onus falls on anyone who wants to put forward a proposition that is not currently accepted by most people (or most experts). Centuries ago, when it was taken for granted that the sun and planets circled the Earth, someone who put forward the 'weird idea' that the sun was the centre could reasonably have been expected to provide good arguments for this. But now that virtually everyone has accepted that the Earth orbits the sun, no-one is under any obligation to prove it. There are a few people around who believe that the Earth is flat, or that the American moon landings were a big hoax (filmed in the Arizona desert by Steven Spielberg). Such people may say things like 'Go on, then, prove that the Earth is round', or 'Prove that humans have landed on the moon', but the onus is on them, not you.

## Issues

Some propositions can be determined to be true or false quite simply. If we want to support our prediction that the next person to walk into the room will probably be right-handed rather than left-handed, we need the single premise that the majority of human beings are right-handed. We would also need to be ready to defend as legitimate our assumption that the next person to enter could be expected to be randomly drawn—in terms of handedness—from the general population. But suppose we wanted to argue that the 2000 Olympics will not benefit Sydney financially. We could resort to an argument by analogy in which our premise might be that the Olympics were a financial disaster for Montreal. This would be pretty weak, though—all kinds of differences apply—and Sydney has had a chance to learn from any mistakes Montreal made.

The proposition that Sydney will not benefit financially is one that relates to a complex set of circumstances. We could hardly expect to be able to prove it with just one premise. To defend the proposition satisfactorily we would need to look at many aspects relating to the economic impact of the Games: the money flowing in directly from ticket sales and media rights, the boost to the city's economy by visitors spending, the possible longer-term improvement in tourism, the foreign investment stimulated by enhanced overseas interest in Sydney, the cost of providing infrastructure, transport and security, possible social problems, the risk of attendance being poor, and so on. Each of these would involve separate arguments.

The outcome of some of these arguments might support the proposition, but others (e.g. those relating to the amount of money earned by selling media rights) might contradict the proposition. So further argument would be needed to show that the negatives outweighed the positives. Some of the subarguments would probably be clearcut—there may already be definite figures for how much money the television rights will bring in. In other cases much less definite predictions might have to be made about trends in interest rates, the amount of overtime wages that will be needed to complete projects on time, the impact of the Asian financial crisis on future foreign investment, and so on. So there might also need to be arguments justifying the inclusion in the overall argument of some rather tentative subarguments. There might be, for instance, arguments defending the arguer's use of some economic theory or model.

We call the different aspects that must be argued about 'the issues'. In the case of a company's decision to buy a new photocopier, there are likely to be a number of different issues involved. The manager might pose a series of questions like this:

- Is the Chipmunk photocopier the cheapest?
- Is there a warranty of at least 12 months?
- Is it simple to operate?
- Can it do double-sided copies automatically?
- Will the supplier service the machine?
- Has it got a good reputation?
- Can at least one ream of paper be loaded?
- Can it do large-size copies?

And the list could go on. We can regard each of these as an issue to be argued about in order to decide whether the proposition that the company should buy the Chipmunk photocopier is to be accepted or rejected. They are all relevant issues. But they are not equally important. The company might regard automatic stapling and choice of ink colour as nice to have but not essential, while it is very important to be able to do A3-size copies. Issues can be major or minor. Some potential issues—such as the colour of the machine—are regarded by the manager in this case as too trivial to warrant attention.

We can go further and say that some issues may be 'necessary' to an extended argument. Suppose the company needs a machine that can do double-sided copies. An employee given the task of making this decision would be very unpopular if he or she neglected to check on whether or not the Chipmunk could do this. Sometimes a single issue is sufficient to resolve an argument. If the company has only $5000 to spend and all brands except one cost more than this, that will end the argument.

Deciding which issues are major and which are minor is an important part of planning an assignment. The evidence you will need to get (i.e. the research you will have to do) needs to be relevant to major issues. It would be a mistake to spend a lot of time getting material that helped you to argue well about minor issues, and have nothing much to back up your arguments on the major issues.

## DEALING WITH THE COUNTER ARGUMENT

In a face-to-face situation you will not be allowed to forget that there is a counterargument. When writing argument remind yourself that there is always, potentially, a counterargument. You have to consider what form the counterargument would take, and decide whether to respond to it. Bev of our dialogue (see p. 67) has only to deal with the counterarguments put forward by Barry. These were easy arguments to deal with (or should have been). However, if Bev was writing an essay defending her position it would not be enough for her to imagine herself arguing against Barry alone. She would have to think what the ideal counterargument would be—the best possible one—and try to deal with that. After all, her reader would be much better informed and more logical (it is to be hoped) than Barry.

While writing an argument, stop every so often and ask yourself what an intelligent opponent would say in response to what you are arguing at present. This will help you avoid being too easily satisfied with your own work. You might realise that some statistical evidence you want to use is out of date and inadequate; perhaps some further research will be necessary.

In extended argument, the counterargument will not necessarily conflict with your argument at every point. In other words, not all issues will be contested. Two people disputing the choice of a new photocopier might agree that the Chipmunk is best for rapid operation, ease of use and optional features, but disagree about its reputation and probable reliability. Or they may disagree about what counts as a major issue. One person might insist that capacity double-sided photocopying is essential, while another sees this as a minor matter and demands that any photocopier considered have variable ink colour.

Extended arguments often involve arguments about which issues are important (or even sufficient). If one person can prove beyond doubt that the company must have double-sided photocopying, this becomes a necessary issue (we still don't know whether a Chipmunk will be chosen, but this will be one of the criteria applied to each brand considered). In the same way, two people disputing the financial impact of the Olympic Games on Sydney might argue about whether certain issues should be regarded as relevant and important. The word 'financial' in the proposition has already excluded some kinds of impact (such as the cultural and environmental impact) as issues to be debated.

## Concession

A responsible arguer will not claim to have a superior argument about every single issue in an extended argument. The kind of salesperson who claims that their product is best in every way is usually naive (or regards the potential customer as naive). The salesperson who is prepared to admit that his or her product has certain shortcomings acquires more credibility and is more likely to be successful. ('Yes, I have to admit that the Chipmunk takes up a lot of floorspace and, yes, it is a bit noisier than the Nashua, but our designers felt it was worth compromising on those aspects to ensure a really fast, yet mechanically rugged machine.') This salesperson has made concessions. He or she has conceded that in some (minor) respects the opposite side has a better case. Being willing to concede shows that you are open to reason. It also shows that you have looked at other points of view, and considered the counterargument.

## Qualification

Occasionally while making an argument you will decide that it is appropriate to qualify some premise, or perhaps even your overall conclusion. That is, you pull back to a more cautious position: for instance, saying 'most' instead of 'all', or 'some' instead of 'most'; or limiting the scope of your claim in some other way ('At least this is the case in this country' or 'This has applied since the late 1970s').

## Refutation

To argue successfully you may also need to show that the counter-argument (or some of the issues it contains) is false. This is refutation. You can refute the counterargument by:

- showing that a premise cannot be accepted as true;
- criticising its logic—showing that individual arguments are inductively weak or invalid;
- pointing out that unfair argument tactics are being used;
- proving that issues critical to the counterargument are irrelevant.

Sometimes you can win an argument simply by refuting the counter-argument. This would be the case if the onus of proof rests with your opponent. If he or she claims to have seen an alien spaceship hovering in the sky last night, and you can demonstrate that the evidence put forward is at best inconclusive, then you have won the argument. It would also be the case if only two alternatives are possible, so that if one is wrong the other must be right. However, this is not always the case. The counterargument (whether made by an actual opponent or made hypothetically by yourself) may be wrong, but so may your argument. The truth might involve some third explanation.

The set topic of an assignment may require you to engage with the counterargument (e.g. 'What are the arguments for and against a flat rate of taxation?'). There may be choice as to whether you support some argument, or treat it as a counterargument ('How does Herzberg explain human motivation? Do you agree with him?'). Otherwise there are no rules about the degree to which you should devote space to discussing the counterargument. It will depend on circumstances.

## ORGANISING ARGUMENTS

We have mentioned that clarification is an important preliminary to argument. It is also important at each stage during the argument. You need to make very clear to the reader just what is being argued at each stage. Argument requires clear signposting. Show that you have finished with one issue and are moving on to a different issue with appropriate language, as in this example:

Thus it is evident that with respect to normal maintenance the Chipmunk is the cheapest photocopier to use. Another issue that must be considered is appearance. This is important because ugly photocopiers are known to cause distress to office staff, leading in some cases to chronic resentment, absenteeism, vomiting and even suicide. How does the Chipmunk rate in terms of appearance? Extremely well!

Note that the 'rhetorical question' at the end is answered. There is no room for ambiguity or vagueness in rational argument. Be prepared to restate and recapitulate. Make it as easy as possible for your readers to pick out your main arguments. Express your premises and conclusions in the kind of sentences that are appropriate to propositions (see chapter 4), and let them stand out from the surrounding mass of detailed factual material which constitutes your evidence.

 To sum up briefly what we have been saying—in an extended argument:

- There will be introductory material where the proposition to be argued is made clear and placed in context, perhaps with some mention of the history of the question and the general direction of the argument indicated.
- Your own starting points and assumptions should be clearly identified. There may be analysis of the assumptions on which the counter-argument rests.
- Different issues will be identified and argued about. There may be arguments to show that certain issues are important, perhaps sufficient. There may be concession that not all the minor issues favour one's own side of the argument. There may be qualification.
- There may be argument that the onus of proof rests with the opposing side.
- There may be refutation of the counterargument, in part or in its entirety.
- There may be arguments or explanations relating to the methods used in gathering supporting evidence.
- There will be an appropriate concluding section, in which you might do some recapitulation, restate the overall proposition that you believe you have proved, and return to the wider context.

There may also be long passages explaining the investigative methods used, and putting the premises in context. Such material may take up more space than the material that is devoted to actual argument.

## ARGUMENT IN CONTEXT

Finally, it is important to remember that there are differences between disciplines. Some disciplines (e.g. chemistry) are empirical. Knowledge in such disciplines is acquired on the basis of observation and experiment. Some of the knowledge relied on in such disciplines, though, consists of theories. A theory is a supposition about what is the case. The theory might be mistaken, and there may be some quite different explanation, hence it is always provisional—otherwise it would be a law rather than a theory. There was a theory that matter consisted of particles called atoms before there was direct evidence of their existence. In empirical disciplines a hypothesis is a prediction, based on a theory, which can be tested experimentally. It is much more limited in scope than a theory.

Other disciplines (e.g. cultural studies) are more speculative or conjectural. They are prepared to discuss ideas that are impossible to observe directly or prove by experiment. Their theories often involve cultural activities and relationships and meanings rather than physical objects. They accept as reasonable starting points for argument ideas or propositions that more empirical disciplines would reject as unverifiable. Freud's notion that much human behaviour is determined by unconscious motives is an example. Although Karl Marx is now seen to have been far less objectively 'scientific' than he thought he was, and although many of his specific ideas have led nowhere, his emphasis on the significance of economic considerations opened up ways of thinking about human experience that have been useful and influential in many disciplines.

To take another example, geography is often empirical, as when dealing with climate and geological factors (physical geography). But cultural geographers who want to explain why human beings build environments consisting of skyscrapers, shopping malls and theme parks have to be more speculative. The fact that a discipline is relatively 'speculative' does not mean that it does not proceed rationally. In a film studies subject, for example, a rational argument can be constructed based on evidence. The evidence is not derived from a laboratory experiment but from careful textual analysis of relevant films. There may be certain regularities and recurrences of themes and images. This textual analysis must be related to some theory that makes sense of it.

Your arguments will vary somewhat according to the discipline involved. You will become familiar with the kinds of assumptions that are expected or allowed, and the sort of evidence that is appropriate. The scholarly articles published in relevant journals usually provide a general guide to what is appropriate in the discipline, though they are likely to be much more specialised and dense than anything an undergraduate would be expected to write.

Unless you are told otherwise, you should assume that every essay or oral presentation is essentially an argument. It should set out to defend rationally a particular point of view—that is, to show that a proposition is or is not true (or is probably true). It should make its purpose clear in the ways that we have discussed. It does not matter that it is a viewpoint shared by many or most other people who have thought about the topic. It is still your argument. Others may have come to a similar conclusion, but you are putting together your own extended argument to support it.

## CONCLUSION

In this chapter we have looked at:

- logical fallacies (bad argument); and
- the proper procedures for conducting argument.

Logical arguments are one way of dealing with ideas and facts. Another way often used in academic contexts (and often combined with argument) is exposition, which is the subject of chapter 6.

### Activity

Find a short letter to the editor that contains an argument (see 'Identifying argument' in chapter 4). Put the argument in standard form. Evaluate the argument. Is it clear? Are there any fallacies or violations of good argument practice?

## chapter 6

# Dealing with ideas: exposition

Here our focus is on 'exposition', another way of working with ideas commonly used in universities. **Exposition** has a different purpose from argument—it aims to inform or explain. You tell your reader or listener about something (e.g. ancient Rome, cancer, the theory of evolution, the cause of a downturn in the economy) to give them a better understanding of it. You are not asking them to agree with a particular proposition.

But argument and exposition are often found together, and can even merge. The person talking about the economy may go beyond simply surveying possible reasons for the downturn—he or she might suggest what they think the main reason is. Similarly, a long argument will include passages of exposition. For instance, in the course of arguing that smoking causes cancer, the arguer may include some explanation of the nature of cancer.

There are two other types of writing which are common outside academic contexts but are occasionally found within them: **description** and **narration**. These sometimes get confused with exposition. Description means telling your reader/listener what something looks like (or sounds, tastes, smells like). We encounter this in advertising and travel journalism. Narration means relating a sequence of events in time—that is, telling a story (whether factual or fictional). Be careful not to use these kinds of writing when you should be engaging in exposition. If you have been asked to analyse the causes of the 1987 stockmarket crash, for instance, you should not get caught up in narrating the events of the time (first this happened on Wall Street, then this happened in Paris, the next morning this happened at Tokyo, and so on): a mere 'chronology of events' does not constitute an analysis.

## EXPOSITION TECHNIQUES

The main techniques used in exposition are:

- classification;
- definition;
- illustration;
- comparison and contrast; and
- analysis.

### Classification

This kind of exposition involves putting things in categories or classes. Suppose we are interested in the vehicles humans use to travel in. We could classify them according to how they are powered (Figure 1): by gravity (bobsleds); by wind (sailing boats); by animal power (cart, coach); human effort (bicycle, canoe, wheelchair); steam (some trains, some ships); petrol (motorcycles, cars, trucks, buses, aircraft); electricity (some trains, some cars, trams). Such a classification might be quite useful

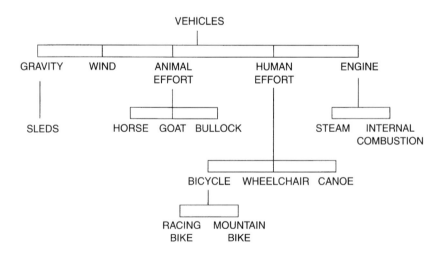

**Figure 1** Vehicles classified according to their source of power. (Not all members of classes are shown.)

because it focuses our attention on the question of power source, and other aspects of the vehicles, which might otherwise have distracted us, stay in the background. We can notice similarities that might otherwise have escaped us (e.g. a bicycle and canoe can be seen to have something in common—both are propelled by human effort). We notice that one class (the petrol-powered vehicles) is by far the biggest. This makes us aware of the dependence of humans on oil resources for their transport needs.

Classification can also make us aware of useful distinctions. To consider another classification, the sociologist Max Weber suggested that there were three types (or sources) of authority in human political affairs. These were:

- charismatic authority, where a leader is believed to have exceptional qualities and is therefore obeyed;
- traditional authority, where authority comes from a belief in the rightness of established customs and traditions;
- rational–legal authority, where authority is based on the acceptance of a set of rules or laws.

By making these distinctions we can better understand authority as it operates in the world. We can see more clearly how political systems differ from one another. A particular political situation may be more complex than we thought and involve a mixture of all three kinds of authority.

To return to our classification of vehicles, note that (like Weber's) it is a simple one. There are some issues it does not touch on. If we are interested in the kinds of animals used to move vehicles, we would need to divide the animal power class into a range of subclasses: horse, ox, donkey, goat, dog, and whatever other animals have been used. Going in the other direction, we could say that the whole group of vehicles is just one class among many in the category 'machines'.

Classification shows two important intellectual processes. If we talk about classes, rather than individuals, we are generalising. Thus we talk in general about bears—all the creatures belonging to this category. We concentrate on what they have in common (they all have fur, they all hibernate) rather than their differences (e.g. size, aggressiveness, habitat). Or we might go further and talk about animals, grouping together lions, pigs, impalas, yaks and rabbits. It can be useful to generalise, but it is worth remembering that in doing so we are ignoring individual distinctiveness.

**Some important points to remember about classification**

- People, things and concepts can be classified in an infinite number of ways.
- There must be a single, consistent classifying principle. (It would be absurd to divide your fellow students up as follows: these four students are Korean, these three have pet ducks, these two eat sausages, these three love to play tennis, these four are studying journalism.)
- The classifying principle is arbitrary, and is imposed by whoever does the classifying. It may be useful in some way, or it may be trivial. Also, the fact that a person can be placed in a category on the basis of one thing (e.g. musical ability or shoe size) does not mean that they share other attributes (three people who play the piano won't all necessarily like eating spinach). Classifying sometimes says more about the classifier than about the persons who are classified. An example of specious (or false) classification was the attempt of some 19th-century European scientists to divide the human species into distinct races.
- Classifications are often hierarchical—that is, they start at the top and work their way down. We can classify drinks available at a bar, for instance, first into the two main divisions of alcoholic and soft, and then break each of these into more specific groupings (alcoholic into wine, beer, spirits) which get more specific as we go further down (Heineken beer sold in a stubby); see Figure 2.

In classifying we are often engaged in a process of *abstraction*. From the complex total actuality of a conveyance such as a bus we have separated out (abstracted) one element: what makes it move. We can then talk about motive power *in the abstract*—that is, without reference to any particular vehicle (though we may occasionally have a mental image of a tram or bobsled). Look again at the Max Weber classification of authority. Weber talks about authority as an abstraction. He leaves actual human beings out of the picture. He does not discuss the concept 'authority' in terms of particular times, places and people because he wants to understand authority *as such* and not have it confused with other issues. (Later, once he has explained the concept, he may provide examples from real life.) Dealing in abstractions is one of the challenges of university study.

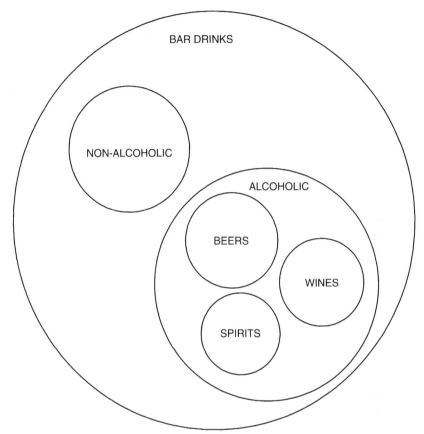

**Figure 2**  Classification of drinks sold in bars. Diagrams of this kind are a useful way to understand the relationships between classes.

## Definition

This kind of exposition is easy to understand because it follows naturally from what we know about groups of things. When we define something we:

- put it in some appropriate group or category; and
- show what makes it different from the other members of that group.

Defining literally means setting limits—marking off the characteristics that belong only to the thing being defined. What we define is normally

a class, not an individual thing. The class of beers we have defined can of course contain various subclasses (e.g. different kinds of beer).

In the definition of a flute provided by the *Concise Oxford Dictionary*:

| | |
|---|---|
| A flute | [thing to be defined] |
| is a musical wind-instrument, | [general characteristics—its class] |
| being a long wooden pipe with | [qualities which make it different |
| holes along it stopped by fingers | from other items in this class] |
| or keys, & blow-hole in side near | |
| upper end . . . | |

Note, though, that there may be no single, fixed, agreed **definition** of something. There is also the difference that must be understood between a definition of a thing and a definition of a word. Dictionaries define words. They tell you what most people in some language community (e.g. American speakers of English) accept as the ordinary meaning of a word at some point in time. But the meanings of words shift, and a single word is called on to do different jobs. Think of the name 'Europe'. In some uses 'Europe' is meant to include Great Britain; in other contexts it excludes that country (because some of the British consider themselves different from 'Europeans' such as French and Germans).

Definitions in dictionaries are brief, but definitions as a way of explaining something can go on for pages. We call this *extended definition*. In this kind of exposition, most of the space is devoted to explaining the characteristics that make the thing different from others in its class.

One kind of definition is called *stipulative definition*. The writer or speaker stipulates what a term shall mean for present purposes. This is often preferable to using some definition from an ordinary dictionary which is inadequate to the use of the word in a specialised academic sense. For instance, you might say: 'By "the Asia–Pacific region" I mean here . . .'; on some other occasion you might use that term differently.

## Illustration

**Illustration** is probably the commonest kind of exposition. It means explaining some idea or thing by presenting an example. If I am giving a lecture on the power of volcanoes, it will help to refer to one or more actual examples of volcanic eruptions. I might talk about the eruption of Vesuvius that destroyed Pompei in ancient Italy, or show photographs of more recent disasters. I might hand around a piece of lava, so that my audience could see and touch it. In the present debate about Australia becoming a republic, people on both sides of the argument often give examples of how things are done in existing republics, such as Ireland or the United States, in order to suggest what Australia could copy or avoid.

Illustration is the opposite of classifying or categorising. Instead of generalising and dealing in abstractions, we show the reader or listener an individual case. It is as if we have reached in and picked an item out of the class. Instead of continuing to talk about the idea of 'authority', we could refer to a ruler in an actual country (President Clinton in the United States) to convey the idea more clearly. Illustration is a way of returning to the particular and everyday.

Sometimes illustration is brief, with just a few words inserted in a sentence:[1]

> When recently hatched birds such as ducklings are hand-reared for a few days, they strongly prefer the company of their human keeper to that of their own species.

Often the general principle or idea to be explained (the proposition) is stated in a sentence or two at the beginning, with the rest of the paragraph devoted to illustration. The following example is from a book about life in the 14th century,[2] when people knew much less about the world than they do now:

> For [people in Europe in the Middle Ages] the earth and its phenomena were full of mysteries: What happens to fire when it goes out? Why are there different colors of skin among men? Why do the sun's rays darken a man's skin but bleach white linen? How can the earth, which is weighty, be suspended in air? How do souls make their way to the next world? Where lies the soul? What causes madness? Medieval people felt surrounded by puzzles, yet because God was there they were willing to acknowledge that causes are hidden, that man cannot know why all things are as they are; they are as God pleases.

Note how, after providing examples of questions for which the 14th century had no answers, the writer restates the basic idea by using the word 'puzzles'.

Sometimes illustration can go on for page after page. When you are reading, be alert to the signpost words and phrases that indicate that the author is using illustration. There are words like 'for example', 'for instance', 'such as', 'this can be illustrated by'. Use these signposts in your own writing.

---

### A few more points about illustration

- Make sure you explain the principle that is being illustrated. Do not rely on examples only.
- Don't let the example take over. This sometimes happens when the example is a story. The speaker or writer can become more interested in telling the story than explaining ideas.
- An example should be a good example—that is, typical of the group of things it is being used to illustrate (schnapps would be a poor example of a drink in the Australian context). The point of using an example, often, is to bring in something familiar.
- Don't use illustration unless it is needed. You will be wasting space.
- Use several examples from the group if there are significant differences between them.

---

## Comparison and contrast

Exposition often involves **comparison** or **contrast**, or both. Usually something that is unfamiliar is explained by relating it to something that is well known. We show how it resembles, or differs from, the familiar thing.

Sometimes assignment topics will direct you to use comparison or contrast. Even if there is no such requirement, it can be a useful strategy. A whole essay can be structured around some systematic comparison or contrast. Even if the final essay doesn't do much comparing or contrasting, you might use the strategy for exploring the subject yourself at the research stage. If you are going to have to write about the Kodiak bear, you can begin to understand it by thinking about how it differs from the grizzly, if the grizzly bear is something you already know about.

A procedure of comparison, however, makes sense only if the two things compared are different enough in some respects to make it interesting to note what they have in common. It might not achieve much to compare Sydney and Melbourne, as you would expect these two Australian cities to be very similar. If you were able to establish significant parallels between Melbourne and Moscow you would be doing something more worthwhile. Similarly, there is no point in contrasting two things unless they have at least one thing in common. We already know that a psychologist is different from a giraffe, or even from an accountant, but we may not know how a psychologist differs from a psychiatrist or a social worker.

We could put this in terms of classes. In comparison we are finding reasons for putting two things (which would normally be placed in different classes) together in the same class. In contrast we are showing that two things, even though they belong to the same general class, need to be placed in separate classes in terms of certain characteristics (ordinary beer and light beer may look and taste much the same but differ significantly in alcoholic content).

A special kind of comparison is **analogy**. An analogy is a striking or unexpected comparison which appeals to the imagination. The term is also used for the kind of inductive argument that relies on drawing a conclusion about something because it is similar to some other thing.

## Analysis

**Analysis** involves explaining something by considering its parts—that is, by looking at what it consists of. The thing could be an event, a process, a mental state, a physical object, an idea. In some cases the term becomes interchangeable with classification.

Analysis is not always merely a matter of explaining or listing the parts of something. In some contexts the term is used to refer to the process of bringing out the meaning or significance of something, or showing how it works. If we are asked to analyse a book or film we are normally expected to point out its meanings and how they are produced, and not simply to identify all the characters and list the separate scenes.

An important kind of analysis is *causal analysis* (sometimes referred to as cause-and-effect). Here is an example from a discussion of the evolution of the modern horse:[3]

> As horses got larger their faces grew long, again because of their new food. In the forests the short-faced ur-horses (small ancestors of the horse) ate with their heads raised, alert for danger as they browsed the leaves that screened them. But on the steppes, the ur-horses' larger descendants ate in full view with the heads down and their eyes buried in grass, making it easy for predators to sneak up on them. But as horses' faces lengthened, their eyes rose above the grass so they could watch for danger while grazing.

In another example of cause-and-effect, from a book about ancient Rome:[4]

> The Roman houses, moreover, caught fire as frequently as the houses of Stamboul under the Sultans. This was because, in the first place, they were insubstantial; further, the weight of their floors involved the introduction of massive wooden beams, and the movable stoves which heated them, the candles, the smoky lamps, and the torches which lighted them at night involved perpetual risk of fire; and finally, as we shall see, water was issued to the various stories with a grudging hand. All these reasons combined to increase both the number of fires and the rapidity with which they spread.

It is worth noting how this is organised. The author separates out the different reasons with words and phrases like 'in the first place' and 'further'. He uses the words 'fire' or 'fires' three times, not just one, to ensure that the reader is clear about what effect follows from the causes, and he distinguishes two kinds of effect, referring to both 'number' and 'rapidity'.

The signposts writers use when explaining cause-and-effect include:

- consequently (therefore);
- as a result (is caused by);
- determines (leads to);
- results in (produces);
- because (this is why).

Causal analysis requires you to have a good understanding of the thing you are attempting to explain. Some complex events have several contributing causes, not just one. And the fact that one event occurred after another does not mean it was *caused* by the first event.

## TWO OTHER KINDS OF EXPOSITION

Less important as thinking procedures but worth mentioning, these may be the main structuring principle for a whole paragraph, although probably not for anything longer.

**Restatement** means repeating the same basic idea, although in different words, or perhaps from a different point of view. We again go to Rome for an example:[5]

> The conditions under which the Roman man worked recall the most advanced Western practices of today. The Romans were wide awake and well organised and not overwhelmed by their tasks. They were not wholly

absorbed in work. They had learned to compress it within limits which were strictly observed.

Note how every sentence here continues to make what is essentially the same point.

Restatement should not be confused with repetition. Use it only if it helps your reader or listener to understand what you are trying to say. Repeating words and ideas simply to fill up space will work against you.

**Qualification** occurs when a proposition is followed by sentences that set limits on what has been said. These may refer to exceptions to the rule, or in some way caution the reader about the truth of the idea. Consider this example:

> The ancient Romans, then, enjoyed a lifestyle we can envy. Of course, life was less pleasant for women and children, cats, geese, and the poor. It is worth bearing in mind that most of what we know about life in Rome derives from the writings of the privileged, educated class. A significant proportion of the population were slaves. In the last few centuries of the Empire life became increasingly uncertain, especially for those in border regions.

Sometimes students make good points in their assignments but fail to develop them. After one or two sentences setting out the idea they move on to another. Good academic communication involves exploring ideas thoroughly and explaining them in detail. Readers must get the point and know they have got the point, not be left wondering whether they have guessed correctly. You should also remember that, although a sustained piece of writing may be characterised by one or other of the techniques we have looked at, they are often mixed. An expository paragraph, for example, may begin by stating a proposition (an idea, a main point), follow it with some restatement, and then provide an example, before moving on to some causal analysis.

## CONCLUSION

In this chapter we have looked at the way in which exposition differs from other modes of writing, and have explained the main techniques of exposition. Being aware of these will help you to communicate your ideas. And, as these are also techniques for thinking about concepts, it will help you to find things to say in the first place.

## Activities

1. Choose one of the following and do a classification:

   My time-wasting activities     Neighbours
   Sports     TV programs
   Morning noises     Simple pleasures

2. Write an extended definition of one of the following:

   Action movies     Techno music
   Monarchy     Desks
   Any sport     Tourists

3. Choose any of the topics in the previous two activities. Write a few paragraphs on an aspect of the topic using cause-and-effect analysis. Also use some illustration.

4. Write a few paragraphs that explain any of the topics in the first two activities by comparing and/or contrasting them with whatever seems appropriate.

5. Find a magazine article or passage from a book. Try to identify the main kind of exposition involved. Locate the signpost words relevant to the expository mode being used. Repeat this exercise with other passages until you have closely studied examples of each kind of expository writing.

# part III

# LEARNING STRATEGIES

# chapter 7

# Effective reading

Among the most important of all academic communication skills, **reading skills** entail the ability to use printed resources effectively, not just the ability to understand written language.

There are two ways in which your reading might need improvement. First, you may not read as efficiently as you could (you may take longer than you need to). Second, you may not 'take in' what you read very well (i.e. you don't fully absorb or understand or remember it). The two problems are interrelated. If you are having trouble understanding an academic text, this will slow you down and perhaps demoralise you. On the other hand, if it is important to understand the material fully, enough time must be given to the task to allow for this. It does not make sense to save time merely in the interest of efficiency.

Sometimes, however, the time spent and the information absorbed have different priorities. We may, quite reasonably, decide to trade off 'taking in every detail' against 'not wasting too much time'. This happens when we scan a newspaper so quickly that very little 'sinks in'. Someone asks 'Anything in the paper today?', to which we respond 'No, nothing much, just the usual Kodiak bear stories'. Little has been absorbed, but we have used our time efficiently, quickly working out that there was nothing in today's paper of any real interest to us.

What we did, in dealing with the newspaper so efficiently, was to use a perfectly appropriate strategy, in this case one involving rapid scanning. Without thinking about it consciously, we used a certain kind of reading behaviour. This strategy has been learned over years of becoming more and more familiar with newspapers. Only someone skilled in knowing what to look for and how to interpret various cues—headlines, photo captions, and so on—could have done this. Part of the strategy involves relating the contents of the paper to a wider context: for instance, connecting a headline in the paper with something you already know about from the television news, which allows you to skip that item.

Using strategies is the key to effective reading. Usually a technique that improves your comprehension also helps with efficiency. This applies even to strategies that are time-consuming. In the long run it is worth investing extra time in using a strategy that helps you understand a text, rather than returning to that text again and again because you still don't understand it.

One of the main problems that students, especially beginner students, have with reading is the anxiety that they will not be able to remember what they have read. If this sounds like you, calm down. No-one expects you to remember every word and every detail. What matters is that you begin to get a 'feel' for the concepts. Understanding is built up over a period as you read the text again, or read other texts, listen to lectures, and so on. University education is not a matter of 'parrot-fashion learning'.

Although reading is an important basic skill, reading behaviour is difficult to change because:

- people take their ability to read for granted, and don't accept that they need to do anything differently; and
- people pick up unconscious reading habits.

You already use some strategies (such as scanning a newspaper) without realising it. Other strategies can work for you too, but you will need to learn them and consciously apply them.

## FOUR FUNDAMENTAL PRINCIPLES

Four principles are fundamental to improving reading.

### Components

Writing consists of words combined together to form whole sentences. Sentences are combined into paragraphs, paragraphs into sections of chapters, sections into whole chapters, and so on.

The ideas in the text are also built up from smaller parts. Certain facts are stated as the premises of arguments, and certain conclusions are drawn.

Individual arguments are combined into extended arguments. Background material and further speculations, examples or predictions are added.

Sometimes we need to move from the parts to the whole. There are weak readers, who can understand each word in a sentence but have trouble understanding what the sentence as a whole means. Even quite good readers can become bogged down among the individual words when reading difficult material. Or they may be too distracted (or overwhelmed) by the complex details in paragraphs to work out which is the main idea—not seeing the wood for the trees. Good writers do what they can to help: they use signpost words and phrases (e.g. 'similarly', 'on the other hand', 'in conclusion'). They clearly state, and restate, key ideas. You should be alert to the different methods the author has used to make things clear.

### Context

Reading is made meaningful by context. The newspaper reader makes sense of a headline like 'Suspended Bronco to Miss State of Origin' in terms of its being in the sports section of the paper and through a knowledge of Rugby League football—what we have called cultural literacy. We also make sense of words in terms of their sentences. The words in this headline could have other meanings: a 'suspended bronco' could be a horse dangling from a rope, and there is nothing in the words 'state of origin' that would suggest a football match to an American or British speaker of English (it could refer to the winner of a beauty contest—'Miss State of Origin').

The other words in a sentence provide clues to the meaning of an unknown word. These sentences, in turn, exist in the context of some unfolding story or discussion, which provides further clues. Part of being a good reader is to be prepared to relate what you are reading to some context (other books you have read, lectures you have attended). It is a mistake to read a text in isolation. The more 'cultural literacy' you are able to bring to bear on a passage of writing, the better you will be able to understand it.

### Purpose

Reading should have a clear purpose. If you have a definite idea of your purpose, you can choose an appropriate strategy to achieve that purpose. You need to keep in mind the relationship between your reading and your purpose. You have to think about what you are doing, and why.

## Choice of material

Perhaps the best way of reading more efficiently is to avoid spending time reading unnecessarily. This is not to say you should be doing as little reading as possible: university study is all about reading. Undergraduates should be soaking up all kinds of things from printed sources, not just those they are obliged to read. However, you must have a clear sense of priorities. There is never as much research time as you would like, and your reading must be disciplined and selective if you want to get the best return on the time invested. It is easy to spend a lot of time on a book—or on the Internet—that will contribute very little of value.

Choosing what to read involves both evaluating likely resources and locating useful information in the text. Before committing our time to reading something, we should devote a few minutes to determining what it can do for us. A quick browse through the book can pay off. Suppose you have to write an essay on *Terminator 2* in a science fiction film subject. A book that doesn't even mention this film but includes a good discussion of the genre of science fiction, and analysis of similar films, could help you to write on *Terminator 2*.

 **Things to consider when choosing a text**

- How much relevant material does it contain? Use the contents page and the index to determine this.
- What is its purpose? Does the text provide a new angle on the subject, or a comprehensive treatment of all the main theories and approaches? Is it aimed at the expert or non-expert reader? The preface of the book will probably explain why the book was written, and for whom. Sometimes the introduction does this.
- How easy will it be to read? Are there lots of short paragraphs, subheadings, summaries, and a glossary to explain unfamiliar words? Read a paragraph or two to get an idea of the style. A dense and difficult book with few 'reader-friendly' features will be slow-going.
- Is the theoretical approach appropriate? The date of publication will tell you if the book or article is up to date or not. You could also do a quick check of the bibliography and index. If there is no mention of authors and concepts that you know are important to the assignment topic, you may decide that the book won't have much to offer. A quick look at any introductory material may be worthwhile as well.
- Are there illustrations and/or other graphics that may be useful to you?

There is no obvious right or wrong book or article to use. It depends on what you need. The main thing is to evaluate a resource first.

## GENERAL STRATEGIES

There are four basic reading strategies. You have probably used each of them, without giving it much conscious thought, to suit various purposes you had:

### Scanning

This means moving your eyes quickly over a text to find something, or to see whether it contains anything you want to read.

### Skimming

This means moving very quickly through the whole passage or text to get a general sense of what it is about. You read as little as you can, while still picking up some idea of what is being discussed. Read any subheadings and a couple of sentences from each paragraph. Paragraphs often have a topic sentence which contains the main idea. It usually comes fairly early on, although it is sometimes at the end. One method is to read just the first and last sentence of each paragraph. Alternatively, you could go a bit further into each paragraph, looking for the topic sentence but being ready to skip ahead at any moment. All you want, usually, are the main ideas of the paragraph. You should skip over any material which develops, further explains, qualifies or illustrates, or provides evidence for the main idea. You don't want to read examples, so you should be alert to signpost words that introduce examples ('for example', 'for instance', 'such as'). Skip any qualifications ('but on the other hand') or comparisons ('similarly').

### Key reading

This means scanning or skimming most of a text but reading relevant passages or paragraphs carefully and in full. Alternatively, you might locate them by using the index.

### Reading in full

Sometimes this is necessary. With some material unless you work your way through the ideas in the order in which the author has arranged them, and take in the examples or other explanatory material provided, proper understanding will be difficult.

## Reading speed

There are books (and occasionally short courses) which claim to be able to improve your reading speed, perhaps by a factor of three or four. But there are no magic solutions. Becoming a faster reader involves:

- being selective in the way described above, so that you speed up whenever and however it is possible to do so—that is, you learn to be alert to opportunities for missing out or skimming some of the material;
- speeding up the rate at which your eyes move through a page of text. This involves reducing the number of side-to-side eye movements. You practise limiting your vision to the centre of the page, taking in a whole line at once.

Techniques aimed at increasing speed can help you to overcome the bad habits that are slowing you down. These include regression (the tendency to keep glancing back at what has already been read, often because you're anxious about failing to understand or remember), and subvocalisation (the tendency to read aloud, even if so quietly as to be inaudible to others). However, it is unrealistic to expect that reading can always be fast. The main thing is to move fast when you can.

## MAKING SENSE OF A PARAGRAPH

There is a difference between 'reading for understanding' and 'reading to find' (ideas and information). The former occurs when we need to absorb the full meaning of what an author is saying; the latter when we are already familiar with the subject, and need only to get a bit of further evidence from a few paragraphs in a text.

The main topic or central idea of a paragraph is often expressed in a topic sentence. This usually comes early in the paragraph. If you look at paragraph 2 in Appendix 1, you can see that it has a definite and obvious topic sentence—the first sentence.

Now look at paragraph 1. Does it have a topic sentence? Not really. The sentence which contains the words 'interest group' in bold type provides a definition of this term, and is the most important sentence. Interest groups turn out to be the general topic of the next five paragraphs. However, paragraph 1 also involves an explanation of why there are such things. It begins by setting up a contrast between the United States and Australian parliamentary systems, to demonstrate that American politicians are less bound by the political party they belong to. It goes on to show that an outcome of this relative freedom is organised efforts by interest groups to influence the way politicians vote. There is no quick and easy way to pick up the core content of such a paragraph.

Below are some hints on how to work out the meaning of a paragraph. For an example to work with, we can use paragraph 5 of Appendix 1 (though it isn't in fact a difficult paragraph).[1]

*Step 1.* Ask who or what the paragraph is about. You can work this out by identifying key terms. The words that help you identify the content of paragraph 5 are terms like 'political sociologists', 'interest groups', 'democracy', 'Congress', 'unorganized citizens', 'shoreline pollution', 'child abuse'. But how do you know whether this paragraph is not really about political sociologists or shoreline pollution? How do you know that 'interest groups' is the important term? First of all you can make use of the idea of context: if you are not reading the paragraph in complete isolation, if you already know that it belongs to a section of a chapter discussing interest groups, you already have a lot to go on. Another clue is repetition: the term 'interest groups' (or 'these groups') occurs five times in the paragraph, the other contenders only once.

*Step 2.* Ask what aspect of the thing the paragraph is about. You know it is about interest groups, but what particular characteristic(s) or effect(s) of interest groups is under discussion? The first sentence tells you that it is the activities of interest groups that are being considered. This idea of 'activity' is picked up in the paragraph by words such as 'operating' and 'win favours'.

*Step 3.* Ask what you are being asked to believe or understand about this aspect of the thing. An author will do more than concentrate on one aspect of the thing discussed. The author will make some point about it, raise some question, assert some proposition. Be on the look out for sentences that do this. The first sentence is a good example: it points you clearly to the problem to be addressed by indicating that opinion is divided. The opposed terms 'beneficial or harmful' in the first sentence organise what is to follow. The rest of the paragraph goes on to address each of these (in reverse order). Looking for signpost words and phrases can help you to work out what an author is trying to get across. These are the words that organise and connect ideas and facts ('on the one hand', 'thus', 'also', 'on the other hand', 'furthermore', 'for example').

---

If the meaning of a paragraph is not immediately obvious, you should ask:

- Who or what is the paragraph about (what is the general topic)?
- What particular aspect of this topic is it about?
- What are we being asked to believe or understand about it?

To answer these questions we can:

- relate the paragraph to its context;
- look for key content words;
- look for repetition of such words;
- look for signpost words and phrases;
- look for sentences that express general principles or raise issues.

---

## READING AS A THREE-STAGE PROCESS

Now, let's put it all together. You have a long chapter or article to read. How do you go about it? We suggest that you look at reading as a three-stage process:

- First stage—what you do before reading in full.
- Second stage—reading the text, or a section of it, in full.
- Third stage—what you do after reading in full.

Exactly what you do in each stage will depend on your purpose and the difficulty of the text. The main thing is to stick to the three stages.

In the *first stage* you think about your needs, use your prior knowledge, and decide what you want from the text (book or article) to be read. You could begin by making a list (mental or quickly jotted down) of questions you want answered. If you were researching Australian history and wanted to know about Australia's first European immigrants, the convicts, you might jot down questions like: Were they really bad criminals? Were there any women prisoners or just men? How long were they kept as prisoners? Did they go back to Britain when freed or stay in Australia? Are most Australians descended from these convicts and their guards?

Most of these are questions that can be answered by facts. There are historical records that you can check. But you might have other questions which facts will not answer, such as: Were convicts a significant factor in the economic development of the new colony? Did Australia's convict origins influence the kind of society that developed? Make use of any questions like this provided in textbooks and study guides.

Instead of asking questions, you can review what you know—draw on general knowledge, other texts you have read, and lectures and tutorials in the subject. Concentrate on main ideas rather than specific details. Draw a simple concept map, or jot down the answers to Who? When? What? Why? questions. It doesn't matter that there might be a lot of gaps in your existing knowledge. The important thing is that you are bringing to the 'front of your mind' whatever existing knowledge you have. The new knowledge in the text you are about to read then has something to attach itself to.

Before reading in full, inspect or preview the text to be read. Read the introduction and conclusion. Make use of any previews, summaries and abstracts, and take note of any section headings and subheadings. Skim through paragraphs, and have a quick look at illustrations, diagrams and graphs. If the material is difficult, reread the introduction.

Most of our childhood reading involved stories where it made sense to begin at the beginning, and let the narrative unfold. This is how most people prefer to read novels (though there are those who skip ahead to the end of a detective or mystery story because they are impatient to know the outcome). In academic reading it helps to survey the ground in advance.

At Taronga Park Zoo in Sydney you can look down from a high position and get an idea of the whole terrain: monkeys here and kangaroos there, giraffes down there, tapirs hidden away, and elephants over that way. You can see in advance where you will be going, and what to expect. You get some idea of the way the various parts of the zoo relate to one another. You see where it all ends. Some zoo visitors, on the other hand, might be just as happy not to have a preview of what is to come—to let each bend in the path bring its own surprise.

Once you have previewed the text, you could subdivide the material (unless it is already reasonably short). Making use of existing divisions and subheadings in the text, divide it into smaller units for reading in full. How many subdivisions you make will depend on the length and difficulty of the material.

You could also make predictions. Think about what seem to be the main point(s) or overall argument of the text. On the basis of what you now know about the text (or the section of it you are going to begin with), ask yourself some questions, and/or make some predictions, about what you will find in the text. If there is a subheading 'Crimes for which convicts were transported', you may predict that these were mainly murder, rape and armed robbery. It doesn't matter if your predictions turn out to be wrong (in this example you would be wrong); the point is that having made a prediction, you will be interested to see whether or not it is confirmed. You will therefore find what the text has to say more meaningful and probably remember it better.

With the *second stage*, some of our advice may sound contradictory. This is because different readers have different bad habits they need to overcome, and because texts and purposes can differ.

- Be alert to the main or central idea in a paragraph. Examples may be provided that help to explain these, but look out for propositions expressing general principles.
- Keep moving forward. Read the whole paragraph before pausing. Don't be anxious about taking everything in—you can read it again later. Don't worry if you cannot seem to identify the main ideas. This can be difficult on a first reading.
- Don't start making detailed notes; you can do this later. If you make notes now you will waste time writing down material that is not essential. When you have read everything in full you will have a much better feel for what is essential and what is not.

Taking notes prematurely is often merely a way of coping with the anxiety you are feeling because the text is difficult to understand. Try not to let unfamiliar words slow you down. There is a good chance that you will pick up the main meaning by the end of the paragraph or the end of the page, even if there are words you don't understand. If you start hesitating at every difficult word you will never get to the end. Now is not the time to be looking up dictionaries. If you are fairly sure that a particular word will keep recurring and is important to know, then make a dot with a soft pencil in the margin opposite the word whenever you come to it and look it up later. After you have come across it a few times its meaning may become clear, and there will be no need to look it up. When you think you have identified the answer to one of the questions you posed at the outset, or something you think is especially important, mark it, but keep going.

Note that you must not leave any marks in library books. If you own the book or are working with a photocopied text you have more scope for marginal notations, preferably using a soft pencil you can easily erase. Occasionally scribbling something down in the margin is a good way of reading actively. Talk back at the text a bit. You might jot down comments like: 'interesting point'; 'wicked'; 'differs from what Jones says'; 'don't get this at all'. Put a mark against anything you are sure you will want to come back to. But avoid a lot of underlining—especially the use of fluorescent highlighters. We suggest that you do not have a highlighter in your hand for the first reading. There is a strong temptation to use it—and this usually means overusing it. It is often difficult to decide on the first reading precisely what constitutes the main idea, which might deserve to be marked. You mark one sentence. Then you mark the next because it seems important too. And so it goes on until most of the page is bright yellow or pink—quite defeating the purpose. Look at graphics such as maps and diagrams if the text has them. You may be in the habit of reading around them, but they can help you to grasp concepts.

When you get to the *third stage*, you have finished reading in full. But that doesn't mean you have yet got the full benefit of the text. A little time spent reflecting on what you have read is useful. Now is the time to do the following.

- Jot down the main points from memory, perhaps in the form of a concept map (see Appendix 5). Then go back and check the text. Alternatively, verbally recite the main points to yourself ('Smith is saying here that a small proportion of the convicts were political agitators rather than criminals. They led some rebellions in the colony, but these were all defeated. Their radical political views did not influence politics in the colony as it developed').
- Write brief answers to questions (your own or those of the study guide)—in your own words, of course: you want to review the ideas, thoughts, concepts behind the words of the text, not the exact words of the text.
- Review the text—that is, skim it again, perhaps rereading important bits in full. Do some free writing to express any thoughts or new questions you have after reading the text. You may begin to see new implications or perhaps new ways of applying the knowledge. If you

have read something important and have someone who is prepared to listen, tell them about what you read. Or write down some questions or comments you could take to the tutorial.

* Make an assessment of your current project. You might want to modify your plans now that you have read the text. For instance, you may realise that another book you planned to read is now unnecessary.
* Make notes if they are needed for research or revision purposes.

## VOCABULARY

We suggested that you not allow unfamiliar words to slow you down when reading. However, it has to be acknowledged that sometimes you won't get far with texts unless you understand the meanings of key terms. We can make a distinction between those unfamiliar words which are part of the specialised terminology of the discipline, and those words which are ordinary but perhaps not often encountered. Academic writers tend to have larger vocabularies than most people, and enjoy using them. There may be little point in looking a word up in the dictionary if it is so rare that you will encounter it only twice in the next five years. Look up words you keep encountering or which seem to be important to the relevant discipline.

You should be aware that ordinary dictionaries do not usually provide the specialised meaning of words used in academic disciplines. Specialised dictionaries and other reference books are needed. Some books contain glossaries where you can look up such words. Words included in the glossary will often be identified in the text by being printed in bold type. Definitions provided in lectures and study materials will also be helpful. Sometimes a chapter in a book that comes earlier than the chapter you are using will define a technical term that is unclear. Use the index to locate the page(s) where the word is first used.

Even definitions provided in specialist dictionaries and glossaries are not always fixed and final. You may come across a text which uses the word in a slightly different way. This applies more in the social sciences, humanities and communication studies than in disciplines like chemistry and biology, where it is easier for all concerned to agree on what words shall mean. In the former there are conflicting theories about, and different ways of conceptualising, the phenomena to which the terms refer. What one writer understands by terms like 'class', 'modernity' and 'globalisation' may be different from what others understand by them.

When they want to identify some new category or thing, writers tend to push existing words in some new direction instead of coining a new word. Normally they will explain what they mean by the term (in fact, their whole text might be an argument about what you should understand this term to be). Thus context will help to make the meaning clear.

In fact, context is the main way in which we learn the meaning of words. That was how you learned language as a child: when people used the word 'cat' there was always a small, furry, four-legged animal with whiskers and claws around (or a picture of one), so you began to guess what 'cat' meant. When you learn a new word—either by reading a definition or from the context—try to use it yourself in some way. You will then be much more likely to remember it.

## CONCLUSION

We have seen in this chapter that it is important to select reading matter carefully, and to relate reading to your specific purposes. Active readers connect the parts to the whole. They read a sentence in the context of the paragraph, a paragraph in the context of the text (e.g. article, section or chapter), and a text in the context of the subject.

## Activities

1. Pick up any non-fiction book you haven't seen before, preferably an academic one. Without reading more than one or two paragraphs in full, evaluate this book. What purposes would it serve? How comprehensive and authoritative is it? How easy to use?

    Write down which specific features of the book allow you to draw your conclusions about it. (Example: 'boxes in text with information on important theorists—gives reader option of finding out more about where theories discussed come from.')

2. Select a chapter of the book (or a long self-contained section of a chapter). Read only the first and last paragraphs (the first two if they are short) plus the first and last sentences only of every paragraph in between. Put down the book. Write down or tell someone what it is about.

3. Select any short chapter in a textbook you will have to use (or something similar). Read the first two paragraphs only.

   (a) Write down briefly what you think the chapter will go on to say. Also jot down any current Australian issues and news items to which the concepts of the chapter can probably be applied.

   (b) Now read the whole chapter. Mark what seems to be the topic sentence in each paragraph.

   (c) Write down what seems to be the main idea of the chapter in under 30 words.

4. Read through a few pages of this text and mark any words which are new and unfamiliar. Then try to work out what they mean from the context (other words in the sentence, or the sentence before or after might give clues to what they mean). Check whether you are right by consulting a dictionary.

## chapter 8

# In and out of class

Outside formal classes your greatest challenges are to stay motivated, avoid distractions and use time efficiently. Inside class your greatest challenge is to overcome being passive. It is all too easy to 'tune out' in lectures, and be a mere 'onlooker' in tutorials.

You may have carried over from your school days the notion that organised classes are all that matter, and that what you do at home is something added on. Turn this idea around. The main game is the learning that is going on in your head—whether you are in class, discussing academic matters with a friend, reading a book on the bus, or thinking about an essay while jogging or washing up. Classes are there to help your overall learning program.

At school, when the buzzer sounded to signal the end of a lesson you could relax—you were 'out of class' (also out of learning and concentrating mode). Now that you are an adult who has elected to pursue a certain course of study, avoid such distinctions between 'in' and 'out'. You don't have to switch your thinking and learning on and off according to your schedule of classes.

Tutorials and practical classes help by giving you a chance to *do* things—not just to be told things. They give you a chance to practise being an alert, active listener; to articulate ideas in speech; to engage in debate; to work productively with others in group situations. These are all important communication skills that you will need in your future career.

## ORGANISING YOURSELF

In degree courses that don't involve laboratory work, formal classes take up only a minor portion (no more than a third) of the time you are expected to devote to academic work in any week. This is an important difference from school: students are more likely to fail or underperform because they cannot structure their work outside class effectively—and commit themselves to doing it—than because they lack 'brains'.

There are at least two 'balancing acts' you must perform. First, you have to juggle the demands of the different subjects in which you are enrolled. Although subjects are timetabled so they don't clash, each subject normally operates independently of the others. This means you could have several important assignment deadlines falling in the same week. A well-organised student begins work early enough to prevent this becoming a crippling problem. It is important to devote an equal amount of time to each subject until you are *certain* that some variation from this can be justified. Obviously you will find some subjects easier, and some more interesting, than others. Some may make more regular demands on you—for instance, having a test every week or so, rather than assessment at the end of semester only. Be careful not to allow such factors to starve other subjects of the time they need. Even a 'high distinction' in one subject will not compensate for a 'fail' in another.

The other balancing act is to devote sufficient time to assessment tasks (such as essays, reports, presentations and class tests) while still doing the general weekly learning in the subject (reading textbooks, preparing for tutorials, reviewing lecture notes). There may be a strong temptation to devote time to the former at the expense of the latter, especially if you have been managing your time poorly. Allowing this to happen is a serious mistake.

Detailed attention to the important topic of time management is outside the scope of this book, but many books (or chapters of books) are devoted to the subject.

## TAKING NOTES IN LECTURES

Notes are just notes; they should be brief. If you try to write down everything said in a lecture you are less likely to follow the relationship beween concepts the lecturer is trying to explain.

**Two important points about time management**

1. You must be clear about what has to be done, how long it will take, and when it has to be done by. When you receive assignment deadlines, put them in a prominent place above your desk. Work backwards from the due date, setting yourself earlier deadlines for completing the main stages of the overall task.

2. Time management involves allocating a reasonable amount of time to all normal activities (you need *some* time for recreation, as well as for sleep, meals and travel). The amount of time devoted to particular activities depends on your priorities. Your priorities are determined by your goals. If the goal of getting a degree is more important than the goal of becoming great at netball, cards or learning to dance, then study will have priority. It's as simple as that.

They are *your* notes. No-one else is going to read them, so they don't have to be neat. The more abbreviations you can use the better. For instance, write 'C20' for 20th century, 'v. imp.' for very important, 'sim.' for similar. You can have your own personal way of abbreviating frequently used terms.

## Purpose

You should have a reason for taking notes. If the lecturer is giving you information that is not available in your textbook or other sources, then it is important to take it down. However, if the lecturer is explaining the ideas found in a chapter of the textbook, it may be more useful simply to listen and try to understand, jotting down occasional key points. Read the chapter before you go to the lecture. Even skimming it will be better than nothing.

## Listen actively and think

Be alert to signposts. Lecturers will usually give some indication at the beginning of the main topics to be covered, and signal the key ideas in one way or another.

Your notes can include your own occasional comments on what is going on. That is, you can *talk to yourself* in your notes—'See txtbk on this'; 'Will need for exam'—which will remind you that you need to get the details from the textbook, or study a topic for the exam.

## Focus on the key concepts

A paragraph usually contains one main concept or idea. One or two sentences will state the idea, the rest will reinforce it (e.g. by restating it, providing examples or evidence of it, mentioning exceptions to it). Lectures are the same: you don't need to copy down *all* the supporting detail, as long as you have got the main points. Some supporting detail may be worth noting. Abstract concepts are often easier to understand when related to a practical example, diagram or graph. The main ideas or topics of the lecture should stand out clearly in your notes. You can signal this in a number of ways—with a highlighter pen, an asterisk, or by underlining sections.

Notes do not have to reflect the sequence of the lecture. You could use arrows to show that event X ('the massive consumption of pizza by the population') had the consequences Y and Z ('nationwide juvenile truancy, and mass indigestion'). A concept map could be built up after the lecture to help you to link the ideas, relate them to earlier material, and so on. (See Appendixes 5 and 6 for examples.)

## Consolidate

You should look at your notes soon after the lecture. That is the best time to fill in gaps and make sense of anything that has been scribbled down quickly. Rewrite your notes if this suits you, as a way of keeping the concepts fresh in your mind. You may want to add information from other sources. If you know you will need a comprehensive and legible set of notes for exam preparation, rewriting might be worthwhile. We can call this note-*making* as opposed to note-*taking*.

Should you take notes only in lectures? No. It may be a good idea to jot down some notes during or soon after a tutorial if there is good discussion which helps to clarify some issue for you, or raises new ideas. That doesn't mean that you should expect a tutorial to consist of the tutor speaking and writing on the board while you take notes. During discussion another student might shed light on something. Note it down. You make notes because they may be useful to you later, not because it is the 'expected thing' in certain institutional settings.

## DISCUSSION

You may think of academic learning as reading textbooks, making notes and doing tests, rather than as talking. In fact, *talking* about academic concepts is just as important. Talking is the basis of tutorial discussions and debates, oral presentations and collaborative work in groups. Talking helps your thinking.

Talking comes naturally. As young children we learn to talk, and in the process we test and improve our understanding of the world. Young children are not inhibited by the fear of 'getting it wrong'—the words come tumbling out. But school inhibits this. Some kinds of knowledge become 'schoolwork' repeated in the classroom on command. Moreover, children become anxious about giving the 'wrong answer'. There is the added problem that the language used in books is different from that used in speech—it is denser, more complex, abstract and 'correct'. But academic subjects are not just words on paper—they are about thinking, learning and talking as well.

Talking is active rather than passive, and it helps to keep ideas in your memory. Putting concepts into your own words can also help you to understand them. People often say 'It wasn't until I had to teach something to another person that I really began to understand it'. And you may realise, as you try to put the ideas into words, that you don't really understand things properly—that there are gaps in your knowledge that need to be filled.

Talking about academic topics doesn't have to be something that goes on in a formal setting, such as a tutorial. Two or three students getting together to talk over a lecture they have just heard, or to help each other make sense of a chapter in the textbook, are doing something very useful. If there is someone at home who is prepared to listen to you talk about your studies (e.g. a friend or flatmate), make use of them. They don't have to have studied in the same field themselves, but it will help if they are interested and can ask the occasional intelligent question.

Do not confuse talking in academic contexts with 'performing'—that is, reciting what you think the tutor wants to hear. Anxiety about saying the wrong thing and looking foolish, and excessive eagerness to impress the tutor, are both counterproductive. Talking is a way of communicating with other minds. Your tutor is not watching you for signs of whether or not you deserve good marks. His or her interest is not in mentally classifying you as bright or dumb but in helping your learning by encouraging you to explore ideas in speech. Your tutor wants to know what you do and don't understand. What he or she might find irritating is to discover later, from errors in your assignment or exam answer, that you were hazy about the ideas but didn't say anything.

## The value of discussion

Discussion is more than merely talking. Talking, while useful, can involve merely reproducing verbally something you read. Discussion and debate require you to operate at higher levels of thinking. For instance, a class discussion may explore the consequences of something, or compare two points of view ('The Kodiak bear—friend or foe?'). The group may work towards the solution of a problem that has been posed, applying the knowledge they have of different relevant issues. A debate involves a group considering two opposing arguments in order to decide which is most reasonable or practical. It can provide a trial run of the more complicated skills required in your written work.

Good discussion involves useful exchanges of information and viewpoints. It helps you to 'get into' the subject. It can prod those who are complacent into doing more thinking and reading. You may realise that some of your opinions are based on assumptions that you can't really justify.

Academics use many abstract and specialised terms, and they may be so familiar with a topic themselves that they forget others are not. It can help to listen to another student who 'translates' the idea into more familiar words, and who will then provide an example, or relate the idea to a concept dealt with earlier in a way that is more useful to you than anything a tutor might have said. Discussion between students is not a trivial activity, a diversion from the 'main game'. It is increasingly recognised that students have much to offer each other. Some universities are developing peer tutoring programs, where senior students who did the same subject a year or two previously are used to help teach current students.

## Getting the most out of tutorial discussions

Students have to take a share of the responsibility for ensuring that discussions are effective. If you are unprepared, don't participate or can't focus on the issue being discussed you can sabotage a tutor's attempt to help the group learn through discussion.

Discussion can take different forms. There may be discussion involving the whole tutorial group, or a smaller subgroup —or some switching back and forth between the two. Discussion may be free and informal, or there may be definite ground rules (e.g. speaking when allowed to do so by the tutor or chairperson). Sometimes your own opinions are invited. At other times you may be asked to adopt a role or point of view on one side of an argument, whether or not it reflects your private opinion. Different formats and procedures all have their particular advantages; be aware of what these are. Think about the purpose of any discussion or activity. Is this just to go over the material and ensure that it is understood? To apply the principles to new examples? To analyse and evaluate the ideas? To explore the consequences the ideas might have?

> *Be prepared to move your position in the room.* Rows of tables and chairs facing forward are not good for discussion, and some furniture moving often helps get a discussion going. If the class is divided into subgroups, take the trouble to rearrange yourselves so you can face each other comfortably, without being distracted by your neighbours. You wouldn't try to work at a computer where you had to keep twisting your head to see the screen.

Read whatever you are expected to read before the tutorial, and do some thinking about the concepts coming up. Jot down any questions you think could be asked about the material, either to get an answer you need or to get others thinking. Your input might be useful.

## To speak or not to speak

People have different talents and tendencies, all of which can help a discussion in their own way. Some people speak easily because they are extroverts, others because they are confident and particularly interested in the week's topic. Others are reluctant to speak for three main reasons: (a) they have not done whatever prior reading was necessary; (b) they expect learning to be a passive experience and expect the tutor to do the talking; (c) they are uncomfortable about speaking to a group.

Even if you have a negative self-image, remember that others are less likely to find fault with you than you think. Often, people are more critical of themselves than of others. If you have real difficulty participating, consider seeking advice from a counsellor. (You don't need to have major problems before getting help from the student counsellor.)

Students can be reluctant to speak because they think they'll *attract* the disapproval of the tutor. But it is always a mistake to keep quiet for fear of sounding stupid. The tutor wants people to talk. It's not an oral exam. You may be worried that other students will disapprove of you: perhaps you have been one of only two or three people doing nearly all the talking. One option is to shut up altogether, but unless you have actually been 'hogging' the discussion this won't help. After all, one of the things that has been inhibiting others has probably been their worry that, compared with yours, their contribution will sound feeble. You could try posing a question for others to grapple with. This won't work, of course, if they see you as 'performing' for the tutor. Help to jog your fellow students out of their dependent habits. You probably know their language, and what 'makes them tick', better than the tutor.

If you're not sure about a point, it's all right to admit that you are undecided or confused. Others may feel the same. Your response may reflect the complexity of the topic better than those who pretend they understand. If you are unsure about how to express the concept in words, make some sort of beginning (e.g. 'I'm not quite sure how to explain this'). Someone else may be able to supply a few phrases that will help to clarify the idea. When you do speak, talk to the group, not just to the tutor.

## Debating

This involves an argument about whether some proposition is true or false. Sometimes a debate may be held in a tutorial, with individuals assigned specific roles (defending the proposition, refuting the opposing side's argument).

 Remember that:

- Argument involves *rationality*. There is no place for emotional manipulation or personal attacks.
- Argument demands *clarification* of each side's position: for instance, if both sides agree about what 'multiculturalism' means, they can go on to argue about whether or not Australia is truly multicultural.

## COLLABORATION

Collaboration occurs whenever you work together with one or more other persons. We are mainly concerned here with students working on an assignment which takes the form of a joint project in a small group, perhaps for a week or two, or for a semester. Normally each member of the group receives the same grade for the work.

Group projects are becoming more common. In certain disciplines in some universities—notably medicine, nursing and engineering—students do most of their learning in this way. The rationale for such 'problem-based learning' is that students are forced to be more active and thoughtful, and are exposed to 'real-life' situations. It is increasingly recognised that students need more opportunities to develop skills in collaborating. Even when employers express general satisfaction with graduates, they often single out collaboration as a skill that is lacking.

An ability to collaborate will be more important than ever in the workforce of the future. Often employees with different skills work together in teams. The trend towards flatter management structures means employees are expected to know more about the wider context and to take more initiative, instead of being told exactly what to do by their immediate superior. In such a climate, employees have to liaise effectively with others, and attend regular meetings. Organisational structures, for various reasons, are less stable. People need to be more adaptable than in the days when they remained for decades with a fairly stable 'family' of co-workers. In many jobs, then, it will be an asset to know how groups work, and how to get the most out of them.

People are social creatures, and many students enjoy working in a group, but some find collaboration frustrating—at least to begin with. Working together has distinct advantages: 'two heads are better than one', and six can be better still. Groups have more problem-solvers to put to work and a larger pool of knowledge to draw on. Sometimes the enthusiasm generated through group interaction stimulates individuals to produce better work than they would if working on their own. Group work allows students to practise discussion skills.

There are disadvantages too. Group work is time-consuming. Groups can waste human resources if one or two members do most of the work. Even if there are no problems, such as some members trying to dominate or others avoiding their responsibilities, it can be difficult for people to make the kind of compromises that are needed. You cannot expect to have everything done the way you imagined, or as you would prefer.

Some people are reluctant to have their own hard work used collectively. This can be a particular problem in academic environments, where traditionally it is individual effort that is rewarded. These problems can be overcome. An efficient group will not try to accomplish every single thing in a collective way: instead, members will work on aspects of the task individually or in pairs and then report back to the group.

Many of the benefits of collaboration, and many of the problems, occur because a group is a more complex environment than a pair. When things do not work well in groups, it's usually a result of group dynamics. It is more productive to analyse the group dynamics than to find fault with people's characters. Among other things, the way the group works will be influenced by its members' attitudes towards the group. Are they in fact committed to making the group work well? Or are they trying as far as possible to carry on as individuals, virtually pretending that the group isn't there at all? The box gives a comparison of two small groups.[1]

 **Group A**

- Members don't see the point of working in a group, or expect it to achieve much.
- Members do not become involved in planning the group's goals and tasks. They work on their own, or with one friend, as much as possible.
- Opinions and expressions of disagreement are regarded as divisive or as annoying complications.
- Members are cautious and reserved. They keep their true feelings and opinions to themselves. They may join forces with some others in the group to 'gang up' on the rest.
- No-one knows how to resolve the conflicts that arise.
- Members resent anyone exercising what can be regarded as a leadership role. The group lacks direction because no-one volunteers to take on a coordinating role.

**Group B**

- Members understand that both personal goals and the group goals are best achieved by working together as a group.
- Members help to establish the group's goals. This gives them a sense of 'ownership'.
- Everyone is encouraged to express ideas, opinions, and disagreements openly.

- Members communicate openly and honestly. They genuinely try to understand everyone else's point of view.
- Members recognise that conflict is normal and can result in something better than either of the two contending alternatives.
- Members accept that certain roles or functions are necessary to ensure that the group completes its task effectively and efficiently and that such roles can be exercised for the good of the group.

Obviously Group B members will produce better work, and enjoy themselves more. Group B does not achieve its harmony without plenty of discussion and negotiating of ground rules, roles and approaches to the task. Group B members allow everyone to have their say, even if they are critical of what has been done so far. Such openness is democratic, but it takes time. It is up to the student participants to accept responsibility for trying to make their group more like B than A. Don't expect the tutor to do this for you.

## Making small groups work

First of all, groups need a clear sense of purpose. Do not assume that other people's concept of the finished product is the same as yours. Talk about it. Personal goals should be consistent with the group goal.

One student in the group might have the goal of getting as high a mark as possible for the project whatever that takes, while another wants to spend a minimum of time and accept a lower mark. Both will need to compromise. However, both could make a useful contribution to the group. The first person can put his or her energy to work inspiring the others to 'lift their game'. The second person can look for ways to use time efficiently.

Goals determine tasks that must be accomplished. Some of the required tasks have to do with 'group maintenance'—all those things that ensure that members of the group are comfortable and cooperating well. It will be necessary, for instance, to allow time for everyone to express their opinion about how things are going. Be prepared to spend time considering how you will operate as a group, especially at the beginning. Work out some ground rules. The tendency is to rush into the task itself, but time spent discussing procedures will save problems and possible trouble later on.

There are usually different ways of achieving a goal. Don't reject other approaches just because they are unfamiliar and different from the way you are used to working. On the other hand, don't assume that others know best: explain what *you* think should be done.

## Roles

If the group is to succeed, its members must take on certain *roles*. A role is a specialised set of activities or functions that influences the way the group operates. Some kind of specialisation among members of a group is both natural and useful. In soccer, for instance, there is a goalkeeper, a sweeper, midfielders, wingbacks and strikers. And when the football club meets to raise money, someone acts in the role of chairperson so that the meeting can proceed in an orderly way.

Two main kinds of role are useful: first, roles relating to the task the group is working on; second, roles relating to group building and group maintenance.[2] Below are some examples of each kind. Group **task roles** include:

- *initiator–contributor*—offers new ideas or different approaches;
- *information-seeker*—asks for clarification (says things like 'we need to get facts on this' or 'what is our evidence for this?');
- *information-giver*—contributes relevant information ('I can tell you about that');
- *elaborator*—clarifies and further explains another member's ideas ('I think what Joe is saying here is that we need to get information on Kodiak bears—and quickly');
- *coordinator*—tries to clarify and keep track of relationships between the ideas and facts being discussed;
- *orienter*—attempts to summarise what has occurred and tries to keep the group on track;
- *evaluator–critic*—judges the evidence and conclusions the group produces;
- *recorder*—makes a record of the group's progress, and takes notes.

The other main kinds of role are called **building and maintenance roles**:

- *encourager*—praises others' ideas;
- *compromiser*—attempts to resolve conflicts by finding a solution acceptable to everyone;
- *gatekeeper*—keeps the channels of communication open, and ensures that everyone has a say;
- *group observer*—evaluates the mood of the group and monitors progress.

This list is not exhaustive. Depending on the task and the personalities involved, other roles might emerge or be required. Also, roles overlap: any one person is likely to fill several of these functions simultaneously. Note that the list shows behaviours that people tend to display once a group begins to operate, whether they have been asked to or not and probably whether they realise it or not. However, there is no guarantee that there will always be a member who acts as, say, an effective coordinator or compromiser. It may be worthwhile for the group to appoint people to some of these roles, temporarily or permanently. Roles can be filled when needed. In some cases they can be rotated. It will probably be important to have someone acting as recorder, for instance. A chairperson who does the job well will combine a number of these functions, including opinion-seeker, orienter, compromiser and gate-keeper. A chairperson is not necessarily the 'boss' or more important than others; he or she serves the group by facilitating discussion.

It should be obvious from the lists above that *there are many ways of making an important contribution.* Be aware of the kind of contribution that you are good at making, and try to make that contribution more consistently. If you realise that others tend to fall into useful roles, you can encourage them in this; similarly, if you realise that certain members are becoming 'self-centred' or unfocused, you can do something about it. While factors like personality and experience determine the role you are suited to, you can only be what the rest of the group allows you to be. That's why it can be useful for the group officially to assign people certain roles (if those roles are needed). People cannot perform useful roles if the group ignores the contribution they are trying to make. Even people who are obnoxious and counterproductive are acting this way because the group lets them get away with it: it is not so easy to dominate a group that isn't willing to be dominated.

## Making decisions

While all points of view must be listened to, the time comes when a group has to make a decision. There are a number of ways in which this can happen.

- *Majority vote* is a useful though not ideal solution. The minority who disagree with the majority decision may not be happy. There will be losers.
- *Compromise* is where everyone makes concessions until what they want works in with other people's preferences. Everyone is a winner

and a loser to some extent. The danger is that the outcome will be 'the worst of all worlds'.

- *Arbitration* means calling in some impartial outside person (such as the tutor) to listen to the alternatives. This will restore objectivity. If the group cannot move towards compromise or consensus, the arbitrator makes the decision.

- *Consensus* occurs when all in the group genuinely reach the same conclusion. There are no losers. While desirable, consensus may require a lot of time. It is important not to distort the outcome simply for the sake of achieving consensus.

If there is conflict, do not panic or try to evade it. Being desperate to avoid the situation, or to resolve it in a hurry, can make things worse. Put the emphasis on open communication and begin working through the problem. Conflict is normal. Remember too that conflict doesn't go away just because people try to keep it suppressed. Buried anger and resentment will affect productivity, and it may be healthier to have open disagreement. The following are some guidelines for dealing with conflict or preventing it altogether.[3]

- *Seek out differences of opinion.* The greater the variety of opinions and information it has to work with, the more likely it is that the group will find a solution.

- *Involve everyone in the discussion.* People are more likely to support the group's final decision if they have been able to voice their opinions, even if these are different.

- *Make sure all contributions are fully understood.* Insist on explaining your own position so that people really understand what you mean. Ask for clarification from others if you don't understand what they mean.

- *Don't evaluate other people's contributions—simply describe your difficulty with them.* Don't tell them they are wrong.

- *Focus on the problem, not on controlling people.* Don't issue orders or try to manipulate people; instead, try to explain the problem the group faces.

- *Regard all suggestions as 'group property'.* This includes your own. Don't keep arguing for something just because it was originally your suggestion. Avoid becoming emotionally involved.

- *Don't assume that there must be 'winners' and 'losers'.* Think in terms of group goals. Each suggestion should be evaluated objectively on its own merits—in terms of whether it will help to achieve the group goals.

- *Use group pronouns rather than self-oriented pronouns.* Avoid 'I', 'me', 'my idea'; use 'we', 'us', 'our'.
- *Signal that your ideas are provisional, not fixed.* If people see *you* as flexible, as only provisionally committed to something, they will be more willing to abandon their own fixed position, and not to 'dig in'.
- *Don't take disagreement personally.*
- *Listen attentively.* Give a speaker both verbal and non-verbal feedback.

In group situations the individual must be prepared to work with others, but that doesn't mean 'giving in' to the group. You owe it to the group to explain your point of view as fully as possible. If you don't, you are not making the best possible contribution. A group will need to come up with some rules or plans to guide its work, but as long as everyone is objective and tolerant this can be done in a flexible way.

Collaboration has advantages and disadvantages. It requires a range of skills and a degree of self-awareness. If you and your colleagues are able to make use of these skills, you will be surprised at how effectively you can work.

## CONCLUSION

Your success at university depends in large part on the work you do outside formal lectures and tutorials, so we began this chapter by looking at the importance of organising yourself. Then we considered things you do in class, such as taking notes in lectures and discussing ideas in tutorials. Finally we looked at collaboration, which means working with other students in a small group, whether inside or outside scheduled class time.

### Activities

1. Think of a conflict in a small group situation that you observed or were involved in. What was the conflict? How did it arise? How was it resolved? Was this a good way of resolving it? If not, what alternative could have been used?

2. Non-verbal communication (e.g. tone of voice, 'body language') can provide useful clues to how others are feeling. Give examples. It can also be very misleading. Give examples.

3. Identify two or three task roles and group maintenance roles that you feel you would do well. Repeat the process for someone in your tutorial group that you know well.

# part IV

# ASSIGNMENTS

## chapter 9

# Academic genres

There is no single assessment genre. The commonest genres are the essay, report and the exam. Each of these has its own requirements—its own way of doing things. Different disciplines tend to have their own set of assessment genres: in the humanities, business, social sciences and education you are likely to do mostly essays and reports, while in the sciences you will probably have to do laboratory reports and exams.

Some assignments ask you to reproduce genres used in certain occupations. For example, a journalism student might be asked to write a news story on an actual event, following the same procedures that would be used by a working newspaper reporter. How to do this is taught in journalism subjects. Some assessment tasks involve producing notes, short reports, or summaries—or doing tests, where the demands are relatively straightforward. The most challenging kinds of assignment can be the written essay or oral presentation, which require you to do a number of things—demonstrate research, evaluate research material in terms of the assessment task, think critically, and put arguments together.

## APPROACHING THE ASSESSMENT TASK

Perhaps the key to success with assignments is making good use of your time. Many students do not worry about a piece of assessment until it is nearly time to hand it in, then work furiously the night before it is due—and it shows. But it makes more sense to start work on assessment tasks as soon as you know what they are. Do not think that having a piece of assessment due in a month's time means that you can switch off for four weeks. There are many reasons why it is risky to delay making a start.

First, lecturers tend to schedule assessment tasks around about the same time. If you have two major assessment tasks for each of four subjects, you could have four assignments falling due within the same week or so in the middle of the semester and another four in the final week. Trying to finish one piece of work at the last minute is difficult—trying to finish four is asking for trouble.

Second, there are a limited number of resources (such as library books and journal articles) and maybe a few hundred students competing for them. The smart students will grab those scarce resources as soon as they know what they need. The rest will have to make do as best they can.

Third, too little time means poor work. Poor work here does not just mean a low mark for the assignment. Sometimes you may get away with it: despite minimal input, you may manage to scrape a pass. But what kind of benefit was derived in the sense of developing literacies and growing intellectually? One student, Candy, might put in twice as much time as another, Ben. This may translate into a slightly better mark, though not twice as many marks. However, Candy—having grappled with the concepts more intensively—is now on the brink of getting real insight into some aspect of the discipline (even if this hadn't quite arrived in time to benefit her assignment much). Candy has discovered a couple of library searching tools and is becoming experienced in using them. She is developing some good strategies and habits relating to organising research notes, doing the bibliography early rather than at the last minute, and so on. All this means that Candy will be in a better position to face the next assessment hurdle. By the time the students move into their next year of study, the gap between them will have become wider. Marks do not always measure the learning that is going on (or, in Ben's case, not going on) under the surface.

A bigger problem is that once you get behind with your work and start doing badly, you become stressed, and you may be tempted to drop out completely. A bit of time management not only helps you get better results, it gives you a cushion during difficult times of personal problems or illness.

You have to treat your time as a valuable and limited resource. Time may fly when you're having fun—but it rockets along when you have assessment tasks due. You have to allocate your time carefully. It's simple: if you have six weeks, and four tasks that require the same amount of work and are of the same value and importance, then you have the equivalent of about ten days to devote to each task. You may want to vary this: if one piece of assessment is worth 50% and the other three are worth only 10%, then you should give extra time to the more valuable piece.

## Strategies

It's easy enough for us to tell you to start work early and show why it makes a difference. It's not so easy for you to put such advice into practice. There are at least two things you can do.

First, always break up a big task into smaller tasks. Once you begin to break the overall task up into its different parts it becomes more manageable. We suggest (in other chapters) that there are *at least three* distinct stages in producing a written assignment:

- First stage—planning and researching.
- Second stage—drafting (writing a full version).
- Third stage—rewriting better drafts; proofreading and correcting the final draft; completing the bibliography, title page etc.

Second, start doing some kind of work. You can get hold of some useful books even if you haven't quite decided how to respond to the topic. You can begin compiling your bibliography even though you have not yet got beyond the rough draft stage.

Avoid being a perfectionist or too pessimistic. Even if you are uncomfortable with the topic of this assignment and you are not going to get the fancy mark you got last time, it is better to hand in a poor assignment than none at all. Ask for help if you need it—the earlier the better.

While some forward planning and sensible allocation of time to tasks is important, avoid spending time on elaborate study schedules that you intend to follow starting tomorrow. Instead, take a few minutes at the end of the day or week and write down what you have actually done during that period. This will be a more effective way of changing your behaviour.

## ASSESSMENT GENRES

The three main assessment genres you are likely to encounter at university are the essay, the report, and the exam.

### The essay

An essay is usually an extended piece of written work (undergraduate essays vary in length from 1000 to 5000 words), and is supposed to involve analysis, clear argument, and research. In the essay you bring these literacies together. You are supposed to respond to your question or task by researching as widely as time and resources allow, in order to be able to come up with evidence, and perhaps different viewpoints, which you then analyse or subject to critical thought. An essay is not just about providing a 'right answer', or demonstrating what you know. In most cases what is being assessed is the process—of researching, analysing and evaluating your material, and producing an argument which reflects both the evidence provided and your ability to think critically about it.

The essay is probably the commonest form of assessment at universities. It is now used more than exams, and it is not specific to any discipline area: you will be writing essays if you are doing subjects in economics, business, health science, tourism, engineering or education. Essays are such a popular form of assessment because they are useful for determining how well you have understood—not just memorised. Whereas exams of the short-answer kind assess the ability to learn facts, essays allow you to demonstrate important literacies, such as being able to research, select evidence and use examples, and evaluate different points of view. In essays, you demonstrate your ability to use the discourses of the discipline. These kinds of literacies are those which university students are supposed to have, and employers want.

Usually essays will be returned to you with written feedback from the tutor. They differ in this respect from exams, which can be marked more quickly. There are two main problems with written feedback:

- Students may not distinguish between the comments and corrections referring to relatively minor errors of style and language use and comments on more fundamental aspects, such as the quality of the argument, structure, and depth of understanding.
- Students are mainly interested in the mark awarded. They may not take much notice of the comments, nor make use of them to improve their next assignment.

---

 Essays have the following general structure:

- *Introduction.* This prepares your reader for what is to come. It orients your argument to the set topic (e.g. by explaining what you understand by the question).
- *Main body.* This is where you bring in the evidence of your research, and put together your arguments.
- *Conclusion.* This brings the essay to an end. The reader is reminded in some way of every major point you made or issue you considered. (Introductions and conclusions are discussed in more detail in Chapter 14.)

---

> • *Bibliography.* Any piece of work that contributed to your essay should be included. This does not include only books—films, magazines and newspapers should be included if you have made use of them, even if you didn't quote directly from them.

You will need to find out what requirements there are about format and style in the particular discipline (or unit). For instance, you will probably be told that you must have a separate title page and use a certain referencing convention (e.g. the Harvard system). Some disciplines, notably the humanities, tend to disapprove of such devices as subheadings or lists using numbers or bullet points.

Note that oral presentations, too, should have a distinct introduction, body and conclusion (in your mind, even if the transitions between them are not noticeable to the audience). Oral presentations do not have bibliographies, but you should not use other people's ideas—or provide contestable facts and figures—without briefly indicating their source.

## The report

Reports are different from essays in that, while they also assess the process of evaluating information and communicating effectively, they are usually tightly structured around finding a solution or sets of possible solutions to a specific problem or question.

>  Reports normally include the following sections:
>
> • *Title page.* This includes relevant information, such as your name, status, the person and/or organisation the report was prepared for, and the title of the report. The title of the report should match up with what you have produced.
> • *Table of contents.* List all sections with their headings and subheadings, and the relevant page numbers.
> • *Introduction.* This explains what the report is supposed to be doing, and why it is important.
> • *Methodology.* Here you provide an account of what methods you used to collect your data, and why you chose to use them. You might need to provide a rationale for choosing one method of data collection over another.

- *Results.* This section should provide a matter-of-fact account of what you found rather than interpretation or evaluation of your findings, although you might draw attention to any particularly interesting or important results.
- *Discussion.* Here the results outlined in the previous section are interpreted—what it all means, what patterns have emerged, what findings were particularly relevant. Here you explain the significance of the findings (e.g. how they relate to certain theories, and how they help with your particular problem or question).
- *Recommendations.* In this section you are meant to outline, in order of preference, the different courses of action available. These options should arise out of, and follow from, your results and discussion section.
- *Bibliography.* Here, as with an essay, you should provide details of any texts used in your research.

Some kinds of report (e.g. those relating to case studies) may have somewhat different requirements; these will be explained in the relevant subject.

There is another kind of report that is commonly used in the sciences—the laboratory report, or 'lab' report. Lab reports usually have the same structure as other reports, although they sometimes include or require an abstract after the title page, and they don't always have bibliographies (there might be no need to reference anything). Abstracts are brief (usually no more than 300 words) summaries of what happened: what you were trying to do, how you did it, what actually happened, and what the significance of the work is. The main feature of lab reports is that they are supposed to provide a minutely detailed description of an activity (e.g. an experiment). Generally, lab reports are not assessed on the actual experimental results but on a student's ability to follow, and document, the appropriate steps and procedures.

### The exam

Perhaps the form of assessment that students find most difficult or daunting is the exam. Academics use exams as a way of testing the breadth of a student's knowledge of a subject, but they are aware of the stress exams place on students—they do not expect the same quality of work here as they would in an essay or report.

There are three main types of exam—closed-book, open-book, and take-home.

- The *closed-book exam* does not allow you access to any resource materials—it forces you to rely on your memory.
- The *open-book exam* allows you to consult your notes and any appropriate reference material (such as a textbook).
- The *take-home exam* normally allows you two or three days (often over a weekend) to respond to the questions.

Take-home exams require just as much prior preparation as the others. While they may seem less intimidating, there will not be much time to obtain and consult books and other resources. There should be time to do more than one draft of your answers but no time to begin learning the material. The first two kinds of exams usually last for two or three hours. This means that you cannot afford to change your mind, think about things for too long, or waste words.

## Preparing for exams

- *Make time available for revision.* This is a good reason for getting all your other assessments finished early—you don't want to be too busy, or too tired, to revise for exams. The more you have kept up with the topics in the unit on a week-by-week basis the better position you will be in.
- *Go over your notes.* Identify any areas you do not understand or are not sure about. Seek help if you need it. Understanding the material is more important than just memorising. Concentrate on main points and key ideas. Reading lengthy material in full, especially if it is unfamiliar, may not be a good use of revision time.
- *Be as active as you can.* Do not read passively—stop and see if you can verbalise what you have been reading. Test yourself by, for instance, constructing a concept map on the topic you are revising (see Appendixes 5 and 6 for examples). Resist the temptation to make lengthy notes from books: this gives you the illusion of working but is of dubious value. Compiling brief summaries and mnemonics, though, will be worthwhile.
- *Do not overlook the value of examples.* While you should concentrate on key points, examples can make abstract ideas comprehensible and vivid. It is a good idea when making notes in class to note

examples briefly. Then you have an image to attach to the concept when revising. In a media studies lecture, for instance, you might note in relation to some point that has been made, 'e.g. Princess Di funeral'.

- *Find out all you need to know.* First, make sure you know where and when the exam takes place. Make sure you know all the rules pertaining to the exam and what you may need to bring with you. (This may seem elementary but year after year, in every university, some students get mixed up on these basic things.) You also need to know, well in advance, what form the exam will take (e.g. how much choice there will be), and whether you will be tested on all the topics or modules covered in the unit or only some of them.

- *Get hold of exam papers from previous years.* This will give you a good idea of what to expect—though it is worth verifying that there have been no significant changes to the unit. Do not expect exactly the same questions to be used again.

One of the best things you can do to prepare yourself for an exam is to practise answering exam questions. Try to answer them in the allotted time. Do this a few times. Answering exam questions is not the same as any other form of written assessment, but once you have practised a few times you will become more confident about answering exam questions. For a start, your sense of timing will improve and you won't need so long to get started.

## In the exam

Get to the exam room early. Once you have read the questions, and selected which ones you will answer, decide the order in which you will answer them. Do not blindly follow the order on the exam sheet; if you are confident about any particular questions, do those first. Normally you get ten minutes' reading time. This should be long enough to choose which questions to answer. Stick with your decision; don't be tempted to switch to another alternative when you are halfway into the time available for a question.

Some initial planning of the answer will be worthwhile. Jot down any mnemonics you devised relating to the topic (e.g. the word 'ELVIS' might be a device for remembering the first letter of each of five key points). Do a quick concept map or outline in point form. Note the time at which you will have to move on to the next question.

Be simple and straightforward. Don't get bogged down in elaborate or complex discussions. As long as your handwriting is legible don't worry about neatness. Leave space between paragraphs so you can come back and add any points that may come to mind later.

You must answer the question that has been asked. Carry out whatever operations have been asked for (e.g. 'compare and contrast'; 'explain why'; 'argue for or against'; 'outline the reasons for'; 'evaluate'). Do not simply reproduce chunks of unorganised information. Usually an essay-type exam answer is an argument defending some proposition or other. Although students worry about not remembering, their ability to recall detailed information is often surprisingly good. But the material must be relevant to what has been asked. Some students do poorly because they stop thinking in exams. They barely take note of what the question actually asks for before regurgitating information.

Even if you are unsure, try to write something. A marginally relevant response is better than nothing at all. (This at least is the case in essay-type exams. The marker will give you credit for anything with some sort of relevance and will ignore what is not relevant—as long as it is not actually false. In some kinds of short-answer exams, though, you will have to produce precisely the right answer.) One advantage of putting *something* down in response to the question is that while writing down minor or marginal points you may begin to recall major points.

If you find you are running out of time, you may need to abandon full sentences—just put thoughts down in point form. You will get some credit if they are valid points.

Open-book exams give you the opportunity of bringing in notes or texts, which means that more is expected of you. The best way to prepare for an open-book exam is to ensure that your information and reference material is organised and accessible. Highlight the most important sections or points using a coloured marker, and have a summary, in point form, at the end of your notes or reference text that lists all the main information and where it can be found (number your notes). Don't get carried away by the opportunity for searching out information. Most of your time will have to be spent writing, not reading.

If you have serious problems with 'nerves' before or during exams, you should consider seeking help from a counsellor. There are simple and effective strategies for reducing tension. Many books on study skills or exam technique have useful suggestions on relaxation techniques, as well as strategies for memorising material.

## CONCLUSION

In this chapter we have introduced you to the main written assessment genres—the essay, the report and the exam. Assessment tasks are one of the biggest challenges facing students at university, and it is important that these tasks be approached in a coherent, organised and time-effective way.

We have given you some suggestions about strategies to adopt, and there are more suggestions in the following chapters. What will make most difference to your success, however, is your attitude to assessment tasks. If you are the dependent, institution-centred student described in chapter 3 you will regard assessments as irksome duties imposed on you by punitive staff. For assignments, for example, your focus will be on the finished product and the grade it gets rather than the process of researching and thinking needed to deal with the topic effectively. When the assignment is finished you will forget all about it, and you probably won't make good use of the feedback you get. The independent student, on the other hand, realises that assessment tasks are valuable means of learning the subject, developing intellectually and acquiring useful skills. These skills, vital for any worthwhile job, include the ability to manage demands on your time and meet deadlines.

### Activities

1. (a) Think of a typical weekday in your life. Draw a rough pie chart representing this typical weekday, with divisions showing the proportion of time devoted to various activities (e.g. about a third will probably be for sleep).

    (b) Now write down two or three of your most important goals for this year.

    (c) Does your time chart seem consistent with achieving your goals? If it does not, what areas could be modified? What needs more time and where can you save time?

2. Construct a mock exam paper (or at least a few questions) for a subject you are studying, conforming to the exam subgenre used in the subject (e.g. multiple choice, essay). If past exam papers are available, use them as a guide to the way questions can be framed. You will find this a useful and different way to study the subject. Give the exam to a friend to practise on (he or she can prepare one for you!), or else put it aside for a few weeks and write answers to it, allowing yourself the same amount of time you will have in the exam.

## chapter 10

# Planning an assignment

In the early stages of preparing a university assignment, whether oral or written, one of the most useful general strategies you can adopt is to divide work on assignment tasks into three distinct stages.

| Task | First stage | Second stage | Third stage |
|------|-------------|--------------|-------------|
| Written assignment | Planning & research 'prewriting' | Drafting 'writing' (writing the first full draft) | Revising 'rewriting' (writing improved versions, proofreading the final 'fair copy') |
| Oral presentation | Planning & research | Preparing notes, visual aids etc. | Delivery (giving the talk) |

Some of these stages can be further subdivided, and it might suit you to think of the task as having four or five distinct stages. The main thing is that you allocate your time appropriately. It is all too common for students to do one or other of the following: (a) to spend too long on the research stage, leaving insufficient time to write the paper or prepare the talk. The result is poorly expressed and perhaps poorly structured work that is boring and difficult to follow; (b) to put off doing any work on the assignment until the deadline is close. There is then no time to do anything well. The first stage, especially, will be skimped, with the result that the essay is likely to have serious defects. It may be insubstantial, shallow, unfocused—and perhaps full of irrelevant material.

Here we are concerned with the first stage, where the ground is prepared. If you take the first stage seriously, the second will be much easier. Preparing a written or oral assignment is a complex activity. It is better not to have to think about too much at once. If you have already mapped out a clear direction in the first stage and come up with ideas as a result of both research and your own thought processes, then writing full sentences and paragraphs will be more straightforward. The first stage is made easier too because you postpone the task of writing in full. You are then free to concentrate on ideas, to get an overview of the whole essay before getting caught up in the details of each of its sections. You are also free to change direction.

When you come to the second stage, it is best not to be too worried about correctness. Don't keep revising and polishing every sentence as you write it; you can do that in the third stage. When the third stage is reached, most of the work has been done. You now have a full draft in front of you and all you need to do is to improve it.

It is not always easy to devote time to thought and planning. There is a natural tendency to want to get on with the activity. This may be because you are feeling confident. Or it may be because you are feeling anxious. But the person who takes time to plan, whatever the task, usually does a better job. There's another kind of unfortunate response: when you sit down to begin the task, you may find yourself unable to do anything at all. You freeze up—you cannot think what to do or where to begin—the job seems impossible. At this point you find an excuse to postpone the task. Here again, if you have decided that there will be a distinct planning stage, you can overcome this tendency to freeze up.

Some find it hard to begin because they are overwhelmed by the size and complexity of the overall task. In their anxiety they become pessimistic about any ideas they get. If you have broken the task up into stages, you can be more tolerant of the first ideas that come to mind because in the planning stage everything is *provisional*. You can try out ideas without feeling in any way committed to them. You make a note of even a 'silly' idea in case it ties in with something else or turns out to be useful after all. And then you find you have started. One thing leads to another and ideas begin coming. What you began with may not be used in the final version, but it helped to get you going.

## MEETING REQUIREMENTS

First, thinking about the characteristics of a good assignment, what criteria must the finished product satisfy? Depending on the subject in which an assignment is set, some of the criteria might be more important than others. The criteria we deal with here are for a written essay, although many of them apply equally to oral presentations.

Remember that assessment requirements vary, not only across universities but even at the level of subjects. Usually the department, school or faculty you are working in will provide you with a document (a sheet of paper, a booklet) which will outline what is expected of you; if there are individual differences at subject level, these will be indicated in the subject outline. Read them carefully: if you do not reference properly, or ignore other requirements (for example, some disciplines specify a minimum number of citations per essay), you will lose marks.

### Typical essay criteria

Presentation and format requirements vary between disciplines; be sure you know what is expected in each subject. Whether or not these are specified in instructions or marking criteria sheets issued to you, you can expect certain requirements to apply.

#### Presentation and format

You will need the following:

- separate title page showing required details (tutor's name, subject);
- separate bibliography page;
- numbered pages;
- adequate spacing and margins (2.5 cm all round, one-and-a-half or double-line spacing).

#### Compliance with directions

Make sure you do what the topic asks. Your essay must carry out the procedure which the set topic (explicitly or implicitly) requires. If you are asked to:

- analyse,
- provide reasons for, or
- argue for or against something,

then you must do so, and not merely discuss the subject in a general way.

## Relevance

Your discussions, evidence and examples must all be relevant to the set topic. You do not get credit for irrelevant material, however much research effort it involved or however brilliant it is. An essay is not just an exercise in gathering facts printed in books: it should reflect a process of thinking about the issue and carefully preparing a response to the topic.

## Use of theory

Essays require you to make use of various concepts, principles or theories specific to the discipline. It must be clear to the reader that the subject matter is being examined by, for instance, a historian or economist or communications theorist. An essay is more than a light, general-interest magazine article. Make use of your tools. Use the specialised theoretical language of the discipline appropriately, defining terms when necessary.

## Clear explanation

The important issues (ideas, propositions) must stand out clearly and not be buried in the detail of the essay, or simply taken for granted. Be prepared to draw conclusions—to show what the facts indicate or prove. Make generalisations when appropriate.

It is not always enough to state important points in a sentence or two—you may need to explain, expand or elaborate to bring out their significance.

## Coherent structure

The essay must have a definite introduction and conclusion, distinct from the main body. The ideas should be arranged systematically and logically.

*Adequate research*

You must do enough research to be well informed on the subject. Further research may be necessary to provide relevant evidence and examples, and to cite authorities.

*Accurate documentation*

Quotations should be relevant, contextualised, properly formatted and documented. They should not be used excessively. Other authors' ideas should be cited in accordance with the referencing convention (e.g. Harvard, MLA) you have been asked to use. There should be a bibliography in the correct format.

## ANALYSING THE SET TOPIC

Having looked at the general kinds of requirements you will have to meet, you can turn to the specific topic that has been set for the assignment. Before you do anything—researching or writing—you have to be sure that you understand what it is you are supposed to be doing. The set topic must be inspected closely. Look for the three kinds of words that make up the set topic: these are topic words, limiting words, and direction words.

**Topic words** identify the content or subject matter that the assignment must deal with. In the following three examples, the topic words are italicised:

- What is meant by *the term 'chocaholic'*?
- Analyse the *impact of British colonialism on the chocolate trade* in the Asia–Pacific region from 1800.
- Describe *the policy of the Chinese government in regard to foreign television transmissions by satellite of the series 'Bananas in Pyjamas'*. Compare and contrast *the policy of China* with that of either *Malta* or *Monaco*.

**Limiting words** are those which specify that only one particular aspect of a subject should be discussed, or which set limits of time and place. The limiting words in the following sentence are italicised:

- Analyse the impact of *British* colonialism on the *chocolate* trade in the *Asia–Pacific region from 1800*.

In this case it would be easy enough to forget about the last two words in the sentence and to write an essay that devoted 40% of its length to the impact before 1800. It might also be easy to overlook the fact that you are being asked to consider only British colonialism (not, for instance, Dutch or French), and trade in chocolate (not marzipan or jelly).

**Direction words** are those which tell you what to do with the topic:

- *What is meant by* 'chocolate poisoning'?
- *Analyse* the impact of colonialism on trade in chocolate in south-east Asia from 1800.
- *Describe* the policy of the Chinese government in regard to foreign television transmissions by satellite of the series 'Bananas in Pyjamas'.
- *Compare and contrast* the policy of China *with* that of *either* Malta *or* Monaco.

Note the word 'either' in the last sentence. A student who forgot it was there and treated both would be making a serious error.

'What is meant by' asks you to define and explain. 'Analyse' asks you to talk about the various effects or consequences of colonialism. 'Describe' means 'provide the facts about something, outline its characteristics' (it does not require you to interpret or evaluate).

The following are other common direction words:

- *Evaluate* asks you to form a judgement, or to provide an opinion about the worth of something.
- *Argue the case for* means provide the best reasons you can find as to why something should be believed (whether or not you personally believe it is another matter).
- *Outline* means provide the main features, or explain just the key points or principles.
- *Examine* means investigate an issue or event in a careful, detailed and critical manner.
- *Discuss* is the most open-ended kind of direction. Usually you would be expected to give the subject general consideration, for instance mentioning the different points of view which exist (not just one, as in *argue the case for*).

In all cases you are expected to respond to the material in a *critical* way. That doesn't mean you are condemning everything. It means you are assessing propositions in the light of the evidence or logic that supports them, rather than taking them at face value.

Having identified the topic words, your first task is to make sure you understand them. You might need to look up terms. Remember that a general-purpose dictionary will not always give you adequate definitions of specialised terms. For instance, it wouldn't help a student of communications to look up the word 'discourse' in an ordinary dictionary; this student should consult a specialised reference book, like *Key Concepts in Communication and Cultural Studies*. Textbooks often have glossaries of terms. Or you might use the index of a textbook to find a definition or discussion of term.

When planning, it is useful to write down some *synonyms* for key topic words. You can find synonyms (words similar in meaning) in a thesaurus or dictionary of synonyms. You might also check the *Library of Congress Index of Subject Headings* in the library. These are reference books which guide you to the words used to classify topics in the library's subject catalogue. If you look up 'colonialism', you are told that you should use the general headings 'Colonies', 'Imperialism' or 'World politics'. The entries usually supply a broader term than the term you looked up, and one or more narrower terms. In this case, under 'Colonies' the broader term is 'Imperialism', and narrower terms include 'Decolonization' and 'Protectorates'. If you look up 'Marketing' you are given the broader term 'Industrial management', and a lot of narrower terms including 'Merchandising' and 'Product life cycle'. As well as suggesting terms to use in searching library catalogues for useful books and articles, having some synonyms will help you to think about the topic.

It is unrealistic to expect to find books and articles on the exact topic set for your assignment. There may be good material that uses different terms ('imperialism' rather than 'colonialism'). On the other hand, you would need to be aware that because imperialism is a broader, more general concept, not everything will be usable (your topic specifies colonialism). You might be able to think of a related field even if synonyms do not suggest it: for instance, if you had difficulty finding published material on the effect of violent computer games (a relatively recent thing), you could make use of the vast amount of material on television violence and children. At least some of the arguments about TV can be applied to computer games. You would need to remember the significant differences (e.g. the greater interactivity involved in computer games, and the inability of parents ignorant of computers to supervise their children). Sometimes the set topic involves certain assumptions. It is assumed that you will understand what a word means in the context. In the examples above 'colonialism' *presumably* refers to the whole period of European settlement until Australia became a federation in 1901, rather than merely the period of direct rule from Britain in the first 50 or so years. If you are in doubt it is worth asking for clarification.

## THE SET TOPIC AND STRUCTURE

You will note that the set topic usually determines whether you will be writing argument or exposition. It might well indicate the kind of exposition—comparison and contrast, say, or causal analysis. Students often fail to realise that as well as directing them to the *content* of their assignment (the ideas and facts), the set topic often provides them with their general *structure*. Although you may not yet know just what you will say in the essay, you can begin to see the structure it will need to have. Put down this structure in outline form.

Suppose the set topic is: 'Discuss the factors that could affect Australia's international tourist industry in the first quarter of the 21st century. What steps should the government take to assist this industry?'. As the topic does not specify whether it wants you to discuss adverse effects (which reduce tourist numbers) or favourable effects (which would increase them), you need to take both into account. The structure of an assignment responding to this question would be something like that shown in the box below.

Introduction
    (followed by)
Body
Factors which might have an adverse effect:

* First adverse factor .....................................
    ............................
* Second adverse factor ...............................
    ............................
* Third adverse factor ...................................
    ............................
    (followed by)

Factors which should have a favourable effect:

* First favourable factor ...............................
    ............................

- Second favourable factor .................................
  ...........................
- Third favourable factor ..................................
  ...........................
  (followed by)

Discussion about the above (e.g. whether favourable factors outweigh the adverse ones).
  (followed by)

Steps Australia should take:

1. to counter adverse factors ..............................
   ...........................
2. to promote favourable factors ...........................
   ...........................

Conclusion

Writing the essay is now essentially a matter of filling in the blanks. At this point you may not know much about tourism—or even Australia—but you can see the general pattern of the essay. This is only a rough plan, but it is a plan that comes from the set topic. What fills the blank slots still needs to be worked out, and you may eventually decide to have more or fewer than three factors. Early in the research process you might come up with these adverse factors: (1) people overseas might get bored with Australia due to overexposure during the Sydney Olympics; (2) epidemics of dangerous new viruses might force governments drastically to limit movement of people between countries; (3) the development of 'virtual tourism' allows people to experience other places electronically from their homes. These are not necessarily the three most likely factors, and you would be well advised to keep looking for more. Because you have your three 'slots' ready, you can think carefully about what should go into them. If you do not think and plan you will be more likely to throw anything in as long as it seems vaguely relevant. The topic will not always give you a neat structure, but your work will be more manageable and efficient if you approach it in this way.

## PLANNING AND RESEARCH

You cannot write a complete assignment using only what is already in your head. While it is important to do your own thinking, you are going to have to read books and articles, and perhaps carry out other kinds of investigation. Here we discuss different aspects of the task in different chapters, but you are the one who must integrate all these activities and procedures.

There are particular things to avoid in written assignments. One is the 'magpie syndrome' (the magpie being a bird that decorates its nest with all kinds of small, bright, colourful objects), where bits and pieces are pulled out of a range of printed sources and assembled in an incoherent way. Another is the kind of assignment that reads as a simple survey; here the student makes the obvious general points that can be made on the topic but takes it no further. That kind of work might get a pass, but nothing more. Most importantly, however, you have to avoid **plagiarism**, where sentences or ideas produced by the author of a source are reproduced but not identified. This is a serious violation of academic convention.

In the first instance research is about informing yourself. Once your knowledge on the topic has been enlarged, you are in a better position to write your own discussion about it. You will produce something more intelligent, interesting and coherent if it is your work, rather than if you simply transfer information from books to your notes, and from your notes to your assignment. We have stressed that you should evaluate sources before committing yourself to using them, and that you should read a text (or section of it) before beginning to make notes. If you follow this advice you will be less likely to become a magpie. And although it may take some self-discipline to follow such procedures, in the end your use of time will be more efficient.

The thinking and planning you do influences what you choose to read, and make notes from. What you read, in turn, influences what you think, and may cause you to change your original plans. Your new thinking and plans then cause you to look for new sources. All this may sound obvious and logical, but it is good to start with what you know, and do some thinking and planning (having analysed the set topic) before you start researching.

Without a plan, you tend to let information-gathering take over. You may find what seems to be good information, make a lot of notes, and convert your notes into an assignment without considering whether the material is really relevant, whether various subtopics are getting more or less space than they deserve, whether all the subtopics fit together, or whether they are being presented in the best order. Using some kind of outline of your assignment can control these problems. The outline can be developed and refined as your research progresses. Have an outline you are satisfied with before going on to write the first draft (the first version in full sentences and paragraphs).

A simple example is given in the outline for an essay below about the willingness of many people in Western countries to believe that aliens have visited Earth. At first you might not have many ideas, but if you think about it you may come up with an outline like this.

---

### 'Belief in Visits by Aliens'—Provisional Outline

INTRODUCTION

BODY

I. Description of the topic (800–900 words)

- The main kinds of ideas people have about aliens (maybe two or three examples).
- History of this topic (is it a recent belief?).

II. Explaining the topic (900 words) (why people have such beliefs).
- More cases of 'unidentified flying objects' because there are more planes, weather balloons, and rockets in the sky (is this a major reason?).
- Mass media sensationalism.
- Mental illness and drugs—hallucinations.

CONCLUSION

---

Although this isn't much, it has already begun to give direction to the research. For instance, I have decided that I want to sum up only the main categories into which beliefs about aliens fall—I don't want to get bogged down in too many accounts of individual 'sightings' of hovering lights or whatever. I have decided I need to know whether such beliefs are recent, or whether they have always been around. Note that I include in the outline questions I want answered. I indicate my uncertainty about whether 'more objects in the sky' is really a major reason. The outline also includes an estimate of the word length of each main section.

As you read, keep the outline in mind. It will be useful in helping to select the sources (and sections within sources) to concentrate on. However, this outline is only provisional, and things can be reconsidered. After extra reading, I decide that the idea about objects in the sky can be dropped (see box on the next page).

---

## 'Belief in Visits by Aliens'—Outline 2

INTRODUCTION (150 words)

BODY

I. Describing the phenomenon of belief in aliens (600 words).
   A. The main kinds of beliefs. People vary in how they think of aliens: what their degree of involvement is (just observing us, or interfering?). Belief in aliens often accompanied by belief in conspiracies.
   B. Historical trends.
   • Belief in visits by 'flying saucers' begins after World War II.
   • 1950s–60s mostly just reports of objects in sky.
   • 1970s–90s more reports of encounters, abductions.

II. Explaining belief in aliens (1200 words).
   A. Influence of mass media.
   • Sensational news stories.
   • Fictional narratives: TV—The X-Files; film—ET.
   B. Eccentric individuals: attention-seekers, mentally ill.
   C. Cultural factors.
   1. Decline of orthodox religion—need for substitutes (compare New Age mysticism?).
   2. Need for new kinds of myths due to: anxiety about nuclear war, the dangers of science, paranoia about increasing power of governments (compare other kinds of 'urban myths').

CONCLUSION (50 words)

---

This is still not necessarily the final outline: it might be worth reorganising the concepts. But you can now assess what further research needs to be done—you know you need to get further material on TV and film, for instance.

If you have difficulty producing an outline it may be because you are wanting to do things back-to-front. You are trying to imagine the final, fully fledged essay and deducing from that what the main idea of each paragraph would be. But the whole point of outlines is that they are ways of groping your way towards the final result. Outlines are things you play with, tinker with. They can start off consisting mainly of empty slots to be filled in later (look again at the section on *The set topic and structure*). Perhaps at school you had to hand in an outline with your essay and therefore think of it as a final product, to be judged, rather than as a thinking tool. If you can do that thinking in your head, fine;

but doing it on paper is often easier. If you prefer to move more quickly to the first full draft, do so. It is a good idea, though, to go through it and construct an outline of the key points (subtopics) so that you can see it all on one page and check such things as the logical connections, relevance to the set topic, whether the important aspects are getting the space they deserve. Note that the kinds of outline we are talking about here are conceptual frameworks, not paragraph summaries. In the example above, point II. B might be a single paragraph, while point II. C. 2 may need four paragraphs. But each division at the A, B, C level would begin with a new paragraph. Note that you are constructing a hierarchy of ideas—a kind of **classification** (see chapter 6).

If you don't review your plan for the assignment at least once during the research process, there is a danger that you will lose control of it. The student who controls and directs their research with this kind of planning and reviewing will get a much better result than the one who just goes out and makes pages and pages of notes in an unorganised way, and then goes straight to the writing-in-full stage.

## CONCLUSION

Let's briefly recapitulate two important points about planning. First, a vital part of the planning process is to ensure that you understand what is required. Closely examine both the set topic for the assignment and any general guidelines or criteria that apply. Second, make sure that you incorporate a stage in your planning in which you can explore possibilities and treat everything as provisional. This is the best way of generating a good final product.

## Activities

1. Identify the topic words, limiting words and direction words in each of the following:
    (a) How, and to what extent, is the press regulated in Australia? Outline the arguments for and against such regulation.
    (b) What have been the main trends in the profitability of Australian newspapers in the 1980s and 90s?

(c)  How successfully has the advertising industry responded to social change in Australia in the past decade?

    (d)  What were the main features of Australian urban development in the colonial period, and how did these differ from urbanisation in Britain?

2. Draw a concept map which relates to the problems of (a) overseas students, (b) mature age students, or (c) students who need to earn extra income. See the example of a concept map in Appendix 5.

3. Construct an outline (about as elaborate as the one on p. 145) for an essay which will argue for or explain one of the following propositions:

    (a)  Exams should be abolished altogether.

    (b)  New technology will (or will not) radically change tertiary education.

    (c)  The pace of change in Australia has been too rapid.

4. Find a self-contained piece of exposition or argument of say 1500–2000 words in length and construct the outline that appears to govern it. First try to identify its thesis (central idea), and write this at the top of the page.

## chapter 11

# Research: finding resources

Most university assignments have to be researched. You have to produce informed discussion and argument. You cannot rely on your existing knowledge or make wild, unproven statements or claims. You have to:

- search out and accumulate relevant evidence;
- go through the results of your research and decide which parts are important;
- develop an argument which demonstrates your ability critically to respond to the evidence.

A term often used for research skills is 'information literacy'. Just as much as the other generic skills (e.g. critical thinking), research skills are:

- necessary for successful university study in most subjects;
- the basis of future intellectual development (or 'lifelong learning');
- valued by employers and transferable to a wide range of employment situations.

We live in what is called 'the age of information'. The ability to access electronic databases and other computer-related information sources will be essential. Finding your way to information is only part of it: you need to be able to select the information that is most useful and manage it effectively.

## THE NATURE OF RESEARCH

Research means finding out the answers to questions in a thorough and systematic manner. In a way your research is similar to the process found in detective stories or films. In Edgar Allen Poe's short story *The Murders in the Rue Morgue*, for instance, Dupin the detective is faced with a difficult problem. People have been murdered, and there are lots of witnesses who heard things, but the witnesses (who are from different countries and backgrounds) contradict each other: the Italian thinks he heard a Russian speaking, while the Englishman thinks it was a German. There is a mass of information but no obvious solution. Dupin takes all the evidence, makes sense of it, and uncovers the killer—which turns out to be not a Russian or a German but an escaped orang-outan. But Dupin makes an impossible task look easy, not just because he is very good at making sense of the clues but because he knows where to look for evidence (he interviews neighbours about what they heard and saw, looks for marks in the house, checks out how the murderer entered and left, and even carefully reads the local newspaper story about an orang-outan that escaped from its owner).

In your research tasks you are not investigating a murder, but you are expected to look for sufficient evidence to put together to back up an argument, or to come up with a solution to a problem.

## Research at university level

The amount of research required varies. It may be simply a matter of getting information about a couple of straightforward issues for a short assignment, where you know exactly what you need to find and perhaps where to find it. Or it may be a major exercise in which you have to respond to an open-ended assignment topic, and where you know almost nothing about the topic until you have done some research. To get an overview of what a research process can involve, consider an example of the second kind of task (see box).

Suppose you have to write an essay on universities and Estonian politics since World War II. You know next to nothing about Estonia, and it is not going to be easy finding material on the subject. This means allocating plenty of time for searching. You might spend half your time researching, and the rest of the time writing. It is important to allow adequate time to locate and use materials; it is also important to ensure that you do not run out of time for the writing part. The amount of time you can devote to the assignment will be influenced by the assessment weighting it carries.

There may be specialist books or articles which treat aspects of Estonian education in detail, and you might find material in comparative studies of education in Eastern Europe. But as you will need to locate education within the wider field of Estonian society, history and culture, you will have to find more general texts. You would probably consult books on Estonian history and society that explain how and why educational systems have developed in Estonia. You might not find as much specific information about education as you hoped, but by now you have learned that Estonia was part of the Soviet Union until the 1980s. So you decide to consult works on Soviet education. Even if there isn't much specifically devoted to Estonian education and culture, there might be comparative studies of the different Soviet republics (including valuable statistics on levels of literacy or the percentage of the population with secondary and tertiary qualifications), which would enable you to start building up a picture of tertiary education in Estonia.

If library books and journals did not have sufficient information, it would be time to start thinking of alternatives. A key-word search on the Internet could turn up articles, or details of recent studies. You might find a couple of Estonian university web pages on the Internet (in English) containing brief histories of the institutions.

Next it might occur to you that an obvious place to seek information on Estonia would be the Estonian Embassy. You might even look in the phone book for Estonian organisations ('Friends of Estonia', 'Estonia–Australia Friendship Society', 'The League of Estonian Patriots') and give them a ring. They would probably be flattered to find people interested in their country, and might have lots of information.

Thus, to be a successful researcher you should:

- plan and schedule your research time;
- work out what you need to know;
- not expect all the information you need to be available in the first place you look;
- use your imagination to think of other sources of information.

## PLANNING

In the planning stage of the task (and indeed throughout) you must do a lot of *thinking*. Although this may seem obvious, many students (especially those who tend to be dependent, surface-oriented learners) get hold of books or other research materials and begin making notes without doing much thinking—just as they might attend a lecture and take down notes without thinking much about the topic.

*Begin with what you already know.* Try to work out what the set topic requires and begin formulating the outline of a rough answer in point form (see chapter 10). You might do some brainstorming at this stage or use other techniques to generate a list of questions you need to answer with your research. The danger of going straight into research is that you might spend a lot of time finding out about things that are irrelevant, and/or lose sight of all the aspects that need to be covered. A rough plan of the assignment that indicates how many words will be available for each subtopic or separate issue will help you to allocate research time. Suppose the assignment requires you to discuss buses, trams, ferries and trains. You may decide that ferries deserve only 20% of the space available. In that case it would be silly to spend 80% of the time available finding and reading material on ferries—yet this can happen if you do not think and plan first, especially if there is a wealth of fascinating, easily available material on that subtopic.

An important aspect of planning is *setting priorities*. This means deciding what you should do first, what you should do next, and so on. Begin with your lecture notes and the set textbook(s). Then read materials that provide a general overview. Books written as introductions to the field for first-year students or the general public will be useful here, even though you may need to consult more specialised materials further on in your research. Encyclopaedias and other reference books are sometimes useful too. Only after you have some familiarity with the general topic you have to treat, should you devote yourself to more specialised and detailed resources.

Having said that, it must be acknowledged that in practice you do not always have the luxury of consulting resources in what might be the ideal order. In units where many students do the same topic there may be heavy demand for a small number of library resources. Work out what will be most useful and borrow or order them while you can. Borrowing privileges are usually restricted for sources in high demand; you may be able to have a book for only three days, or overnight, or you may have to use it in the library. You may then be tempted to do a lot of photocopying, but while photocopying can be useful it can also waste time and money. Be sure you really need the material you propose to photocopy before you join a long queue. In the time spent queueing and copying, you might have been able to skim through the whole article or chapter, locate the three relevant pages, read these closely and note the key points. Then you can walk out of the library having achieved something.

Note that libraries normally allow you to reserve items currently on loan to someone else. The fact that something is not on the shelves when you first check doesn't mean that you cannot eventually get it. But if many other students (who also have the right of reserve) want the text, do not expect to be able to borrow it more than once. If, on the other hand, you know that an item cannot be borrowed and will be available in the library, you can defer using it until you know just what you want from it.

## LOCATING SOURCES

Head for the library when you have to do research. If the library does not have the material you're looking for, library staff can alert you to other sources of information. Probably the most useful thing you can do in your first few weeks at university is to familiarise yourself with the university library—its staff, information systems, hours, rules and regulations. Most university libraries offer guided tours, and some subjects include library visits, lectures and small assessment projects or activities which are meant to provide you with a basic working knowledge. After that, the more you use the library the more productive it will be for you. Do not be afraid to ask library staff for assistance—they are usually very helpful. Collect any brochures that explain library services you may need to use.

While first-year students tend to rely mostly on books, journal articles are another useful resource. Scholarly journals are far more up to date (during the time a book is being prepared for publication, six or eight editions of a journal might be published). They cover a much wider range of topics, though articles are often highly specialised. While the titles of useful books can be found directly from the library catalogue, a different procedure is needed to find individual journal articles (see below).

Most of the printed sources in libraries are texts which conform to high academic standards. Before work is accepted for publication by academic publishers or journals it is scrutinised by experts in the field. This is called peer review. On the basis of the peer(s) decision, an editor will reject the paper, return it to the author for modification if they are not satisfied with it, or accept it in its present form. Books for the general reader or school children, in contrast, may package information attractively but are less reliable. The same applies to articles in ordinary magazines.

There are other texts kept in libraries that provide valuable information, such as audiotapes, videos, films, reference books, yearbooks, directories and encyclopaedias. Another useful resource is newspapers. Libraries usually keep electronic or microfilm copies of selected major or local newspapers. If you know a topic or issue was making the headlines the previous year, it might be worthwhile searching around that time for relevant reports, editorials or opinion pieces. Although newspapers don't have the same intellectual credibility as books or articles, and issues are not likely to be covered in any great depth, they may provide quantitative material (figures, statistics), examples from everyday life, and the opinions of politicians, businesspeople, bureaucrats and others involved.

 **The Internet**

Libraries should be the first place you visit—but there are other possibilities. The **Internet** is accessible in university computer labs and perhaps libraries, or from home if you have a modem. It is an exciting source of material just because of its size, but that is also its main drawback. Most of the information you get from 'the Net' is difficult to verify, so you have to be careful about what you use. To use the Net, you need the same search skills that you use on your library catalogue—except that you will have far more 'paths' to choose from and it will therefore be more time-consuming. Also, the Net can be seductive: you are tempted to try a few more websites, or you become intrigued by material which is interesting but irrelevant.

Generally it is best to use conventional sources (books, journals) first, and make use of the Net only if these have not worked. We do not want to discourage you—the Net can be extremely useful if you need the most up-to-date spin on things—but a great deal of material on the Net does not meet academic standards. It is unverified and/or trivial, so you should be wary of basing too much work on such research. If you do use material from the Net, make sure that you bookmark the site or take down its details, and reference it properly when you use the material.

Government institutions do not normally come to mind as sources of information, but they can be useful. The most obvious attraction is statistical information: government institutions collect and publish statistics on every aspect of life—economic, social, political, cultural. But there is more than just statistics: making sense of a particular situation (in education, welfare, trade and development, industrial relations, finance) often depends on knowing what policies the government has put in place in that area. Then, government institutions do a lot of their own research on important social and cultural issues, which is published in the form of reports. These can provide useful models for putting together your own reports.

Local (town or suburban) libraries will not have the same breadth of holdings as your university library, and a much smaller proportion of their holdings will be academic texts than is the case with university libraries, but they can be useful. Do not overlook them.

Businesses don't do the same amount of research as government departments, but they do publish material—reports, brochures, financial viability studies—that might be useful. They will not let you have anything sensitive, but if you approach them they might think it a good public relations exercise to help you out. Occasionally media organisations will be prepared to assist. When you contact such off-campus sources be polite—that will increase your chances of eliciting co-operation. Keep a record of what you found, its date, and where you got it from so that it can be properly referenced.

## Where do I start?

There are five steps a student might take to find materials. It is not an exhaustive list and would not apply in every case.

> Five steps to finding material:
>
> - what you have;
> - bibliographies;
> - subject catalogues;
> - indexes;
> - browsing.

### What you have

Begin with reading material you already have or have been told about. The set textbook may have only a couple of pages relevant to the topic you have to research, but at least read these pages as a starting point. Do not overlook recommended readings for the unit, which may be provided in the unit outline.

## Bibliographies

Make use of the bibliographies in the set and recommended textbooks. Take note of books mentioned within chapters (in references or lists of further reading), also other relevant resources listed in each new book or article you make use of. Entries in reference books sometimes include bibliographies. Some reference books, in fact, are bibliographies—where a whole volume is devoted to listing works in some field. If someone has recently compiled a bibliography of recent relevant works in a particular field you might as well take advantage of it. Occasionally what proves most useful about a particular item will be that it refers you to something else.

Bibliographies specify author and title. The next step is to search for the book in a library by looking up either the author or title in the catalogue. You cannot search for a journal article in the library catalogue; you need to use an appropriate index (see below). But you can look up the title of the journal itself to check whether the library holds it. If the library has the book, the author or title catalogue will provide you with the book's call number, which will enable you to locate it on the shelves (or to reserve it if it is currently on loan). (The catalogue provides other information too: see Activity at the end of this chapter.)

## Subject catalogue

This allows you to find books according to their subject matter. You can use subject catalogues to find potentially useful books for which you have neither an author nor title—that is, books you didn't know existed at the outset. Obviously the number of subject categories is finite, so don't expect to be able to enter *any* word as a subject word. Even if there were such things as books that dealt with the influence of rock music on polar bears, there might not be a subject category 'Polar bears and rock'. The relevant category would be more likely to say 'Popular music, ursine' ('ursine' referring to bears as a species). To find appropriate headings to look up, consult the *Index of Subject Headings* (these are reference books held in the library).

It is usually a good idea when analysing the set topic for your assignment to note some **synonyms** of the key words. If your topic was, say, 'Discuss the significance of conservation for leisure activities', some obvious synonyms for 'conservation' would be 'heritage', 'environment', 'environmentalism', 'ecology'. Synonyms for leisure would be 'recreation', 'amusement', 'sport', 'tourism'. Some of these words (e.g. 'tourism') are not synonyms in the strict sense, but they can probably be regarded as related (or cognate) words within the context of a discipline such as tourism studies. Your knowledge of the unit in which you were given the assignment topic would allow you to infer that the term 'conservation' here included the preservation of interesting historic sites, beaches and national parks. These are places used for leisure purposes (e.g. Sunday picnics) by people living near them. They are also places visited by tourists. So it would make sense to assume that there might be published material relating conservation to tourism that was worth looking for.

Synonyms for words can be looked up in a thesaurus. This is traditionally a kind of reference book, though many word-processing programs on computers now include a thesaurus. Synonyms may provide better starting points for subject catalogue searches than the original word in the topic. However, a thesaurus will usually supply many synonyms that are not relevant or useful, and they will not necessarily give you cognate words specific to an academic discipline. You must also be careful not to get side-tracked; a word's synonyms have different shades of meaning and can sometimes point you in the wrong direction. In the example above, although 'tourism' is a useful synonym for research purposes, we must be careful not to substitute the word 'tourism' for the word 'leisure' when writing the assignment. Presumably there is a good reason why the latter word was used in the set topic.

Another potential problem is the fact that a single word may have a range of different meanings. One example is 'culture': as well as the meaning we understand the word to have in this unit, it is used to refer to artistic products and practices of a certain kind and to the growing of biological cells and tissues in laboratories. The word 'communication' can pertain to the production of meaning, or to the behaviours associated with sending messages, or to the technologies used to send messages. Each of these different meanings is associated with a distinctive field of academic knowledge.

There is an important moral in all this. You cannot expect to handle assignments well if you are not taking interest in, and keeping up with, the general conceptual content of a unit as it proceeds from week to week. While marks may be allocated for specific tasks (e.g. essays and oral presentations) and not for general study (listening to lectures, reading the textbook), the latter is important if you want to produce good assignments.

## Indexes

The ordinary library subject catalogue allows you to find books on the basis of their subject, but not articles in journals. There are certain specialised indexes, however, which allow you to locate articles on specific subjects. Some of these indexes can be found in libraries in hard-copy form, but increasingly they are accessed electronically (e.g. on CD-ROM). They are usually grouped in broad discipline categories (e.g. physical sciences, education, social sciences, humanities). A useful index to be aware of is APAIS (Australian Public Affairs Information Service), which allows you to locate articles in a wide range of Australian periodicals.

Slightly varying procedures are needed to search different indexes. Library staff will be happy to help you become familiar with them. After finding in the index an article that looks useful, the next step is to get the call number of the relevant journal (if the library holds it) from the title catalogue. In some cases you may be able to access the full text of an article electronically. Libraries may also make available photocopies of articles likely to be in demand by undergraduates.

## Browsing

Sometimes you can find a useful book by looking on the shelves in the vicinity of a book you know is relevant to the topic. The advantage of browsing is that you can quickly inspect a book to see if it will be any good. But you should not rely on browsing as a way of finding resources: cataloguing systems are such that similar books are often far apart on the shelves. Remember too that a book may be absent from the shelf because it is on loan, and unless you consult the catalogue you will not know that the library has the book.

## GETTING HELP

Do not lose sight of why you are expected to do research. You are developing information literacy, not just getting a bothersome assignment out of the way. Open-ended research tasks (as in the Estonian example)

## Evaluating sources

Not all the books you pluck from the shelves will be equally valuable. Sources can differ from one another in many ways:

- whether or not they have been screened before publication by academic experts (i.e. peer-reviewed);
- the extent to which they engage in arguing and theorising rather than merely providing facts;
- their purpose and intended audience (e.g. whether written for the general reader, aimed mainly at first-year university students, or written primarily for people who already have a lot of expertise in the field);
- their ease of use (e.g. readability);
- their comprehensiveness; whether or not they have aids like illustrations, graphs, maps, suggested further reading, index, glossary;
- their accessibility (i.e. whether they can be located using library catalogues and indexes. Articles in newspapers usually cannot be located in this way, though some libraries have indexes for some newspapers). Availability also varies (e.g. an item may not be available for loan to undergraduate students);
- the medium (print being the main one, videotapes and audiotapes being much less common). Print can take many forms—'hard copies' (i.e. material printed on paper), also microfilm/microfiche (used to store old copies of newspapers and other periodicals) and electronic (which can sometimes be downloaded and printed in hard-copy form).

Whether something is valuable or not depends on your purpose. If you need a quick and simple introduction to a subject, you will not choose the most substantial and rigorous text; if you need something very up to date, you may have to go to a newspaper article.

are challenging, but they also help to develop your skills in accessing and utilising information.

Do not be afraid to ask for help. Failure to seek help when it is appropriate to do so does not reflect credit on you. Librarians are there to help people access information using library resources. It is their job; they generally enjoy doing it. However, you should regard library staff as people who can help you to improve your information literacy, not simply as people who can help you cope with your current assessment task. When they show you where something can be found or some procedure to follow, make a note of it so that next time you can do it on your own. Don't become dependent on librarians for what should be routine tasks. If you use a big library, make yourself a map of where things you need are located (e.g. showing the location of encyclopaedias, specialised reference books relevant to your disciplines, current periodicals, a hard-copy serials index you have found useful, newspaper microfilms). This means you can go straight to what you need on future visits to the library.

If you are genuinely in doubt about whether or not to make use of a particular resource that will require a fair amount of your time, it may be appropriate to check with your tutor.

## CONCLUSION

A particularly important part of your university work is research. In this chapter we have talked about what research is and where it fits in. Then we looked at how to find the materials we needed for research. In chapter 12 we look at how to make use of what you find.

### Activities

1.  You can often determine whether a book is 'academically respectable' rather than light and trivial simply by inspecting the information on the book contained in its on-line catalogue entry. You may find out other things too (e.g. it may be good to know that the book contains illustrations). What can you tell about the book from the following data provided on an electronic catalogue?

    ```
    YOU CHOSE: Popular music—Analysis, appreciation.
    Call Number: 781.63 11
    Author: Brackett, David.
    Title: Interpreting popular music/David Brackett.
    Publication: Cambridge; New York: Cambridge
    University Press, 1995.
    Material: xiv, 260 pp.: music; 24 cm.
    Note: Includes index.
    Note: Includes bibliographical references and
    discography.
    Subject: Popular music—History and criticism;
    Popular music—Analysis, appreciation; Musical
    criticism; Musical analysis.
    ```

2. Use an appropriate library index or CD-ROM catalogue to find the title and location of an *article* which looks as if it might be useful for an essay on the subject of pressure groups in politics. If the periodical containing the article is not in the library catalogue, find another article.

3. Again using the topic of pressure groups, conduct an Internet/World Wide Web search to find information on any aspect of the topic. Spend about 30 minutes. Briefly describe this search: what search engine(s) you used, and the main stages and results of the search—including noteworthy 'dead ends'. The purpose of this exercise is to practise using the Internet and to get a feel for how worthwhile it is as an academic research tool.

4. Locate five separate reference works in the reference section of a library that would be useful to you in researching this essay topic. For each of the five, provide the title and call number and briefly explain in just what way it would be useful.

5. Find and view the front page of a major newspaper published on or near the date of your last birthday. You may be able to find back issues of the newspaper on the World Wide Web, or in archives stored on microfilm or microfiche.

## chapter 12

# Research: using resources

We have explained that research activities should be directed by a clear sense of purpose. It is important that your research effort is properly integrated into the overall task of working on the assignment. You have to be clear about your purpose. What do you have to achieve in the assignment task? If you are vague about the ultimate purpose of the exercise you will not know what kind of research is needed, or how much is appropriate.

The *primary* reason for doing research is to find out more than you already know. Researching an assignment should not be something you do in order to 'dress up' a mediocre assignment with a few quotations from published authors and a bibliography. In the first place you do it in order to be a more knowledgeable writer on the subject, so that your *own* thoughts are more penetrating, precise, interesting, thoughtful. Having read what four authors have had to say on a certain topic, rather than just one, you are likely to develop a better understanding, which will be reflected in what you proceed to write.

The *second* reason is to obtain evidence for a credible argument. Without research your argument would be just a series of vague assertions.

A *third* reason is that research can provide useful examples to help you illustrate what you have to explain. It can make your essay, report or presentation more interesting and informative.

## MAKING NOTES FOR RESEARCH PURPOSES

You don't have to make notes every time you read something. Whether you do or not will depend on your purpose. You may be reading a source simply to develop your understanding of the topic. Or, already having collected a lot of information, you might be reading a source to check whether it has anything new to offer. However, when the reason for your research is to gather evidence or inform yourself on a large and complex topic (as in the Estonian example in chapter 11), it is important to make adequate notes: memory can easily let you down.

Taking notes from books, articles or any other source means being selective. There is no point in taking everything down—but you don't want to leave out important information. You can decide what to include or exclude by going back to the initial planning stage, where you analysed your task and worked out what it was you needed to find. This might be one of the following:

- general background information;
- specific details;
- arguments for or against a position;
- examples.

If you have done prior thinking and planning, you will have worked out the subtopics or subsections of your assignment—at least in a preliminary way. If you were writing about pressure groups in Australian politics, for example, you might decide to provide answers to these four questions:

1. What are pressure groups (or interest groups)?
2. How much influence do they have?
3. In what ways are they harmful in democratic political systems?
4. In what ways are they beneficial?

Although a single source (e.g. a chapter in a book) might have material on all of these, it will be best to make notes on each of your subtopics separately. Go through the whole chapter noting whatever you need to, about harmful effects. Then go through it again looking for material on beneficial effects. This is preferable to trying to do everything at once.

Have a provisional outline of the essay, which will help you to identify precisely what you need to find to support your subtopics (and sub-subtopics). As far as you can, work out the approximate number of words to be devoted to each part of the essay. Throughout the process of researching and writing, *check that you are still on track*. Look back every now and then at the requirements of the set topic and/or your rough plan or outline. Continue this regular check throughout the whole research process. It is easy to begin drifting in the wrong direction, accumulating irrelevant information. A lot of valuable time can be wasted in this way—both in getting the information in the first place and in trying to make sense of the mass of material you have collected. (See chapter 10 on relating planning to research.)

Most of what we have said about making notes in lectures (see chapter 8) is relevant here, with an important difference. Lecture notes should be comprehensive: your notes cover the essentials of the whole lecture. Similarly, you might even summarise a substantial portion of a text for revision purposes. Research notes are more selective: you go to what you need and ignore the rest.

 **Some golden rules of note-making**

1.  *Identify relevant material* in the text. Having got hold of a book or article, locate the parts relevant to your purpose as efficiently as possible by using the book's index or by skim-reading. Survey a passage before beginning to write anything down. (Observe the three stages of reading suggested in chapter 7.)

2.  *Keep your purpose in mind.* Don't get 'involved' in what you are reading. In other words, stay detached but alert—you are not reading for pleasure but to find useful information. The last thing you can afford to do is get caught up in, say, the book's exciting account of the fall of the Soviet Union when all you want to know about is Estonia's not-so-exciting education policies.

3.  *Use a separate page* for each separate source you make notes from. As far as possible you should also use a separate page for each subtopic of the essay. This will make life easier when you come to organise the material you have collected.

4.  *Label each page.* Give it a number and a heading which briefly notes the topic (e.g. 'Pressure groups—main types'). Then record the source you are using. The author's surname will be enough, provided you have separately noted the full publication details of the text and there is no other source to which that name applies. Do these things before you make any notes. It takes self-discipline to make this a habit, but it can save much time later on, when you may need to cite the source of some important information but have no idea where you got it from.

5.  *Be clear and simple.* Write notes in everyday language, preferably in point form. The source might have a long paragraph about how education policy changed in Estonia under the different Soviet leaders. What you can do

is record a name (e.g. Gorbachev) and next to the name write a few points (e.g. 'Control of education passed to Estonian parliament').

6. *Focus on the essentials.* You need specific concepts and facts which relate to particular subtopics in the plan you have made of the overall assignment. What counts as the 'essentials' of the passage will depend on your reasons for wanting notes. Use abbreviations whenever possible—as long as you will remember what they mean. Resist the temptation to record too much. Notes limited to the main points will be more useful to you later, as it will be easier to organise them. There are two other reasons why you should try to be brief: (a) you are forced to paraphrase rather than merely transcribe. Making brief notes singling out the core ideas forces you to think—you have to use your brain to convert the full version into something much shorter and simpler. This means you will begin to understand better and remember more. Transcribing (copying out large chunks of the text) does not require thought; (b) it will reduce the risk of accidental plagiarism.

7. *Note useful examples* that you can reproduce easily in your essay and that make a point or back up an argument. We have seen (in chapter 6) how using examples is often an excellent way of explaining a concept. Do not overdo this technique.

8. *If in doubt, revisit the source.* If you are not sure whether or not it is worth making notes from a source, and you know you will easily be able to access the source again, write yourself a quick note so you can find the material again. If later you decide it is worth including some statistics from that source, you will know where to find them. Photocopying allows you to revisit the source (but note our warning about being tempted to photocopy too much).

9. *Take care with quoting.* It will sometimes (but not often) be appropriate to note down material you want to include in your assignment as a direct quotation. You must copy the original material exactly, down to the last detail of punctuation. You must also clearly identify it *as a* quotation. It must not be allowed to become confused with the rest of your notes so that it slips unattributed into your assignment: you will then risk being accused of plagiarism.

10. *Note down the page number* of the source against every idea that you may need to cite and every quotation.

If you have worked out a tentative plan for your essay before you began collecting material and followed these rules, things should begin to fall nicely into place. Sort and review your notes, and with the information now at your disposal build up a more detailed outline of the assignment. Use point form rather than full sentences and paragraphs. Although the outline will concentrate on the main concepts and principles it can include notes about how these will be explained or amplified when you come to write the assignment in full (e.g. one sub-subtopic in your outline might be 'increase in political lobbying'; alongside this you might write 'use example of National Rifle Association').

## USING SOURCES

We now look at how you might make use of separate sources to gather information on a particular topic, using examples of actual academic texts. The sample texts are reproduced in the Appendixes section at the end of this book. It is important to read the sample text in conjunction with our discussion so you can follow the points we make. Our examples happen to be from the area of sociology/politics. Although your study may be in other disciplines, the general principles will still be relevant.

You have to write an essay on the topic of interest groups (also called pressure groups) in Australia. You consult four sources (texts) in the order in which we present them. Appendix 1 is the first you get hold of and you make some notes from it, bearing in mind that it is discussing the United States political scene (though it does, unusually for an American textbook, make a reference to Australia). The last two paragraphs, which deal with the advantages and disadvantages of interest groups, may be especially useful if you have to decide whether or not interest groups are undemocratic.

The next source you obtain is Appendix 2. As you come to each new text in the research process you need to relate it to what the previous texts had to say. (In real life you may have read these a week or more before.) There is no point in repeating work you have already done. On the other hand, it would be wrong to assume that the subsequent texts will merely recap what the first one did with the topic. While it can be useful to work with a number of sources on your desk at once, this is not always possible.

More than half of Appendix 2 repeats what you have already learned. Paragraph 1 provides a couple of instances of how interest groups can act (e.g. they can put pressure on the executive branch of government), but the main new material comes in paragraph 2, which raises the issue of relations between members of interest groups and leaders of interest groups. This concept is picked up in the last half of paragraph 4, which suggests that the leaders might have different ideas from the members, and not be able to find out what they want. This is worth noting because it adds a new angle: perhaps interest groups can be undemocratic in their internal workings, not merely in their relationship to the overall political context.

The next source deals with Australia. Appendix 3 offers another definition—very similar to, but perhaps better than, that of Appendix 1. It widens our knowledge of the diversity of interest groups by giving us some new categories in paragraph 2, which tells us that groups can be promotional or sectional. Appendix 3 also gives us some Australian examples. We can note the points made about the way pressure groups parallel the state–federal division of government in Australia, but this is not central to our purposes in this assignment. It is interesting that according to Appendix 3 pressure groups are 'ubiquitous' (present everywhere) in Australian politics. This is surprising, given that Appendix 1 seemed to account for American interest groups in terms of the unusual freedom of United States politicians from party constraints, and specifically cited Australia as an example of a country where politicians were not so open to outside influence.

Finding this apparent inconsistency is not something to worry about. In fact, you could draw attention to it in your essay with a sentence like this: 'It is sometimes thought that interest groups are significant only in political systems where legislators are free to vote as they wish rather than having to follow a party line (here we would cite Robertson, the author of Appendix 1). In fact, though, they are often found in Australia, where there is tight party discipline.' This will impress the reader of your essay. You could push further into the issue to try to resolve the contradiction. This might lead you to conclude that Australian interest groups work in a different way from American ones—not targeting individual members of government as in the United States, but working to influence whole political parties and government departments, and mobilising voters.

Paragraph 3 of Appendix 3 has useful material which allows us to expand our list of the positive and negative aspects of interest groups. We need to note down only the new aspects, not the ones supplied by our earlier authors.

Appendix 4 does not supply much that is useful to our purposes that we don't already know. The final point about *social movements* is worth noting. It develops that idea more than the other sources, and provides further Australian examples.

## ORGANISING THE MATERIAL YOU HAVE GATHERED

When you make notes, never put notes from two or more sources on the same page and, as far as possible, use a separate page for each subtopic (see golden rule number 3 in the box). For example, the definition of interest groups, perhaps with examples of their diversity, would be on a page of its own. This page should be labelled in some way. Having your material on separate sheets of paper has two distinct benefits. First, as you read subsequent sources you can quickly find your notes on this subtopic. If the new source adds to or improves on what you have already got, you can make further notes. If not, you save time which otherwise would be wasted. Second, when you are putting the information together you can easily pick out the pieces of paper with notes on this topic. When you return to your assignment plan you can quickly survey the material you have gathered on a subtopic. And when you begin drafting the assignment in full you can easily consult your notes on each subtopic.

If you worked out a tentative plan for the essay before you began, and if you followed the rules above while taking notes, things should begin to fall into place. Sort and review your notes and use them to build up a more detailed outline of the assignment (see chapter 10). On the expanded outline (which is still largely in point form) you can note what you will use from the material collected. This is preferable to moving straight into writing a full draft. As you play with your outline you may realise that there is simply no space to go into details about United States lobby groups or that they are not relevant.

If you have been researching a large and 'open-ended' kind of topic, as in the example of the essay on Estonian universities in chapter 11, your notes might not fall into neat subtopics and there might not be a well-worked-out plan to relate them to. The process of going through the material you have collected will take more time. You will have to identify main ideas, arguments or trends and cull these from the mass of information. The main thing is that you control the essay that emerges: don't let it be 'driven' by the stack of notes in front of you. As you begin to shape a focused and coherent response to the set topic, you will have to accept that some of the evidence you gathered (despite your sacrifices in time, money and energy) is not going to be needed for this particular essay.

## REFERENCING

Referencing is a necessary part of any assignment, but it causes students more trouble than it should—probably because (a) it involves getting exactly right a lot of fussy details, (b) students can't see why it matters so much, and (c) it is one of the last tasks in finishing an assignment. This means that all too often it is 2 am the night before the assignment is due when you discover that you forgot to note down the publication details of an important source.

Referencing (or 'documenting') your sources refers to the following operations:

- making sure that any material you have quoted from a source is recognised as a quotation by your reader;
- citing the source (author and text) of any quotations used or any ideas that deserve to be acknowledged. Such citations (or 'references') take the form of footnotes or endnotes in some referencing styles; in others they are included in the text;
- providing a list of the works you used (sometimes called a bibliography).

You don't have to memorise the referencing convention used in a subject—you just need guides and models.

---

 **Why use references?**

Referencing serves a number of purposes:

- to show the reader that your writing has not emerged entirely from your own mind and that it is at least partly based on evidence from certain sources and the opinions of authorities;
- to allow your readers to check the same source for themselves (perhaps to make sure that you got it right);
- to avoid plagiarism by identifying quoted material as the work of another person;
- to avoid plagiarism by acknowledging that certain ideas (even if now expressed differently) are ideas for which some other writer deserves credit (or, if they are stupid ideas, deserves blame!). Ideas are a form of intellectual property. Whoever first put an idea forward deserves to be identified as the 'owner' of the idea.

---

The purposes served by referencing are integral to the academic enterprise. They help to preserve the academic values we have discussed (in chapter 2), such as commitment to the exchange of knowledge (so we point our reader to the other sources available) and respect for scholarship (writers and researchers deserve to have their work properly acknowledged). References are relevant to the reliance of academic work on arguments based on good evidence (discussed in chapters 4 and 5).

We have suggested that in many ways students are 'apprentice academics'. Your assignment is in a sense a simulation of a 'real-world' article published by an academic researcher or a report published by some organisation. Knowing how to reference is a literacy relevant to many publishing activities, and these days a fair proportion of graduates, employed in all kinds of organisations, sooner or later have to write or help prepare material for publication (surveys, brochures, information kits, training manuals, handbooks, directories).

## Referencing systems

There are many different systems or conventions. Some important ones are the Harvard system, the MLA, the Oxford–Cambridge (Turabian), and the Chicago style. Individual publishers of books and journals often have their own variations. You might get through your university career having to use only one style, or you might have to use several, depending on the disciplines in which you study. The differences between the styles are usually fairly minor, but it is important to be consistent. Use the style specified in a particular subject. If you have a choice, choose one style and stick to it. Never change styles within a single assignment.

Information on requirements can be found in subject outlines and study materials. The reference section of a large library should also have complete manuals explaining each of the main systems. These provide numerous examples of how to reference unusual sources (e.g. interviews, radio programs or personal correspondence). As well, several websites provide information on citation styles, including guidelines for referencing Internet material.

Whatever referencing guide you use, follow the format for bibliography entries and every other aspect exactly, including all details of punctuation and underlining or italicising. You should also follow directives as to, for instance, whether items are placed in alphabetical order in the bibliography, whether or not they are numbered, the heading used ('References', 'List of works consulted'), and so on. There may also be rules about how to display quotations (typically, a quotation of four lines or more is indented; quotation marks are used only for shorter quotes incorporated in your text without indentation). There may be general rules about style, such as using words rather than numerals for numbers up to and including ten.

Textual references, as the Harvard system allows, are easier to use than footnotes. Normally only the author's surname and page number from which the quote is derived are required in parentheses (brackets) at the end of a sentence like this (Lemonhead 107). Note that the full stop comes after the brackets. If the reader is interested in the source, he or she looks up 'Lemonhead' in your bibliography at the end of the assignment. If you have two sources by Lemonhead, include the year of publication (Lemonhead 1987: 107). Note that your reference specifies an author rather than an editor. If the source is an essay by Lemonhead in a collection of essays edited by Cranberry, then your bibliography should list this essay by Lemonhead as a separate entry. There are many special cases and variations (books written by several authors, particular editions of books, material you want to cite which has been itself reprinted from some other source, and so on). It is just a matter of having time to look up the right format to use.

## Quoting

Quoting means copying down material from a source and reproducing it in your assignment. If you are going to quote it must be a direct quote: every detail must be faithful to the original. If you make any change, or insert any explanatory material of your own, put the differences in square brackets [ ]. If you leave out any part of the original, use an ellipsis (. . .). Make sure you identify the whole quotation with quotation marks (' ') or indention, and indicate the author and source.

Either quote exactly and completely or not at all. If a quotation is not necessary (which is most of the time), you can convey the general meaning by paraphrasing (putting it in your own words). Make sure they really are different words. Merely changing a word here or there from the original is not enough. If you have taken notes in point form, then you have nothing to worry about: the full sentences you generate from your brief notes will be your own work. Even if an idea is expressed in your own words, it may still, of course, need to be cited as the idea of another person (see below).

If you want to use a quotation when making notes from texts, copy down the exact words and punctuation and put it in a prominent place in quotation marks. Otherwise you may lose track of what is quotation and what is not, and find that you are accidently using someone else's words in your essay without identifying them.

When using quotations in your writing you have to contextualise them. The author you are quoting has a somewhat different agenda than you have. Dropping statements into a different text will confuse your reader. Before beginning the quotation, you may need to explain what has led up to it or how it fits in: 'Armstrong, in explaining why the early settlers developed an intense fear of beavers, shows that the Iroquois "cleverly spread rumours about man-eaters who could sever a leg with a single bite" (117).' You must also ensure that any sentence you begin is grammatically complete. Using a quotation midstream must not be allowed to interfere with the logic and sense of your sentence. Look at the way published writers introduce quotations and incorporate them into their sentences.

 **When to quote**

You will not need to quote often and you should avoid long quotations. Only quote if:

- the original expresses an idea in a particularly apt and striking way;
- the reader should be able to inspect the precise way the thought was expressed by the author you are quoting (it may be significant that certain words were chosen rather than others);
- you are closely analysing an idea expressed by an author and you want the reader to be able to keep referring to the precise way it was formulated so that they can follow your analysis;
- the author is an authority, which lends credibility to your argument or analysis.

### When should you acknowledge ideas?

Even when you do not quote a full sentence direct from a source you have used, you might include in your own writing ideas, concepts, facts and figures you have come on in your research. If you wanted to include in an essay any of the facts and statistics from paragraph 2 of Appendix 1, for instance, you would need to provide a reference to the source, page number, and where it was obtained. Essentially, you have to reference anything that is not already well known and accepted.

Reference facts and figures so the reader can check the source, especially if there is any possibility that they are false, incomplete or contested. A piece of information that anyone could readily find and no-one would dispute need not be referenced: if for some reason you wanted to make mention in your essay of the height of the Sydney Harbour Bridge you would not need to provide a reference to the source from which you obtained it. The author of Appendix 2 briefly quotes from the First Amendment to the American Constitution but does not supply a reference. To do so would be fussy, as (at least in the United States) this is a well known and accessible document. You normally do not have to cite the source when you look things up in dictionaries and general reference books, but reference if you incorporate an actual quotation from the source.

Reference ideas for which someone other than yourself deserves credit. These are insights, hunches, theories or conclusions which constitute some advance, however minor or modest, on what was known or thought. Many ideas, though, are so familiar that they are said to be '*in the public domain*'. Credit for these does not need to go to a particular individual. An example would be 'smoking can be a factor in heart disease'. Most of the ideas in the Appendixes are in this category: although they may all be new concepts to a student, it becomes clear after reading a few sources that interest groups are so common that anyone who studies the political scene understands their significance. So you could write a sentence like 'Interest groups are an important feature of modern political life in Australia' without citing any author. But what if the next sentence went: 'So far, very few interest groups in Poland are politically effective'? This proposition is not well known and obviously agreed about, so the author would need to be acknowledged.

What about the first sentence of Appendix 1: 'An important effect of the distinctive American party system is that it encourages people to try to influence the way individual legislators vote on specific issues'? This is a borderline case. It may be that while everyone knows interest groups exist in America, seeing them as 'an effect' of the party system is not a routine and obvious conclusion to draw; so perhaps we would supply the source. Remember, even if the concept or idea does *not* need to be cited, if you reproduce another person's actual words (i.e. if you quote), the source of the quotation must be cited.

Reference ideas when you have other reasons for attributing them to a particular author, even if they do not strictly need to be acknowledged for the other reasons above. You may want to disown the idea (he said it, not me!), or you may want to indicate that a reputable authority shares an opinion you hold. Your reference should cite the author of the quotation or the author whose idea is being acknowledged—not an editor and not someone else who quoted the original author in your source.

If in doubt, always reference. There may be some variation between tutors and disciplines in what is expected. Your markers will let you know if you are not referencing correctly.

---

### Some useful tips

Referencing will be more painless if:

- you record the full bibliographic details of each source as soon as you know it will be used (in an assignment involving many sources, index cards that can be arranged in alphabetical order of surname are useful);
- you never make notes without identifying the source and noting page numbers;
- you follow guidelines exactly and get it right. Avoid using your own typographical gimmicks, such as capitalising authors' names or using special fonts for the bibliography.

---

Check with your tutor if in doubt about requirements. Tutors may have different opinions as to what should be included in your bibliography. You should allow time for proofreading of your assignment before submitting it. A fairly common error is to forget to underline (or italicise) the titles of books and periodicals. This must be done wherever they are mentioned in the text of your assignment, as well as in references. Titles of chapters and articles are not underlined but placed in quotation marks.

## TYPICAL FAULTS IN STUDENT RESEARCH

The following are the errors most often made in research in student assignments:

- *not enough research or research too narrow* (e.g. a lot of material deriving from research on some aspects of the topic, while other important aspects have not been researched);
- *research not relevant* (e.g. taking notes from sources that seem interesting or important and using the material in the assignment regardless of whether it answers the set topic);

- *material derived from sources not well understood* (and/or not well integrated into the assignment);
- *plagiarism* (e.g. not identifying quoted material as having been written by others or putting forward ideas without acknowledging the author who deserves credit for them);
- *research taking up too much of the time available.* After delay beginning work on the assignment, to do even a minimum amount of research means that other stages of the task (e.g. writing improved drafts and proofreading) have to be skimped;
- *research strategy poorly planned*, with time wasted on sources of marginal value, or becoming engrossed in research and failing to move on to the next stage soon enough. Sometimes the urge to be 'perfectionist' must be resisted—there is simply not enough time to track down and read every source that might have some relevance.

## CONCLUSION

In this chapter we have looked more closely at how to use sources such as books and articles, and how to reference that material. While we were mainly concerned with research relating to an assignment, much of what we have suggested about making notes applies also when you are getting ideas and information from printed sources for general study or exam preparation.

### Activities

1. Find a magazine article or short and easy-to-read chapter in a book. Imagine you have to write an assignment on the subject it deals with. Make notes deliberately using every one of the ten golden rules.

2. Write a mini-essay a few paragraphs long about some aspect of interest groups, making use of the sample texts (Appendixes 1–4). Make notes and use these to construct your essay (don't work direct from the sample texts). Include one brief quotation and one longer quotation (say four lines long). Reference this essay fully using the citation style of one of your subjects (e.g. Harvard system). Include a bibliography, title page, and whatever conventions of style and format are appropriate.

chapter 13

# Writing well: the basics

The ability to write well has always been highly valued. In earlier times—and in underdeveloped societies still—the small fraction of the population with this skill derived a great deal of prestige (or cultural capital) from it. Now, when most people are able to write in a basic way, those who can write with confidence and clarity still have a distinct advantage. But writing well does not mean a mere ability to use the language correctly—that is, just conforming to the rules and conventions of the language. A good writer is someone who can deal with ideas: combine ideas from different sources, give appropriate emphasis to the most important ideas, and above all explain ideas so they can be understood, in a form that is appropriate to the genre being used (business letter, company prospectus, minutes of a meeting, government report).

Skill in writing depends more on formal education than does skill in speech. There are 'self-made' businesspeople with a flair for oral communication, who have done well in the world without the benefit of much education. Such people are likely to hire others to do their writing. Now that most people work for large organisations, there is probably less scope for progressing far without good writing skills. Even those employed in technical areas find that their work involves more writing than they expected, especially when they have been promoted to senior positions. Reports, submissions, applications, memos and other correspondence have to be written for the benefit of others within the organisation, or for outside persons and groups.

Many students believe that correctness is what matters most in writing: being able to use the correct grammar, spelling and punctuation is seen as a formula for academic success. It is not surprising that those for whom English is not their native language should have such a view—they are still building a vocabulary, and sometimes have difficulty making themselves understood. But native English speakers are also often preoccupied with correctness, although correctness is not the salient feature of written communication. A perfectly correct example of language can be boring and ineffective.

Of course, correctness is important. First, faults in grammar, spelling and punctuation inevitably reduce the credibility of a writer. The reader may feel the writer has been casual and careless in other aspects too, and therefore that his or her ideas are not to be trusted. Second, defects of expression interfere with your ability to communicate what you mean. Third, serious faults will lose you marks. Some famous authors have been poor spellers, but they had editors to check their work before it was published. Students have to get it right on their own, and their reader—the tutor—will be on the lookout for mistakes.

## THE MAIN FEATURES OF WRITING

There are some ways in which communicating in writing is different from spoken language, especially face-to-face dialogue. (We deal with this difference in more detail in chapter 15.)

 **The main features of writing**

- Writing is premeditated. You normally have more time to think about what will be written and how it should be expressed. A first draft can be corrected before the reader sees it.
- Writing freezes language, giving a permanent record. It can be read at the reader's pace, and reread if necessary.
- Writing takes place in the absence of the reader (while reading takes place in the absence of the writer). To bridge this divide, you need to be careful to write to your audience and provide it with all the help it needs to make sense of your work.

The fixed nature of writing means that any errors or departures from convention will be more noticeable than they are in speech. People do not speak consistently in full, grammatically correct sentences. An unedited transcript of spoken language shows that people tend to speak in fragmentary sentences, and make all kinds of errors that normally go unnoticed.

The writer must anticipate the needs of readers. They are not present to ask questions of the writer, and cannot indicate that they are confused or bored. The writer must supply whatever context may be needed by the reader to understand the meaning of what is written, as well as its relevance and importance.

Writers must realise how difficult it is for readers to follow what they say. Writing does allow more complex ideas to be communicated in fewer words, but while you have been thinking about those ideas for hours, days or weeks, the reader has not. You might have become so familiar with the material that to you the direction in which the argument will go seems obvious. To the reader it may not be obvious at all. Writers need to learn to put themselves in the position of their readers. (In an academic situation you should not rely on the fact that the tutor who reads your assignment has existing knowledge of the discipline. The tutor is probably familiar enough with the subject to be able to work out what a badly written essay is trying to say, but will judge the assignment on how well it would work for a reader who did not have such special knowledge.)

Your reader knows you have had time to prepare your work, so you have to make sure that you take sufficient time to get it right—at every level, from general structure to punctuation. Actually, the reader's expectations will vary according to the genre and particular circumstances. A tutor marking an exam paper knows the student was under great pressure of time and will usually be tolerant of errors in punctuation (in fact, will probably not even notice them). Likewise, if someone making notes during a meeting is asked to write up and distribute a summary within half an hour, allowances will be made for a few errors in grammar and spelling. But if you have had weeks to do an assignment, you are expected to have devoted adequate time to each aspect of the project, from planning to final proofreading.

You cannot expect to scribble down your immediate thoughts in the spoken words you might use in everyday speech. Be straightforward. Your goal is to help someone understand something they did not understand (at least, not fully) when they began to read. If you do not have this sense of relationship with a reader, your writing will suffer.

Writing *is* different—but it is not completely different. Do not think your essays need to be full of big, unusual words and long, ponderous sentences. Mimicking academic writing in this way will interfere with communication, and you aren't communicating effectively if you yourself can barely understand your sentences.

It is useful to imagine writing to a listener, as in face-to-face spoken communication. Another way in which you should maintain some connection between your writing and speaking is to make sure you can verbalise what you write. That is, check that you can express in spoken words the main ideas of your assignment. They don't have to be the same words—as long as they are the same basic concepts. If someone asks you what you said in your essay, you should be able to give them a satisfactory answer (even if you oversimplify things a bit) without having to pick up the essay and read from it. If you *cannot* do this, there is a good chance that you are repackaging material found in your sources without processing it through your own mind—also that the essay will be difficult to make sense of. While it is often easier to deal with complex ideas in written language, good writing depends on clear thinking. If there has been clear thinking it should be possible to voice your ideas.

## WRITING TO A PURPOSE

What goes into any written communication should be determined not by what you know about the subject but by what your audience needs to know on a particular occasion. If the audience needs only a general idea of what a kangaroo is, there is no point in giving it an exhaustive scientific classification of kangaroos. A paragraph or page about kangaroos in an encyclopaedia will be dense with information: it has to be as comprehensive as possible because it will be consulted by readers interested in different aspects of kangaroos. But an encyclopaedia is a special genre. Most communication has a more specific focus, and it is not appropriate to try to be so comprehensive. Writers have to select, from all that they already know or can find out, the content appropriate to the occasion.

You might need to provide an argument, rather than descriptions or definitions. This would be the case if, for instance, you wanted the audience to agree with a conclusion you had reached.

### Purpose and structure

Purpose determines what we say. It also determines how we go about saying it. If we are classifying things, we might have to come up with a number of categories. You might use one paragraph explaining each one of these (in a longer piece of writing, each might get several pages). If you were discussing cause and effect, you would move systematically through the different causes or consequences of something. You will remember from chapter 10 that the set topic dictates the logic of your response to it: that is, it can indicate the structure of the assignment even before you know just what points you will make.

## The argument

Your argument might be: 'Kangaroos originally evolved in southern China and migrated to Australia hundreds of thousands of years ago.' Or: 'Kangaroos should be farmed for their meat and hides.' In these cases your purpose is to convince people of something—to discover what it will take to get them to accept your proposition. You will have to present evidence. To support the first proposition you might argue:

- that long ago Australia was connected by a 'land bridge' to Asia;
- that predators such as tigers eliminated kangaroos in Asia but did not spread to Australia before it was cut off by sea.

The first point is true, and perhaps the second would be accepted, but much more evidence would be needed to make your case convincing, such as proof that kangaroo fossils have been found in China.

To convince your audience that kangaroos should be farmed you might try to prove:

- that there was a good potential market at home and/or overseas for kangaroo products;
- that it would be economically feasible to farm kangaroos, despite the cost of high fences and the difficulty of handling undomesticated animals;
- that the widespread Australian sentiment against farming an animal of such national symbolic importance could be overcome;
- that an alternative to the beef cattle industry should be found because it damages the environment or because of some new cattle disease.

The last two parts of your argument do not have much to do with kangaroos: one is a cultural question; the other concentrates not on what is good about kangaroo farming but on what is bad about the cattle industry. But in making an argument, you need to use anything that might help convince the audience.

Being clear about purpose means considering the needs of the reader, and this has implications for the way you will put together your written work. A basic question, but one which many writers fail to take into account, is what they should do to indicate their purpose to the audience. The fact that *you* know what you want to communicate does not mean your audience knows. Thinking about your task in terms of the effect you want to achieve with the audience will also remind you that you need to do such things as:

- secure the audience's interest in the first place;
- provide some general context for your particular discussion;
- help the audience to follow the discussion (e.g. by providing signpost words and phrases).

## Analysing the audience

Once you start thinking about the needs of your audience, you realise that not every audience is the same. In real-life communication we need to know who it is we are trying to inform or influence. You will want to ask:

- What do they already know about the specific subject, related subjects, general context (to give you a better idea of what to include or leave out)? A good way of making new material meaningful is to relate it to things an audience already knows.
- What kind of literacy do they have in the relevant field? Will they understand specialised terminology, or should I use ordinary language? Which terms need to be defined?
- What is my relationship with them? Should I be formal and correct, or use casual language?
- What do I want the audience to do or think as a result of reading my work?

## Constraints

Just as you have to take the audience into account, it is necessary to ensure that your purpose is compatible with such constraints as word length. You will almost always be given a word length for an essay or report (in the case of exams there is no limit on the number of words, but the time available is limited). This constraint is not something peculiar to academic contexts. Newspapers, magazines, and academic journals all have to ration their space, and contributors are given strict guidelines on length.

Having to conform to a set length is a useful discipline. It encourages you to be focused in your content and concise and exact in your style.

While you must avoid going significantly over length it is foolish not to make use of the space you have. University essays are usually meant to be within 10% of the set word length. In other words, if the set length is 1000 words, try to write at least 900 but no more than 1100. It is better to have a first draft that is over, not under, the set length. In the process of revising it and improving the style, you will usually find it shrinks. Apart from satisfying assessment requirements, learning to write to a specified length is a useful skill for later life.

## ACADEMIC ASSIGNMENTS

What has been said about purpose and audience applies to all serious, premeditated acts of communication, not just to university work. However, you may think that academic assignments are somewhat different from 'real-life' communication, and in a sense you are right. Assignments are exercises. A student writing an assignment about kangaroos is not responding to a request from people who really want to know more about them. His or her real purpose is to demonstrate to a tutor (who already knows a lot about kangaroos, and probably doesn't expect to learn more from an undergraduate) that he or she has learned the concepts of 'Biology I', or whatever the subject is.

University assignments are often 'copies' or simulations of real-world communication, but not always: exams and tests, for instance, are not used outside educational institutions. The trend, however, is towards exercises that approximate what students will have to do in their eventual occupation. Obvious cases of this are assignments in disciplines like journalism or marketing, which duplicate real news stories or marketing proposals for a given product. In other subjects, students may conduct an experiment, survey or investigation and write a report on it. Such reports often conform reasonably closely to what might be published in the outside world. Here guidelines will be provided about format and structure, and there will probably not be much confusion about what is required.

An essay is also a simulation (or imitation): it asks you to use an academic style and terminology appropriate to the discipline, and to include references and a bibliography. It's like an article that might be submitted to a scholarly journal, which suggests that an essay is normally expected to involve argument—just as scholarly articles and chapters do. Scholars in a discipline advance or refine knowledge in the field by putting forward propositions and evidence to support them. Sometimes they argue against some other scholar's proposition. You might have to do this, or you might be asked to review the arguments that have been advanced on some topic, without having to support any of them. Or the set topic might merely ask for explanation of some sort. But essays are not expected to be the kind of comprehensive slabs of information we find·in encyclopaedias and other reference books. They involve dealing with material in a selective, thoughtful, evaluative way.

It is worth thinking about the purpose the lecturer or tutor had in setting the assignment task. Quite likely, he or she is interested in seeing whether you have understood the concepts taught in the subject, can express them in your own words, can make sensible use of published materials, and can demonstrate thinking skills. In other words, you are expected to analyse, synthesise, evaluate, make connections—not simply to reproduce what is printed in the textbook.

Because the essay is an imitation of the real thing (academic argument), there is a sense in which you are not addressing the tutor as your audience. Although most students realise that the assignment should be written so that it could be marked by any qualified tutor in the discipline, others are too conscious of the fact that their actual reader will be their tutor. They take too much for granted: knowing that the tutor already knows the meaning of a term, they don't define it. Or they may seek to impress the tutor by using a lot of specialised terminology and academic-sounding language.

A useful device is to picture your reader as someone who is not an expert in the field. Think of your reader as a student like yourself—as someone who is acquiring a general understanding of the field but who does not know what you do about the exact topic. Explain the ideas or argue the case to this imagined person in language he or she would understand. You can assume that the basic terms and concepts of the discipline are known, so don't define everything, but do explain any terms or concepts specific to your topic. Put concepts in your own words as far as possible. Your priority is to be clear—not to sound 'deep' or 'academic'. The tutor who marks this essay will see at once that you understand the material. You have been able to process the concepts in your own mind, not merely reproduce them.

## Introductions and conclusions

These two parts of an essay need special attention. Always include them in point form in outlines of the essay—even early outlines—so you remember that you need them and that they are distinct from the body. However, they are not something you need to think about until relatively late in the overall process. Remember to reserve some of the word length for the introduction and conclusion (perhaps 10% for the former and 5% for the latter).

Having said all that, it's important to think of the introduction and conclusion as serving certain functions—not simply as spaces to be filled. You may be tempted to fill up these spaces in the essay with formulas and clichés, perhaps carried on from high school days. What matters is that an essay or other written work be introduced in a way appropriate to its subject, audience and purpose. It should also be brought to a conclusion in some sort of way. There is no formula that covers every case; nor is there a set length. If it is possible to introduce something appropriately in three sentences, there is no point in writing more. Some long essays, on the other hand, need an introduction of three or four paragraphs.

The key to writing a good introduction is to think about what is needed in the circumstances. Suppose you are introducing one person to many others at a social function. You might be casual or formal, you might supply some information about the person or you might supply only the name. There is no single way of doing it. What matters is to achieve the purpose.

Actually, you are doing two things in an introduction: you are introducing your reader to the topic (the subject matter); you are also introducing your reader to your particular treatment of the topic. The two do overlap, but they are not quite the same thing. Both need to be dealt with, but one may require more words than the other.

What is required of an introduction will vary from one essay to another. The longer and more complicated an essay is, the more important foreshadowing the essay's structure will be. Suppose you visit a zoo with a guided tour. You might appreciate a chance to look at a map of the whole zoo at the outset. Or you might welcome some preliminary explanation by the tour guide. But too much preliminary announcing can be boring.

Suppose you are writing a proposal for a very fast train (VFT) service between Sydney and Melbourne. Your first paragraph finishes with these sentences: 'The VFT would have distinct benefits for Australia. In particular, it would benefit the environment, stimulate the economy, reduce congestion in Sydney and Melbourne and take pressure off the airports.' The reader can reasonably expect that the essay will now go on to provide evidence for these four points and in that order. It is unnecessary for you to add sentences stating what the essay will do—you have already implied what it will do.

---

 An introduction will have to do the following (in some way):

- get the reader's interest;
- indicate the central idea (in an argument, the proposition you intend to defend), or at least point to the specific focus of the essay;
- contextualise the central idea (and/or the whole discussion) by showing what broader topic, problem or event it is part of; indicate why it is important; indicate the grounds for focusing on the specific aspect chosen; and perhaps mention other relevant theories or arguments;
- orient the reader—provide a sense of the direction in which the essay will go;
- explain anything else that needs to be understood before the reader goes further.

---

First impressions are important, so take some trouble with the introduction. The language will not be as dense as may be appropriate in the body of the essay. Give the reader a chance to get his or her bearings. To return to the example of the social function, your guest might prefer to be met in a lobby and given a chance to get a feel for the place—not be pushed straight into the party going on inside.

A common fault with introductions is the insertion of a lot of irrelevant historical context. High school essays often begin with the 'cavemen' back at 'the dawn of time'. If I am writing an essay about the VFT there is no need to begin with the first cavemen inventing the wheel and human societies being obsessed with finding faster and faster ways to travel. Although the topic (as distinct from your treatment of the topic) will need some sort of introduction, you must set limits on this. Don't succumb to a misguided sense of responsibility to trace the history of the thing from its origins. If you are writing about the influence of former Prime Minister Paul Keating on Australian economic policy, you should not devote the first paragraph to an account of his childhood in Bankstown.

Other common faults with introductions include the dictionary definition which isn't really necessary, and introducing part of the essay rather than the whole thing.

> A conclusion has the job of:
>
> - bringing the essay to an end (providing the reader with a satisfying sense of 'closure');
> - stating or restating the proposition proved or the thesis discussed;
> - helping your reader to draw together the different strands of the essay, to appreciate it as a whole. Some recapitulation of main points may do this (but avoid long, detailed and boring repetition of what has already been made clear);
> - connecting your specific argument or discussion to a wider context in some way.

The conclusion should not add anything new (apart from points relating to the wider context which are outside the scope of what has been discussed in the body of the essay). A conclusion might indicate what further investigation could be made of the topic, or perhaps make predictions. In the introduction and conclusion you may preview what is to come or review what has been said; only in the body of the essay do you do your actual arguing.

Do not expect to get them right on your first attempt. The introduction, especially, will need a lot of reworking and polishing. Treat your first versions as a way to get started. When you've written a satisfactory draft of the body of the essay you'll know what you need in the way of introduction, and how you might conclude the piece.

A good way to learn how to write better introductions and conclusions is to look at how others do it. Get hold of articles or chapters that are substantial but readable, and study the ways their writers have introduced and concluded them.

## GET HELP

Once you have a draft, give it to someone else to provide you with feedback. Your tutor might be prepared to have a quick look to see if you are on the right track. Alternatively, your university may have a language/study skills centre that can offer assistance, especially if English is not your native language. (Note that they will not be able to help you with content.)

Tutors and student support staff will be more interested in helping you if they feel that you are not just 'using them'. Take along a point-form outline as well as the draft. Try to identify potential problems of organisation or expression yourself, rather than just handing everything over. Tell them, for example, that you're having trouble explaining what you mean, or that you're having trouble connecting one section with the earlier material. This saves them time and shows that you are an active learner.

A reasonably intelligent non-expert reader can also be useful. If they cannot make any sense of what you have written, you probably need to do some rewriting. Go over any previous pieces of work you have had returned, carefully read the comments you received, and identify the main (or recurring) areas of weakness. Then check your current draft to see how well it has eliminated or dealt with those weaknesses or problems. You should make good use of feedback provided on earlier assignments.

## READING

One final point. If you are going to improve your writing, you need to read. If you do only a minimum of reading you will not become a good writer. While you need exposure to a range of genres, it is probably especially useful to read material which is clear and well written, and which you really enjoy and find interesting. Read some works closely, and reread them occasionally. That way you will internalise sentence patterns you can use yourself.

## CONCLUSION

In this chapter we have introduced you to some basic considerations relating to effective writing at university. In chapter 14 we go into more detail about how to improve your writing style.

### Activities

1. This exercise is to help you focus on purpose and audience. Think of a topic you know a lot about. Write a paragraph of exposition on this topic to suit each of the following occasions:
    (a) a general-interest piece in an airline magazine (the kind provided free on planes);
    (b) an entry in an encyclopaedia;
    (c) a book for school children.

2. Using the same topic as above (or another if you prefer), imagine you are writing an argument on the topic of about 2000 words. Write the introduction.

3. Find an article or chapter and look at the introduction. Identify every word, sentence and technique that helps the reader to understand the writer's purpose and relates to the reader's interests and needs.

## chapter 14

# Improving your written style

We use the term 'style' to refer to all those aspects of writing which involve choices about words and sentences. The choices we make about how sentences are arranged in paragraphs, and how paragraphs are put together, come under the term 'organisation' (or 'structure') (dealt with in chapters 10 and 13).

As long as someone is reasonably literate in written English, their academic writing is more likely to suffer from inadequate thought and research, and defects in organisation, than from problems with sentences. Style is important, though: poor sentences will frustrate the reader and get in the way of your meaning being communicated.

The term 'style' is sometimes used in relation to whether writing is 'good'—that is, clear, flowing, and easy to read. Sometimes it is used in relation to the personal characteristics our writing has: no two writers have exactly the same style because people tend to have their favourite words, and their own particular ways of putting them together. Actually, we all have more than one style, because different ways of writing are needed for different genres and occasions. An invitation, a postcard, a job application, a letter to a rich uncle asking for a loan, an essay—all require adjustments to style.

Style is tied to purpose. If you are uneasy or confused about your purpose, your style will suffer. You could write quite well in other genres (love letters, abusive notes) yet still have problems in academic essays. Your sentences might not be clear because you haven't worked out what to say, or have failed to understand the theoretical ideas, or because you're trying to sound 'intellectual'. This is why you have to work on organisation first. Only when you have a clear framework of ideas, a sense of direction, and confidence in your understanding of the issues can you expect to write effective sentences.

While you cannot become a master of prose style in a week, once you get an idea of what to do your writing will improve. Perhaps the best way of improving your style in the medium term is by reading. The more you read, the more familiar you become with words and how they should be—and can be—put into sentences.

But what about the short term? How do you improve your style in an assignment due the following Friday? The answer is that you revise. And then revise again. Apart from inadequate planning, the main reason for poor style in student essays is failure to redraft the first version(s) of an assignment. Often this is because students simply run out of time—because they don't start working on the task until just before it is due. An experienced, published writer may produce five or more drafts before the final version. But students often expect that one will be enough. And often they don't see how they can change what they have written.

---

 **Elements of style**

Style can be understood in terms of the following elements:

- *Words chosen.* The English language (because it is historically a mixture of several languages, and has always freely borrowed words from elsewhere) usually offers a considerable number of alternatives (synonyms) for any given word. As well as varying the meaning, these alternative words can contribute to differences in tone (friendly, hostile, casual, official) and level (informal, formal).
- *Sentence pattern.* Variations in sentence patterns can produce changes in meaning.
- *Sentence length.* Generally it is best to stick to short, clear sentences that are not overloaded with information, but at times you might need to use longer sentences to describe or explain things.
- *Punctuation.* Incorrect or overused punctuation gets in the way of your meaning. Punctuation is outside the scope of this book, but many affordable books can be found that provide guidelines. You already know perhaps 85% of what you need to about punctuation; take the initiative and bring yourself up to speed on the rest.

---

## PRINCIPLES OF GOOD STYLE

Good writing has certain characteristics. It is:

- *clear*—nothing is more important than this;
- *precise*—it should show the intended meaning as exactly as possible;
- *concise*—it should be economical, not using more words than are necessary;
- *accurate*—if it does not conform reasonably well to rules and conventions, there may be problems in achieving the above.

It is better to use a lot of words and be clear than to write concentrated prose that no-one can understand. Context can make a difference. Some kinds of writing have to be very precise, even when this involves sacrificing some clarity. An example is a legal document. You might need to read your rich uncle's will three times before you can work out whether he has left his fortune to you or his parrot, and it may be very wordy. But if it was not written in such a way, some legal 'loophole' might be exploited and his night nurse get the lot.

Do not try to get everything right at once. For your first draft it is enough to get the material expressed in full sentences. Then you can go through it again, reworking ideas and choosing other words to get the exact meaning. In going through it again you will realise that you can probably eliminate some 'deadwood', and make it more concise. And then you can start looking for mistakes. Other people (and even computer spelling programs) can check your work for errors before you submit it.

## UNDERSTANDING SENTENCE STRUCTURE

Students are not always good at revising their sentences because, having expressed an idea in one way, they have difficulties finding alternatives. You cannot rework ideas unless you have a grasp of the basics of sentence structure. Nor can you learn those aspects of punctuation which you need to improve your work.

In this section we look at the essential 'building blocks' of sentences and the kinds of sentence patterns that can be constructed with them. This will provide a basic 'model' for all the main kinds of sentences. Each main example below is numbered. Sometimes additional examples are provided. It is not difficult, but it will help if you work your way through it patiently (even if you think you know it already), and do the activities suggested. Grammatical terms have been kept to an absolute minimum.

## Subject and verb

A sentence always has a subject (which can be a person, a physical thing or an idea). It also has a verb. The verb tells us what the subject does (or did or will do), or something about its existence.

|     | SUBJECT | VERB |
|-----|---------|------|
| (I) | Candy | laughed. |
|     | The duck | arrived. |

Usually a sentence also contains something that goes with the verb:

|     | SUBJECT | VERB | COMPLEMENT |
|-----|---------|------|------------|
| (2) | Candy | laughed | at Randy. |
|     | The duck | arrived | at the pond. |

But the most important parts of any sentence are the subject and the verb that tells us something about the subject. Think of subject and verb as 'slots' that have the potential to be filled with many different words. Instead of 'Candy' the subject could be 'Barbie' or 'the old lady' or 'the Vikings'. Instead of 'laughed' in (2) the verb could be 'wondered' or 'hissed' (as in 'The Vikings hissed at Randy').

The subject and verb 'slots' can be filled with groups of words, rather than single words. Instead of 'Candy', we could have a phrase like 'taming wild badgers'. This phrase expresses an idea, and we can say things about this idea, just as we can say things about single nouns like 'Candy' or 'the duck' (e.g. {Candy} is nice; {Taming wild badgers} is nice). Sometimes the verb slot, too, is occupied by a group of words rather than just one:

|     | SUBJECT | VERB | COMPLEMENT |
|-----|---------|------|------------|
| (3) | Taming wild badgers | had always been | my hobby. |
| (4) | What Candy wanted to know | was | how I cooked fish. |

In example (4), you will note that 'wanted' is also a verb. But it is not the main verb of the sentence. It is part of a group of words expressing an idea which is the subject of the sentence. The main verb of the sentence is the word 'was'. (It has to be. Nothing else in that sentence could be.) You must be able to identify the subject and the main verb in a sentence. (If you are not clear about what has been said so far, read it over again before continuing.)

The next thing to understand is that the subject of a sentence—in the sense of the subject 'slot'—is a grammatical entity. The grammatical subject of a sentence is not always quite the same as the main subject in the sense of topic (the person or thing you want to tell your reader about). In the case of example (3) it could be the case that the concept 'taming wild badgers' is the main topic. Perhaps in earlier sentences you have explained that 'taming wild badgers' is a dangerous activity, that 'taming wild badgers' was widely practised in ancient Egypt, and so on. Then you write a sentence adding another fact: 'it was my hobby'. However, if the topic you are interested in discussing is hobbies, it would be more natural to let that be the grammatical subject of the sentence. Thus:

|  | SUBJECT | VERB | COMPLEMENT |
|---|---|---|---|
| (5) | My hobby | had always been | taming wild badgers. |

Example (3) was not wrong if our main interest was in finding out something about the concept 'taming wild badgers'. But if our main interest is in finding out about 'my hobby', then pattern (5) is preferable. Now, considering example (4), although this is gramatically correct, it would be better to let 'Candy' be the subject and write the sentence thus:

|  | SUBJECT | VERB | COMPLEMENT |
|---|---|---|---|
| (6) | Candy | wanted to know | how I cooked fish. |

A single word here replaces the six words that (4) has in the subject slot. Now 'wanted' is the main verb of the sentence. The changes make the sentence more concise and forceful. The subject is easier to identify if it is a single key word, rather than a group of words. Also, sentences tend to be less forceful when words like 'is' or 'was' are the main verbs, with the key 'doing' word in some other slot in the sentence.

Sentences can be longer and more complicated than the above examples but still have the same basic pattern (what is called the 'simple sentence'). There can be plural nouns in the subject and complement slots, or multiple verbs in the verb slot:

| (7) | Sheep, cows, tapirs and goats | grazed | on the hills and valleys. |
|---|---|---|---|
| (8) | The tennis player | swore and walked | off the court. |

Or there may be adjectives and adverbs modifying the main words:

| (9) | Cute Candy | laughed mockingly | at poor old Randy. |
|---|---|---|---|

The basic structure is still the same. Each sentence still has one subject group (Cute Candy) and one verb group (all the rest of the sentence). But not all sentences are like this.

## Other sentence patterns

Look at this sentence:

(10)  Although she was usually nice, **cute Candy laughed mockingly at poor old Randy.**

Here the part of the sentence that conveys the main meaning is shown in bold. It is the same as sentence (9). We can call this part of the sentence the control unit.[1] A group of words providing some further information has been added ('Although she was . . .'). This extra information may be useful, but it is not as important as the idea expressed in the control unit. We can call this added group of words a support unit. A support unit can have its own subject ('she') and verb ('was'). But while the control unit can stand on its own as a meaningful sentence, a support unit can never stand on its own. In this case, the word 'although' marks it as a unit whose purpose is to modify some other group of words. The main verb of the whole sentence is the verb of the control unit, 'laughed'.

In all examples below, the control unit is shown in bold. Note that a support unit can come after the control unit:

(11)  **Candy laughed at Randy,** who had slipped on a banana.

Or it can be placed inside the control unit:

(12)  **Candy,** who was usually nice, **laughed at Randy.**

The test of whether something is a support unit or not is whether it could stand alone as a sentence. 'Who was usually tactful', 'Although she was usually tactful', are not acceptable sentences: they are incomplete. They are what we call fragments. To turn them into sentences that can stand alone you can replace the word 'who' by 'Candy', and remove the word 'although' in the second case.

There are still other sentence patterns. Consider:

(13)  **Candy laughed at Randy** and **Randy lost his temper.**

We cannot say here that one unit provides essential information and the other provides extra or incidental information: they have equal status.

This time we have two control units. They could easily have been written as two separate sentences with a full stop in between. Instead, they have been joined by 'and'. They could also have been joined by a punctuation mark, such as a semicolon (;). In some cases commas can be used, as in a short sentence consisting of three control units joined together: 'I came, I saw, I conquered.' (Note that unless control units are short and simple, as in the last sentence, a comma is too weak a 'stop' to join them; a semicolon is then needed, as in this sentence.)

Sentences can consist of two (or even more) control units, with a number of support units around them:

> (14) Although she was usually nice, **cute Candy laughed at poor old Randy** AND **Randy**, once again, **lost his temper** (which he had rarely done since childhood), for the second time that day.

The two elements joined by 'and' can be called subsentences. Single sentences can be combined, and turned into subsentences, by any of the words known as conjunctives ('and', 'but', 'or', 'then' etc.) and by punctuation marks (normally a colon or semicolon).

You should now be able to identify the control unit and any support units in a sentence. If the occasional sentence is still difficult to figure out, go back over this material or seek help.

## WRITING EFFECTIVE SENTENCES

Make your key words count. Words expressing the key ideas you want to communicate should occupy the important subject and verb 'slots' in a sentence (see discussion following example (4) above). Choosing the best words for the subject and verb can eliminate 'deadwood' and make your sentence clear and exact.

Your main idea should be expressed in the control unit. This ensures that what is logically important will also have grammatical priority. Consider this sentence:

> **Randy slipped on a banana**, causing Candy to laugh.

This is fine if the main idea is Randy's accident. However, if the main point is Candy's laughter you would make that the control unit:

> Because Randy slipped on a banana skin, **Candy laughed**.

Control + control or control + support? Note that the previous sentence could be written in the form of two control units joined together:

**Randy slipped on a banana** and **Candy laughed.**

Here a causal relationship between the two events is only implied. We are told about two things that happened. We do not know for certain that she is laughing at him. Writing that simply hooks one control unit to another can be less clear than writing that arranges ideas in control units modified by support units.

## ELEVEN COMMON PROBLEMS AND ERRORS

The first four examples we deal with are errors of sentence construction, or syntax. Most can be avoided—or corrected—if you use the principles covered so far. The other examples are stylistic weaknesses or problems rather than grammatical errors.

### 1. Fragments

A fragment is a support unit which has been written as a sentence. The writer has set out to write a sentence but (a) has neglected to include a verb, (b) has substituted for the verb a word that seems to be a verb, or (c) has tacked on a word like 'although' used to introduce support units.

In a paragraph on oral presentations we might come across this: 'For example the use of gestures and facial expressions.' Here the word 'use' is a noun. The last five words just provide a bit more information about the word 'use'. In effect the sentence is 'For example the use'. If we take away the first two words, which again serve only to modify, we are left with 'The use'. A subject has been asserted but nothing has been said about it. We can correct this fragment by joining it to the previous or following sentence, so we get something like: 'Mandy doesn't speak much, but she is good at non-verbal communication—for example the use of gestures and facial expressions.'

Fragments can occur when a support unit is added to a subject without a main verb being supplied. In the following examples there is a subject (shown in italics) plus a support unit but no main verb relating to the subject, hence no control unit: '*Sandy* being young and rebellious.' This can be corrected by using an appropriate verb: 'Sandy was young and rebellious.'

Look at another fragment: '*Women* who were ahead of their time in their career plans.' There are two ways of correcting this. One would be to leave 'women' as the subject and put in a verb: 'The women were ahead of their time in their career plans.' Another way would be to supply another subject as well as a verb: 'At the North Pole Andy met women who . . . etc.'

## 2. Modifiers

These involve support units which are separated from, or not properly related to, the words they are supposed to be modifying. The extreme case is the dangling modifier: '**Tramping around a bend in the road,** the house came into view.' Here the support unit (in bold) seems at first sight to refer to the house, because the human being(s) who are actually doing the tramping have been left out altogether. The sentence could read: 'As Candy, Randy, Mandy and Andy came tramping . . . etc.' Grammatically, the example says that a house came tramping along a road. Learn to see what your sentences—as grammatical constructions— are actually saying. It may not be quite what you wanted them to say.

## 3. Parallel elements

In the sentence: 'His favourite activities were hunting and to fish', 'hunting' and 'to fish' are grammatically parallel, because they both have the same relation to the verb 'were'. When two words or word groups are grammatically parallel they must be consistent in grammatical form. Use 'hunting and fishing', or else 'to hunt and to fish'.

## 4. Agreement

Verbs must agree with their subject in number. In one example: 'A pianist who has had lots of different music teachers do not play very well', the verb should be the singular 'does', because the subject is the singular noun 'pianist'.

Make sure that pronouns like 'it' and 'they' agree with the words they refer to. There must also, of course, be agreement of tense in sentences.

## 5. Deadwood

The following is a sentence from a student essay discussing the benefits of having a wide range of radio stations: 'This is only to the listener's benefit because the listener gets to choose the type of news they want to listen to instead of having to put up with the same kind of news all the time.' Note the unnecessary repetition of the words 'listener' and 'news'. The idea could be written as follows: 'This diversity allows listeners to choose their preferred news programs.'

### 6. Demonstrative pronouns

In the sentence: 'This caused a great deal of unrest among the peasants', what is 'this'? Your rule should be to repeat whatever the pronoun refers to, unless it has been clearly identified in the last couple of sentences. Unless you are sure that your reader will understand, do not rely on the pronoun alone: 'This price increase caused a great deal of unrest among the peasants.'

Always restate when beginning a new paragraph. When you are at the editing (revision) stage of the writing process, it might be worth scanning through it just looking for pronouns like 'this', 'these' and 'it', to ensure that there are no problems of this kind.

### 7. Formality, tone and personal pronouns

Assignments should be written in formal and impersonal prose. Simply write your ideas. There is normally no need to start with 'I think that', or 'It seems to me'.

An impersonal style does not mean writing in a stiff and clumsy way. It means that you do not draw attention to yourself or allow your personality to intrude on the text. Suppose you are writing about gambling. You could write that gambling should be made illegal, as long as you produce logical arguments that it is socially harmful. But you would keep out of the essay certain personal objections you may have (e.g. that gambling is against your religion, or that your rich uncle gambled away the fortune that would otherwise one day have been yours).

But you do not have to avoid using 'I' altogether, as it is no longer usual to go to any length to avoid using the personal pronoun in academic work. You should, however, not overuse it. It may be better to write 'as is shown later' rather than 'as I show later', although the latter would usually be preferred to 'as the present author will show later' or 'as this essay will show'. Check what is preferred in individual disciplines. In oral presentations, using 'I' is not a problem.

## 8. Colloquial and 'colourful' language

'Nome, Alaska, is the pits on Saturday night' is slang, and it will be interpreted differently by different readers. Does it refer to lack of attractive nightclubs, congested streets, awful restaurants, groups of aggressive polar bears, lots of drug dealers, too few kebab shops? Everyday language is full of expressions that strongly convey feelings but do not provide exact information: 'Australian farmers have taken a beating', or 'If we don't change our ways, we'll be up the creek without a paddle'. This kind of language is 'colourful', but you should find ordinary words to convey the idea rather than slang expressions. A graduate should be able to communicate in Standard English and not be limited to the language of particular localities or subcultures.

## 9. Jargon and pretentious language

Do not try to sound 'intelligent' by using jargon and long, complicated sentences. Your task is to communicate as clearly as possible, not to confuse people. Jargon is the excessive or inappropriate use of specialised language. Each discipline has its own special new words (or special meanings of ordinary words) so that people within the discipline can communicate with one another more precisely. You should learn the terminology of the disciplines you are studying, and you learn new words best by using them, but make sure you understand them.

## 10. Word choice—other aspects

Try to make sure that your writing is not too general. More specific words will communicate a more exact meaning. Compare the following examples—the general words in the first have been replaced by more specific words in the second:

> As the politician emerged from the aircraft, children began singing a song.
> As the prime minister jumped out of his Boeing, boys and girls from local primary schools started singing the national anthem.

Sometimes it is appropriate to do the reverse. Using specific words will give too narrow a meaning—unless so many of them are used that the sentence becomes chaotic:

> The numerous union members, supporters, security men, police and reporters swarming across roads, carparks and the railway line prevented any cars, vans, trucks, trains or buses entering the docks.

This could read:

> The crowd in the area prevented all land traffic entering the docks.

In the second example we exchanged specific nouns for more general nouns. Occasionally you need to find a word that translates all the particulars of actual instances of something in a convenient abstraction—in other words, an abstract noun. In the following sentence there is too much specific detail:

> After problems with lots of people stealing things the company decided to put better locks on the doors and bars on the windows, install a boom gate and upgrade its burglar alarms.

This is much more compact:

> After a lot of theft the company decided to improve the building's security.

One of the challenges of university study is that you have to read texts that contain many more abstractions than your previous reading. Another challenge is to become more comfortable with using abstractions yourself (see chapter 6).

## 11. Rhetorical questions

These are a device that some students come to rely on too much, and which can be boring for the reader. They are called 'rhetorical' because they are one of the tricks of rhetoric—that is, persuasive public speaking. In a true rhetorical question the answer is so obvious to the audience that it doesn't need to be stated, such as: 'Shall we give in to our enemies and disgrace ourselves?' In oral presentations, rhetorical questions are usually a way of announcing a topic to be discussed, for instance: 'Is creating the perfect burger really such a big achievement?' In an oral situation you can make the most of them; for instance, insert a dramatic pause after asking the question so the audience begins thinking. In writing, the problem is that they are vague. They are used to signal a proposition you want to discuss, but the reader cannot tell exactly what this proposition is, as questions can have different answers. Ask yourself questions in the planning stage, but supply your reader with what you consider to be the answer to the question.

## EDITING TO IMPROVE

You cannot think of everything at once, and improving your style requires you to draft *at least* one more version after the first draft. Redrafting is part of the writing process. When you have become experienced at writing, you may not have to revise quite as much, but you cannot avoid it altogether.

Don't expect to do major editing on your computer screen. Print out a copy and go through it carefully. Double-line spacing is useful so that you have space to write in amendments, though sometimes it is better to start a sentence or paragraph from scratch. Your first changes to the first draft might involve matters of organisation rather than style. For instance, you might have to rearrange ideas, insert extra sentences to clarify meaning, or introduce new subsections. If that is the case, concentrate on those tasks to begin with.

If you feel that your sentences could be improved, the first step might be to underline the key words—that is, the words that express the main idea in a sentence. Take a sample sentence: 'It is fair to say that the current generation of today is the luckiest of any generation yet.' To work out how to improve it, first look for the key words. These are 'current', 'generation' and 'luckiest'. If you had to scrawl a message in your own blood, these three might be enough on their own to get the meaning across. (It is perhaps unfortunate that the telegram is obsolete—being charged by the word was a great incentive for people to fix on the essential words they had to communicate.) Then, check whether key words occupy the important sentence slots of subject and main verb. Finally (once you are sure you have the key words), you can be critical about the other words: What and where should they be? Should they even be there at all? In this case some of them do not deserve to be there. All we really need is: 'The current generation is the luckiest yet.' Simple and clear.

So far, so good. But you cannot always rely on picking out obvious key words. There may not be a single word that expresses each important element. In some cases a pronoun like 'this' carries an idea from some previous sentence, and an abstraction like 'theft', not already in the sentence, may need to be brought in to sum up the idea we are trying to communicate.

Revising does not mean merely replacing and rearranging words within the existing sentences. Sometimes the most useful thing you can do is to rewrite a sentence as two (or more) separate sentences—for instance, you may realise that you are trying to communicate two separate thoughts in one sentence, and it isn't working well. But even if it is not obvious that this kind of problem exists, try improving a sentence that looks wrong or sounds odd by replacing it with shorter, simpler sentences. Take this example: 'Now that the jokes are here to stay, doesn't give much hope to future generations with blonde hair, does it?' One way out of this mess would be to turn it into two sentences: 'The jokes are here to stay. That doesn't give much hope to future generations of blondes.' (By the time you reach the second sentence you may realise other improvements could be made: there was no point in framing it as a question, and the word 'hair' was redundant.) Once you have made a passage as clear as possible by turning it into many short, simple sentences, you can go through and carefully begin combining sentences here and there.

For most students the priority is to simplify. But if your writing is already very clear and straightforward you might need to begin doing more combining of small sentences into larger ones. This can save words, and it provides variation. A passage in which all sentences are similar in length and pattern becomes monotonous.

One problem with revising your writing is that the material is now too familiar. You might not notice errors because you know what you wanted to say. As you read over it, the familiar words seem to confirm that your intention has been achieved. To become aware of what your sentences might really be saying (houses tramping around bends in the road perhaps!) you can distance yourself by reading it aloud, or you can get a friend to read it.

The next stage of the revision process is to go through the latest draft specifically looking for errors you have made in the past. You might do this in relation to use of pronouns like 'this' which are detached from their referent (i.e. the noun for which they are a substitute). Have a list of likely errors—those pointed out to you in feedback on earlier assignments. You may tend to write 'their' instead of 'there', confuse 'it's' with 'its', and write fragments beginning with 'although'. You may have a tendency to use a certain word too often, such as 'actually' or 'just'. If you are working on computer you can utilise the 'FIND' function, but it is quite easy to scan the essay looking for the word yourself.

## A FEW FURTHER POINTS

You want your main ideas to stand out clearly. Anything that is important enough to be on a one-page point-form outline of the assignment probably deserves to be in a sentence that expresses that idea directly. Many of these will be the topic sentences of paragraphs. The sentence should not be too long, or the key idea might be 'buried' in a support unit.

Find out what conventions and expectations the discipline has regarding such features of style as subheadings, enumerated and tabulated points, use of contractions such as 'don't' and 'can't', numerals for numbers under 99, and so on. All of these features should be used with restraint. Avoid gimmicks such as special fonts or capitalisation for emphasis.

Don't 'waffle', or try to say things in as many words as possible to meet word length requirements. The marker will not be fooled. If you are waffling it means you have not done an adequate job in the planning and research stage of the essay. It is likely that your essay will 'shrink' in the revision stage (even if some whole sentences are added), because with each new draft 'deadwood' will be eliminated, so don't worry if your first draft is 20% over the set length. If it is 20% under, you may have a problem; go back and look at your essay plan and see what can be expanded without inflating the concepts you already have.

Bear in mind that a certain amount of restatement of important ideas is necessary. Restatement means expressing the same idea in a different way to make sure the reader understands it. Avoid repetition, which will annoy the reader, but the kind of limited repetition that allows a reader to recognise a point made earlier can be useful. A topic sentence or a sentence in the conclusion that repeats a sentence from the introduction can be acceptable. You must also be prepared to *develop* your important points.

Style makes a difference. Because a tutor marking an assignment is most interested in the way the student is handling ideas and theories, defects in style and presentation are not likely to be heavily penalised (unless they are flagrant). Still, you would probably sooner make a good impression than a poor one. Think of the difference it makes to someone who has just marked eleven essays that were vague and waffly, or turgid, or sloppy. How refreshing to come to an essay whose first paragraph conforms to our criteria: clear, concise, precise and accurate. The same applies to writing you produce for other readers, such as prospective employers.

Universities do not have the time or resources to teach you how to improve your style. You will need plenty of practice in writing, making the effort to improve your knowledge and allowing time to revise.

## CONCLUSION

An effective writing style is clear, precise, concise and accurate. We have provided you with ways of checking that your writing has these characteristics. But effective writing won't happen by itself—to achieve control over your style you have to be prepared to practise, get feedback, read and learn from other writers and, most importantly, revise. Don't be satisfied with the way you said it the first time. You can say it better.

### Activities

1. Find a fairly long sentence you have written and see how many different ways you can find to convey the same basic idea. Do this often and you will get better at it.

2. (a) Take a paragraph or two of writing—your own and/or something published—and rewrite it by turning it into as many short sentences as possible. (It will be a bit tedious to read and may resemble a story for young children, but don't worry about that; just strive to be as clear as possible.)

   (b) Now take a passage which has fairly short sentences and do as much combining as possible: try to turn every sentence into a support unit or control unit of a larger sentence.

3. Read the defective sentences (all from student assignments) below. Try to identify what is wrong with each and then rewrite to correct the fault.

   (a) Ways of not developing boredom can be to have plenty of exercise.

   (b) In life today the life-threatening diseases of AIDS and Hepatitis B are now in existence.

   (c) The generation of teenagers today are thought to be like every other past generation of teenagers.

   (d) Boredom need only be a problem if it is allowed to happen, and to overcome your actions that stem from it.

   (e) Those who argue that history is useful to human beings will say that Columbus discovering America will have many similarities with when human beings first encounter life on another planet.

   (f) Young people today I think live in a much more complex society than those of their parents.

   (g) As the national unemployment rate nears close to 10% every day, obtaining a job or moreso a rewarding job, becomes complicated.

*Comments on the defective sentences.* Read the following only after you have done the Activity above.

(a) Make something else the grammatical subject (e.g. 'Boredom can be prevented by . . .'.

(b) Apart from the redundant words, this sentence says so little that it hardly deserves to be a separate sentence. (It says only that 'AIDS and Hepatitis B now exist'.)

(c) Delete 'are thought to be' (quite unnecessary) and the repetitions ('Every generation of teenagers is much the same').

(d) This is confusing to the reader at first. The idea in the second part of the sentence needs more explanation. It will probably require more words. Eliminate 'your'.

(e) Again, the reader eventually gets the idea but is asked to do too much work. What is the main idea in the sentence? It is a comparison. But each of the things being compared is expressed in a whole group of words. One way to improve things would be to find abstract nouns instead. So we can compare *discovery* and *encounter* (as a noun). We can drop 'to human beings' (to whom else would it be useful?). Hence: 'Those who argue that history is useful will say that Columbus's *discovery* of America will have similarities with the first *encounter* with life on another planet.' It could probably be improved further, depending on exactly what the student was trying to argue. Is the writer really interested in discussing 'those who argue'? Quite likely the student has introduced these ghostly human actors because it did not occur to him or her to employ an abstraction such as 'the *usefulness* of history'. The sentence could also be more specific: what exactly makes these 'similarities' useful? Here is another possible version that no longer tries to cram the concepts into a single tortured sentence: 'The discovery of America by Columbus provides a paradigm for a future encounter with extraterrestrial life. This shows the usefulness of studying history.'

(f) Delete 'I think'; replace the plural 'those' with the singular 'that'. The sentence doesn't say much. Be more specific about how precisely society is 'complex' (the word is too general).

(g) It is unnecessary to have both 'nears' and 'close to'. Because 'nears' is a verb the sentence suggests that the rate moves away overnight and then 'nears' 10% again each day. Replace 'moreso' (not a word in Standard English) with 'especially'.

Presumably none of the writers of these sentences realised just what they were writing. Reading the sentences aloud, slowly, would have revealed their faults in most cases.

## chapter 15

# Effective oral presentations

Have you listened to oral deliveries (presentations, lectures, speeches) that made everyone wish they were somewhere else? The presenter (let's call him Kevin) is clearly uncomfortable and avoids eye contact.

- He reads his paper in a hurried monotone.
- He displays overhead transparencies crammed with unreadable data.
- He loses his place in a bulky script.
- He runs out of time, which leaves crucial aspects not covered.
- There is thus no time for questions or discussion.
- Everyone is too confused or bored to care.

Afterwards, annoyed that all his hard work researching the topic has produced such a poor result, Kevin wants to forget all about it. Consequently, his next oral presentation is much the same.

Kate begins with a few in-jokes, looks people in the eye and smiles a lot. She devotes much of her presentation to showing an entertaining videotape. There is some quite lively discussion and she finishes with time to spare. But Kate does not do a better job:

- The content of Kate's talk is shallow and insubstantial.
- No-one knows quite what the videotape is meant to illustrate.
- Her argument remains hazy and, though people respond to her good humour, the audience discussion has little relevance to her topic.
- The audience is not bored, but no-one gains much from listening to her.

Kate is a natural extrovert, who prefers oral presentations to written assignments because they seem to her free and more spontaneous—and she thinks they involve less work.

Both these students misunderstand the oral presentation genre. Kevin disregards the needs of the audience. His good research is wasted because he is unable to share it successfully. Kate disregards content. Her talent for relating to an audience is wasted because she has nothing of substance to offer.

An oral presentation requires you to bring together different skills in a complex way. Because it happens in 'real time', there are no second chances, and this is perhaps one reason why many people are nervous about 'orals'. Many of the abilities required, though, are ones you already have. Explaining something to 30 people in a room is not *essentially* different from explaining it to one person. If you devote enough time to preparation, you can deliver a good presentation, even if you are not an extrovert. But it must be the right kind of preparation. Kevin spent too much of his time collecting information, and not enough organising it for oral delivery to an audience. There are two basic principles to remember:

1. Preparation is the key to success.
2. The audience must be considered in relation to every aspect of your talk.

 **Why have oral presentations?**

First, in their future occupations most graduates will have to communicate orally to groups. Employers, including those in technical professions, want graduates who can speak effectively. Your aim should be to get better and better as an oral communicator as you proceed through university. You will need your speaking skills to convince a selection panel to hire you in the first place—job interviews share some similarities with oral presentations.

Second, there is an intellectual challenge in selecting and arranging ideas for oral delivery. Having to explain something to someone else clarifies it for you: you understand it better and retain it longer. Orals also allow teachers to determine whether students are dealing successfully with the concepts they have to learn.

## Oral communication in social and business contexts

Even in an age of print and computers, oral communication is very common. The following are some examples of oral presentations that are an everyday part of our society:

- Businesspeople seeking a large loan to build a tourist resort make a presentation to persuade the bank that the project is viable.
- A government engineer explains a new freeway project to a group of concerned citizens who live in the vicinity.
- An accountant presents a paper on changes to the taxation laws at the annual conference of a professional society of accountants.
- A personnel officer conducts an induction session for a batch of new employees to explain working conditions.

In each case the information could have been provided to the audience in written form (in fact, printed material probably *was* made available). But writing, although cheaper and easier, could not replace the speech altogether, for three main reasons:

- Oral delivery provides personal contact between the parties involved.
- It allows feedback, such as requests for points to be explained in more detail. Also, audience members can express their views.
- It allows multichannel communication—not just words but tone of voice, gesture, diagrams on a whiteboard, and perhaps video or computer graphics.

The first point has a lot to do with cultural traditions, and with expectations that the communicator should be present and accountable in certain situations. All societies have ceremonies (weddings, funerals, prize-givings, openings, the exorcising of demons) which would be unimaginable without oral communication. Ceremonies and rituals, being predictable or even stylised events, remind us that speech is not always spontaneous and casual. The speaker has to follow conventions and may need to rehearse the delivery carefully—it can be regarded as premeditated *performance*. (Imagine how many weddings would be ruined, for instance, if the priest or celebrant made things up as they went along!) Oral delivery does not mean leaving everything to chance. Nevertheless, the 'real-time' unfolding of an oral delivery gives you flexibility: you can think on the spot and can change direction; and audience input can help you develop your ideas.

Oral delivery is well suited to 'grabbing' and making use of people's emotions (think of the pep talk to the sports team or sales staff, the sermon, the political speech). There is a story told of a Jewish–American journalist who was covering Hitler's speeches for an American newspaper. Despite the fact that most of the speeches denounced Jews (i.e. people like him), the journalist found himself getting caught up in the emotion generated by the event. The *affective* dimension—mood, feelings—is very significant in oral situations. In business and social contexts, successful speakers realise that often the most useful thing they can do is to introduce the subject and arouse enthusiasm, leaving the detailed information to be conveyed later via some other medium. Less successful speakers allow the informational *content* to interfere with other objectives. If the engineer provides a lot of complicated engineering data which is irrelevant to the residents, and fails to deal with their fears and worries, he or she has not done the job properly. The personnel officer who overwhelms the new employees with more than they can take in on their first day is not communicating as effectively as someone who motivates them to want to know about the job or workplace.

 • Oral presentations provide opportunities for spontaneity, but they should be premeditated and planned rather than free-wheeling.
• Whether formal or informal, they are characterised by social contact between presenter and audience.
• They often involve—and lend themselves to—the modification of people's attitudes and feelings.
• They allow different media to be used simultaneously, but are usually not the best way of conveying a lot of detailed information.

It is surprising how many of the basics of oral communication are ignored in academic contexts, where orals are often dull and hard to follow. Perhaps we can blame the influence of the lecture, a mediaeval genre which originated in an age before print, when content had to be transmitted by speech.

Of course, relevant content is esssential to oral presentations at university. Orals do involve academic discourse, and reason must prevail over feeling. Still, the presenter has to pay attention to effect. You must arouse your audience's interest. You must also be realistic about what your audience can absorb. Both inside and outside academic contexts, content can all too easily take over and ruin a presentation.

## Are there two audiences?

Now to the problem of whether the tutor who will grade the presentation, and your fellow students, constitute two different audiences.

Obviously they have different literacies. The tutor, for instance, is probably already familiar with the theoretical principles; this cannot be expected of your fellow students.

Even in non-academic contexts some speakers try to impress the few experts who happen to be present with complicated content that baffles the majority of their audience. People sometimes get the idea that using complicated language—what is sometimes called 'jargon'—automatically gives their presentation credibility and value. What it often does is to draw attention to the fact that they have little or nothing to say.

It would be foolish to entertain your student audience and leave the marker feeling you had not really engaged with the topic. In the example we gave earlier, Kevin would get a better mark than Kate because he had something relevant to say, even though he delivered it poorly.

However, it is a mistake to imagine you will impress your tutor if you just reproduce material: orals are supposed to demonstrate your capacity to think. Being able to explain your material successfully to a non-expert audience should impress the marker. Few tutors these days will be satisfied with an oral presentation that simply consists of reading out an essay. Indeed, if it were practical, some would prefer to mark you on the outcome achieved: that is, on what your audience understood and retained, and the interest it generated. There is no single standard. Some markers will be looking primarily at your success with the actual audience; others may want the kind of presentation that might be delivered to an ideal audience. If in doubt about this, ask your tutor.

## THE ELEMENTS OF AN ORAL PRESENTATION

Now to look more closely at the different aspects you have to think about. These are:

- *Context:* this includes purpose, occasion and audience.
- *Content:* the ideas, examples, evidence.
- *Structure:* is it logical, and does it make good use of time?
- *Language:* the words and sentences you use.
- *Visuals:* anything you show your audience.
- *Performance:* the actual delivery, as well as how you look and sound.
- *Audience involvement:* anything you allow or encourage the audience to do (ask questions, make comments).

Only the first area, context, involves factors outside your control. Your own input will determine whether the others contribute to, or detract from, your presentation. Think about them at every stage of your preparation. Each one has consequences for the others. For instance, if you want—or are required—to have a lot of audience discussion, you will have to limit the amount of content. Again, if your content is unavoidably dense and complex, there may be a need for visual diagrams.

## Context

You need to start by analysing your task—which means taking into account the purpose of the exercise, your audience, and the occasion.

### The purpose

Your practical purpose is to influence the thoughts of a live audience. Every single thing you do (introducing some humour, displaying a graph, summing up) you do because it helps achieve your ultimate purpose of explaining something to the audience—not just because you've seen other people do it in orals. Naturally, what you say will be governed by the requirements of the set topic. You fail to achieve your purpose if you fail to respond to these. Take account of any marking criteria provided. It helps to know, for instance, that performance (delivery) counts for 20% of the mark, rather than 50%.

### The audience

You have been a member of an audience often enough, and you know what *you* hope for from an oral presentation. One vital fact is that it is hard to keep the attention of an audience. Attention (and with it retention—the ability to remember) falls off drastically after the first ten minutes. This occurs even with a knowledgeable and interested audience. The brain can process information more rapidly than the speaking voice can supply it, and your listeners may begin to attend to their own thoughts more than yours. This doesn't mean they are bored: an interesting point you made may have set off their own trains of thought.

Another important point is that people's own needs and concerns are more important to them than yours. They are more interested in what they want to know than in what you want to tell them.

Always remember that people make sense of new information by relating it to what they already know.

> While bearing in mind the needs that *any* audience has, you must analyse your *particular* audience. Ask yourself these questions:
>
> - What do they already know about the general context of my topic?
> - What do they already know about my specific topic?
> - What do they need to know?
> - How do they feel about the topic?

Audience size is an important consideration. A small group allows you to be more personal (perhaps too much so), while a large group requires a more formal approach, and involves a diverse range of literacies. Think about how you can establish common ground with the audience.

### The occasion

The occasion includes:

- where and when the oral takes place;
- the furniture and facilities in the venue;
- whether your talk will be one of several on the same topic; and
- whether there will be any opportunity to set up visual aids beforehand.

## Content

As in a written assignment, you will need to satisfy criteria relating to the content and organisation of your talk, such as relevance to the set topic, accuracy, evidence of appropriate research and logical reasoning.

Follow the procedures for planning, researching, refining and organising discussed in earlier chapters. With orals, though, part of the exercise is to make your material meaningful to a diverse group, not just to a single reader. You will have to think more about the needs of the audience, and about what you have room for. Put a strict limit on the time you devote to reading and collecting information so there will be time to think about and arrange your ideas.

### Focus

It is especially important that your talk is focused and coherent. Have a single definite *thesis* (a central proposition) which is supported by several clearly defined main ideas. The greater the logical connection between the different parts of your talk (i.e. the more it 'hangs together') the easier it will be to follow. Set yourself this objective: that an average audience member, asked about them afterwards, would be able to understand and repeat your arguments; the person would be able to state in their own words the central issue you had examined, where you stood on it, and the kind of evidence advanced (without necessarily remembering details).

## Timing

The critical factor is time. How long do you have? You should aim to use all your time but not exceed it. Even if there is no strict cut-off point, people usually find it irritating if you go over time.

To decide what you can include, work on an average of 100 words a minute. If you are to speak for ten minutes, you should have about 1000 words if you are reading from a full script. Allow for the fact that questions, digressions and using audiovisual aids will all take up time. In radio broadcasting, speakers were supposed to take three minutes to contextualise and explain one idea. If you are speaking for five minutes you will have time to deal with only one idea in any kind of detail (once you allow for the introduction, repetitions, summaries). An audience that is given too much information will get lost—or while trying mentally to organise the information will miss what you go on to say next.

Perhaps the best way of ensuring that you use all your allotted time without exceeding it is to have spare material—minor points, additional evidence, extra examples—that can be omitted if you find you are running out of time. Mark such materials in your notes with something like 'can omit' or 'optional'. You may want some reserve material available in both the first and second half of your talk.

## Explanation

Remember to consider what your audience already knows—and what it does not know. Use what it already knows as a way into your subject. New knowledge is best assimilated when hooked onto something familiar. For instance, if you were giving a presentation on non-verbal communication, you might start by drawing your audience's attention to the seating arrangements, body postures, facial expressions, clothing and hairstyles present in the room. This transforms something abstract and theoretical ('non-verbal communication') into something concrete.

Background information may have to be provided. Suppose you are talking about changes to drug policies. What the audience needs to know are the:

- principles (what are drugs?);
- historical changes (opium used to be legal, and was used extensively as a medicine);
- current practices (what are considered 'hard' drugs); and
- 'hot' issues (drugs in sport).

While researching a topic it is easy to forget that you are becoming much more knowledgeable about it than students working on other topics. However, do not devote too much time to explaining concepts the class is supposed to be familiar with already.

### Examples and evidence

When doing your research, look for useful evidence and examples. While the tutor and probably some of the students already have a grasp of the theoretical principles, you can always supply interesting new content by providing evidence and examples with which they are not familiar. For instance, to demonstrate that drug policies, and what counts as a drug, are factors that change with different historical periods and cultures, you might point out that ancient civilisations used 'drugs' officially at important religious ceremonies.

Illustration is an indispensable strategy when you are communicating orally. Abstractions can be hard to follow without concrete examples. People relate to everyday examples. The audience will be able to make more sense of the 'drugs' issue if you talk about 'everyday' legal drugs (e.g. alcohol and nicotine) and related issues (e.g. the banning of cigarette advertising from sporting events). Look out especially for evidence and examples that can be presented to your audience visually (e.g. pictures, maps, graphs, television commercials), as long as they are genuinely relevant to the topic.

---

 **Enjoy!**

Look for what is interesting, surprising, useful or amusing in the material. We don't mean that you should trivialise it or use gimmicks. If you develop some genuine enthusiasm for the content this will be evident when you give the presentation. Audiences prefer speakers who seem to care about their material—but you have to understand the concepts. Begin work early enough to get help if needed.

---

## Structure

If you have thought through the relevant concepts, you will have a good *logical structure*. That is, everything will develop smoothly and fit together. You may like to provide an outline which shows the audience at a glance where things are going, and how they are related to each other. Your main ideas should stand out clearly from your supporting material. The *rhetorical structure* refers to all those other things you do to make your material easy to follow: the introduction and conclusion, transitions from one stage of the talk to another, and the integration of spoken word and visual aids.

An old slogan advises a three-stage procedure: 'Tell them what you are going to tell them; tell them; tell them what you told them.' This makes a lot of sense. Rather than just applying formulas, though, put yourself in the listener's place and think about what is necessary for a talk of the length and complexity of the one you are planning, taking into account the listener's existing knowledge.

A good structure is important both for you and your audience. It is important for you:

1. because it helps you to control time. If the material is organised into subsections, these can each be allotted an appropriate portion of the available time;
2. because it allows you to ensure that the key ideas stand out prominently;
3. because it will give you confidence to elaborate on your points, without having to read from a full text, thus allowing you to maintain eye contact and sound more natural;
4. because it helps to integrate visual aids or other media into the presentation.

> The importance of structure to the audience becomes clear if you consider the advantages of the reader. Unlike your listener, the reader can:
>
> - control the rate at which information is conveyed (speed up or slow down);
> - go back and reread;
> - skip ahead to see where the discussion is leading;
> - look something up in another book;
> - linger over an illustration or other graphic;
> - pause for a rest or some reflection.

The challenge for the oral presenter is to compensate for the absence of the advantages associated with reading—or perhaps to go some way to restoring them. Most people have spent many more hours watching television than reading or listening to live speakers. Television caters to a short attention span, and induces a need for variety. It will help if you (a) prepare the audience for what is to come; (b) remind the audience of what it has heard (restatement, recapitulation); and (c) give the audience a chance to consolidate information, and allow time for the ideas to 'gel'.

Restatement means conveying the same idea again in different words, perhaps in the next sentence. Recapitulation means summarising points, or going over something again quickly, perhaps at the end of one of the main sections of the talk. Repetition and restatement are needed more often in oral than in written communication.

As well as being aware of the differences between listeners and readers, be aware of how your listeners differ from *you*. Unlike them, you have been reading and thinking about the particular topic for perhaps weeks. Moreover, you have an overview of your own talk that they lack—you already know (or should know!) where it is all leading.

### Introduction and conclusion

These should be seen as quite separate from the main body of your talk: they have their own special function. The introduction is probably the most important part of the oral, because first impressions usually determine the audience's response. The introduction informs the audience what the presentation will be about, and what the main argument is. It then locates the specific topic within its wider context. You may need to indicate the rationale for narrowing the focus to what you have formulated as the issue for consideration. You may also want to explain why your topic is important.

The introduction also indicates how the presentation will develop. Foreshadowing your structure helps your listeners orient themselves. Keep it simple, though—the more you say here, the less any of it will be retained. No-one needs a long introduction to a ten-minute talk on a straightforward topic. Displaying an outline (of brief points) is useful: you can keep referring to it as you move through the presentation. In other words, your audience needs to know:

- why it needs to listen;
- what it will be listening to; and
- where the presentation is going.

But something more is needed. In the first place it is best to secure the enthusiastic attention of the audience. Something punchy or arresting, such as a surprising piece of statistical information, will help. Anything that shows you care about your listeners' needs, interests and desires will please them. Speakers often begin with jokes, but this is a risky strategy unless you can tell your material well.

In your conclusion:

- Recapitulate your main points.
- Restate the thesis.
- Reconnect the specific topic to its wider context.

You may indicate what follows from your topic, what further research could be done, and what aspects were not covered in your talk. If possible, return in some way to the needs, desires or interests of the audience.

You will have to do more than merely produce a structured argument, with appropriate connections between sections (such as 'signpost' words), in the way you would for an essay. It is necessary to plan in detail the whole experience as it will unfold for your audience. This includes the precise time at which you distribute handouts or display graphics. Have these things written down. Build in places where your audience (and you!) can relax a bit, or where things can be varied. You might use digressions, visuals, recapitulations and summations, or audience involvement. It is unrealistic to demand non-stop close attention.

## Language

Spoken language is different from written language in the following ways:

- In speech, language is less complex. That is, most of the words used are short, non-technical and familiar. After all, an audience needs to take in what is being said very quickly.
- Sentences in speech are much shorter.
- Speech normally does not attempt to explain as many ideas as is the case with writing, and these ideas are usually communicated in a way that does not suggest their full complexity.
- Speech is usually repetitive. That is, while only a few, straightforward ideas or pieces of information are communicated, these are normally repeated consistently so the audience will remember them and understand their significance.

- Speech normally makes extensive use of examples and anecdotes, which gives an audience something on which to base the ideas or information.

We are not saying you *should* do these things, but that this is what we all do already in ordinary speech situations. Any changes from the norm are a strain for the listener. Academic writing tends to be dense and complex, and is hard to follow when read aloud. If you have to write out a full script, make it simple, straightforward and conversational. Read it aloud to yourself to check how it sounds. Avoid long quotations.

 **A few other potential problems with speech**

1. Do not assume that your audience understands all your theoretical and technical terms. Some words may be quite new to them; in other cases they may know the word but not the specialised sense in which you are using it. There is no need for elaborate dictionary definitions. Simply make clear what you mean by the word in the present context.
2. Make sure you can pronounce key words correctly—otherwise you may lose credibility. Find out the correct pronunciation and do some practising.
3. Be careful with colloquial language. Listeners from another culture (or subculture) may be mystified by colloquial expressions such as 'it's a piece of cake'. (Try explaining why 'a piece of cake' translates to 'easy' to people from a different culture!)

## Visuals

We live in a highly visual age. What people see has more impact on them than what they hear. The resources available to you will usually include a whiteboard, charts, overhead projectors, photocopied handouts, and perhaps videotape, projected computer presentations, 35 mm slides, and models. (Use simple props too. If you are talking about economic inflation, you might pull a balloon out of your pocket and begin blowing it up; or if you're talking about drugs, pull out some chocolate and start devouring it greedily. These images will stay with the audience afterwards.)

Diagrams are useful for representing relationships. Written text can supplement the spoken word. It is worth displaying your main points in written form if you keep them simple and brief. For reasons such as poor hearing, lapses of attention and unfamiliar terms, some people will miss some of what you say. As well as providing clarification, visuals can be a way of adding variety.

Visuals—especially simple, arresting images—are not used enough in oral presentations. On the other hand, summaries on overhead projectors (OHPs) are perhaps overused (it is boring to stare at words on a screen for most of a talk). Visuals can *help* your presentation, but they won't do it for you. Be very clear about the intended purpose before using any visual aid: Is it meant to capture attention? To reinforce meaning? To signpost the talk? To provide light relief?

Then think about the practical considerations: Is it available and affordable? How much time and difficulty will preparing the visual aid involve? Is it easily visible (consider the venue and size of the audience)? Will using it delay or distract you?

There is always the risk of irritating your listeners, perhaps because they cannot see what is displayed or do not have time to take it all in. The more elaborate your aids, the more important it is to check that everything will work. Make sure you practise operating the equipment.

 Some general rules about graphics such as OHP slides are that they should:

- be clear, simple and uncluttered with a minimum of information on any page;
- be consistent with other visual aids and the spoken material (same terms used, points in same order);
- be labelled (there should always be a brief heading or caption on a list of points or diagram);
- never be distracting (display only what you want the audience to see at a particular time).

Because people are so visually oriented, they will begin looking at whatever is offered to them and perhaps stop listening to you. Prepare them for what is to come before hitting them with detailed visual material, and tell them how to use it.

## Performance

The actual delivery should be well prepared, not left to chance: no-one wants to listen to a talk that is incoherent or scrambled, with the speaker forgetting things or saying them at the wrong time. Nor will the audience enjoy listening to a speaker who sounds like a robot programmed to grind out information: the point of having a live talk is to benefit from some human spontaneity and naturalness. Both extremes must be avoided.

## Use of notes

Your oral presentation should not be a sloppy, 'off-the-cuff' talk. Obviously it cannot be committed to memory and recited. Of the two remaining options, (a) a delivery that has been thoroughly planned but involves the use of brief prompts rather than detailed notes, or (b) a talk that is written in full and read, which would you rather listen to?

If you are well acquainted with your material, and have a detailed outline that breaks the talk up into sections and subsections, a 'prompted' talk should work well. The understandable tendency is to have notes that are much too detailed and to lapse into mere reading. Students rely on detailed notes because they are insecure; they may be anxious that nervousness will make them forget what they need to say. The chances are that you won't forget, but the solution is to deal with the anxiety about speaking—for instance, by learning relaxation techniques. Students may also feel insecure about the quality of their material; they therefore feel a need to supply a lot of quotations from authorities on the subject, which have to be read. Again, this kind of anxiety is usually groundless. If you have put a reasonable amount of time into working on the assignment, you will probably know more on the specific topic than anyone in the room.

Your notes can contain some of the key sentences, written in full if you wish. Include *signpost* words ('on the other hand', 'alternatively', 'furthermore'), as well as the key concepts. Abbreviate as much as possible, and indicate the time available for each main section.

## Voice

Your voice serves you pretty well in everyday situations, as it will in your oral presentation. However, in an oral, two things are different: (a) you are speaking for an extended period (in a monologue rather than the dialogue of conversation); and (b) most of your listeners are further away than usual.

Try to observe the following rules:

- Let your lips be visible.
- Use your lips—speak energetically.
- Aim to be heard in the back row (wherever you are looking).
- Vary the pace at which you speak (slow down for something important).
- Speak in an expressive way (sound interested in what you are talking about).
- Pause occasionally, and start again with better projection (if you have become too quiet) or with a lower pitch (pitch tends to creep up as we are talking).

It is not enough simply to bear these six points in mind. You must internalise them by practising them before the oral.

### Non-verbal communication

While you are speaking you are communicating in other ways, through your tone of voice, posture, gesture, movement and facial expression. Ideally your 'body language' will reinforce your meaning, but it can impede you by irritating the audience or sending the wrong signals. Non-verbal behaviour is often unconscious. If you get feedback from someone about the distracting way you fiddled with the pointer, you can avoid doing it in your next presentation.

Non-verbal mannerisms become obvious in public speaking. When people speak in pairs or small groups, they continually adjust their non-verbal behaviour in ways that are appropriate to the occasion, for instance by nodding or assuming interested facial expressions. This is not the case when one person becomes 'the speaker' and the rest become 'the audience'. For audience members, the speaker becomes an object of scrutiny, not someone with whom they feel personally involved. The larger the audience, the less any individual feels the need to provide the speaker with the reassuring feedback common in one-to-one conversation. The result is that the speaker begins to feel self-conscious.

Most distracting non-verbal behaviour has its origins in nervousness and tension. If you are reasonably confident and relaxed you will have no problems. Just because you *feel* self-conscious does not mean you have to find 'something to do with your hands'. Almost certainly you look perfectly normal. But if you keep your hands in your pockets throughout, or wave a pointer around, it will become noticeable. (In an episode of the 1950s United States sitcom 'The Phil Silvers Show', a group of soldiers were supposed to listen to an expert talk about something they were interested in—how to make money. The audience should have been attentive, but the speaker kept going 'ahem' every few seconds. The audience didn't listen to what he was saying, and ended up taking bets on how many times he would say 'ahem'.)

Eye contact is perhaps the most important aspect of non-verbal behaviour. You should regularly look at all sections of the audience. Look at someone for a few seconds (but don't begin thinking about that person as an individual), then move on to another person.

---

### Anxiety

The nervous anticipation that goes with any kind of performance is normal, and should decrease once you begin speaking. Some people who are very nervous about speaking in public can benefit from expert advice: relaxation procedures are available. Your anxiety will be much less noticeable than you think—audiences always underestimate the nervousness of speakers. The following are two tactics that should help:

1. Devise a way of beginning so that the transition to being the speaker 'in the spotlight' is drawn out rather than abrupt. If possible, sit near the front during the earlier part of the session. Chat with nearby members of the audience while setting things up.
2. Ensure that within the first few minutes you provide something (perhaps involving a visual aid) that you know the audience will enjoy or find useful. Setting up some audience participation early on allows you to begin with more natural interaction rather than one-way delivery. For example, ask a question and get the audience to respond. Any pauses provided by the use of aids or audience participation will allow you to relax and deal with nervous tendencies, such as overrapid speech.

---

## Audience involvement

Of all the resources available to speakers to make their presentations more interesting and effective, the resource of the audience itself is the most neglected. Getting the audience to think and talk can meet many of the objectives discussed in this chapter, such as establishing a relaxed mood, arousing interest, making concepts meaningful and providing variety. A simple example would be to begin by asking for opinions: people are far more likely to remember a session in which they said or did something themselves than one where they sat passively listening. As always, prior thought is essential. Avoid making requests unless you can predict how people will respond. You would not ask for opinions in cases where most people did not know enough to have an opinion, or where they might be embarrassed.

Audience involvement could include people jotting down their own thoughts in response to a question and perhaps briefly comparing notes with their neighbour; filling in answers on worksheets; having discussion in small groups or the full group; and doing brief role-plays. You must be clear about your purpose.

---

 Whatever you ask people to do, it must be:

- non-threatening and easy to accomplish;
- enjoyable and (ultimately) perceived as relevant;
- easy to explain;
- feasible in terms of available time, audience size and venue.

And you must remain in control—it's your presentation.

---

Decide beforehand whether you want audience questions. If you do, encourage the listeners by directing them to specific issues. Don't just finish with 'Any questions?'. Ask whether someone has a question on a specific aspect of your talk. Or pave the way for questions during the talk: 'I'll move through this secton quite quickly, but will be happy to answer questions on it later.' Respond to questions politely and honestly. If you cannot supply an answer, admit it.

### Feedback

You have resumed your seat after your presentation. It's over. Well, not quite. We would encourage you to regard some process of *evaluation* as an inseparable part of every oral. Think about what you did well, and not so well—and why. Get informal comments on specific aspects from fellow students. Make use of formal feedback provided by the tutor.

## CONCLUSION

We have suggested that students often approach oral presentations in one of two ways—they rely on having detailed facts and figures, or they try to 'wing it', getting by on personality and confidence. Both approaches are flawed. The secret is to do the research that will enable you to speak on a topic, but not to see this as an end in itself. The next challenge is to think of what you want your audience to know and feel. Put yourself in their place; think about what they already know, don't know, need to know, want to know. Be realistic about how much your listeners can absorb; be imaginative about how to plant your ideas in their minds.

Success in academic oral presentations is not a special gift that only some people have. Certainly some people get along well with an audience naturally, but most achieve this with experience. The main thing is preparation—planning every aspect of the activity. *What you have done before you stand up to speak will determine what happens next.*

## Activities

1. Rewrite several paragraphs from sample texts in the Appendixes as an oral presentation, to sound more like speech (e.g. shorter, simpler sentences). Add any sentences you think would be useful (a) to introduce the material, and (b) for the purposes of restatement and recapitulation.

2. Find something easy to read, such as a magazine article or children's story. Alone, or with a friend acting as audience, read it aloud, putting into practice each of the six points in the section on voice. Do it the wrong way and then the right way (e.g. first read in a robotic monotone, as if indifferent to both the subject matter and audience, then read it again with lots of expression). Analyse the passage to work out the appropriate places to pause.

3. Imagine you have to give an oral that will include the material in any one of the paragraphs in the Appendixes.
   (a) Construct brief, prompt-type notes for this section of the talk. Confine yourself to half a page that you can take in at a glance.
   (b) Suggest visuals for use in this section of the talk.

# part V

# BEYOND UNIVERSITY

# chapter 16

# Taking it with you

We saw in chapter 2 that different cultural fields (education, business, the bureaucracy, the military) have their own different practices and discourses. These discourses (ways of using language) carry with them certain attitudes and values. Each of them also has its own genres (in education the lecture, the textbook, the essay; in business the contract, the advertisement, the sales presentation). One consequence is that there is no single, neutral, all-purpose way of communicating effectively. What counts as good communication very much depends on the context, and on specific cultural factors. Another consequence is the tendency of the values and attitudes of the various cultural fields and institutions to influence the communication that goes on within them. Whatever its content, any piece of academic work will reflect the academic field and its values. These include, among other things, being interested in the origins of things, being detached and sceptical, committed to reason, always ready to accept new evidence. Business discourse will focus on immediate economic goals, and value efficiency and practicality. Government discourse will tend to be impersonal, authoritative, concerned with regulations and precedents.

There is sufficient overlap and similarity between the different discourses and genres to enable basic communication skills to be effective across these fields. Writing essays and giving oral presentations at university develops general communication skills, which can be adapted to other purposes and genres. It would be impossible for universities to teach students how to write in all the genres they might come across in their future careers. It would also be unnecessary, as such competency can usually be acquired 'on the job'. An important element in communicating effectively is taking account of things like purpose, occasion and audience. In this text we have tried to encourage you to think about what will be appropriate in the circumstances, and why, rather than merely giving you formulas to follow.

We have to operate within and across these different cultural fields. The picture is complicated by other kinds of cultural difference we come across, such as those deriving from nationality, ethnicity, gender and age. Crossing the boundary between school and university, and later between university and a career, are two important moves in your life. You need to be aware of the kinds of things that will change as you move from one environment to another.

On the other hand, our lives are 'compartmentalised'. We spend much of our time operating in one area, caught up in its discourses and practices and habits of thought. This is natural and inevitable, up to a point. But we tend to isolate different areas of experience from each other more than is necessary. Some students, for instance, do not make connections between the different subjects they study. They also put off thinking about their future employment until after they graduate. And when they find themselves working for an organisation they adapt to its customs and norms, forgetting about the perspectives on the world that were part of their university experience (that was 'uni'—that's all in the past). But perhaps they were hired because the organisation *wanted* someone who could bring some new thinking into the place and not merely go along with things.

In explaining the nature of academic discourse in chapter 2, we reviewed the history of universities and emphasised their relative isolation from worldly affairs. Some university practices derive from long traditions. To look at the other side of the coin—the extensive changes occurring in the university sector—universities now offer a much wider range of vocational courses, such as nursing, accounting, tourism, journalism and social work. And importantly, a much higher proportion of the population (at least in developed countries) attends university. The degree of government financial support, however, is beginning to decline. It is difficult to predict the future affordability of higher education. Some foresee a move towards mass tertiary education in Australia, such that it will come to be taken for granted that almost everyone does some kind of study after leaving high school. This requires society accepting that mass tertiary education is an important social good, worth paying for in the way we are prepared to pay for things like health care. It is by no means clear whether this will happen.

Universities are moving to develop 'flexible delivery' (using summer terms; electronic communication to reach off-campus students; 'resource-based' learning, where students work at their own pace). Closer links will be developed between universities and the workplace, with employees taking courses that have been specially tailored to the needs of their organisation or industry.

There is more competition between universities. Some believe that the use of electronic communication will dramatically increase the number of institutions and courses from which students can choose. Connections and flows between different forms and levels of education are likely to increase significantly. University students will more easily get credit towards their university degrees for courses they have completed elsewhere (at TAFE, for instance). There will be opportunities for capable senior secondary students to do a couple of university subjects while still at school. It will become routine for university study to be followed by courses of the kind taught in TAFE colleges (for instance, a BA graduate will go on to do a computing or book-keeping certificate course).

What are the consequences of these trends and possibilities? One is a change in the kind of cultural capital associated with a university degree. When 40% of the population has a bachelor's degree, such a qualification no longer imparts the prestige it did when only 5% graduated. On the other hand, *not* having a degree becomes a significant handicap (without it you may not be eligible to enrol in a postgraduate diploma course you need or to get to the interview stage when applying for a job). The trends suggest that young people will have to put together a sequence of courses, rather than thinking in terms of a single qualification that becomes a 'meal ticket' for the rest of their lives.

A term often used now is 'lifelong education'. This means that people will continue to study at different times through their careers. They might do second degrees, higher degrees, postgraduate diploma courses, TAFE-type courses or internal training programs run by employers. They will do this to keep up with developments in their chosen field, or to upgrade their qualifications so they can apply for new jobs.

Rather than being confined to quite separate stages of life, education and employment now tend to go on simultaneously. A large number of full-time Australian university students have part-time jobs. Meanwhile many people in their 20s, 30s and 40s who have full-time jobs are pursuing a first degree or a further qualification part-time, often through distance education.

The 'university experience' of today is not quite what it was in earlier times. The world of business is changing too. Companies are less stable, continuing processes of change are almost taken for granted, staff often have a more diverse range of responsibilities and are expected to be flexible. Service industries, including those which are in the business of manipulating or communicating *information* in some way, have become more important than the manufacturing sector in many developed countries. It is difficult to predict what kinds of new technology will arrive on the scene, let alone what sort of effect they will have.

For many people employment will not be secure, and further study of some kind at some point in their lives will be a necessity. If lifelong learning is becoming the norm, then 'learning how to learn' becomes an important part of your first degree. Learning how to learn can involve all kinds of things: becoming more computer-literate, getting used to extracting the main ideas from densely written texts, acquiring a feel for the kinds of resources that can be accessed in libraries, developing listening skills. Above all, it means learning to be aware of your learning behaviour, getting used to analysing what is involved in a particular learning situation, and evolving strategies that work for you.

Clearly the changing world of employment needs people who are flexible in their thinking. As we have pointed out, what you gain from university study is not so much a collection of facts as it is techniques and approaches. You do learn facts about, say, tourism, accounting, tax law or organisational behaviour. But in doing so you also become familiar with the way thinkers and researchers acquire new knowledge. This is characterised by:

- a willingness and ability to survey what is already known and thought about an area;
- an ability critically to evaluate present knowledge;
- a willingness to doubt all views, even your own, until they have been proven conclusively;
- a reliance on good evidence (rather than, say, gossip, rumour or shonky statistics);
- reasoned argument;
- the use of relevant information or procedures from other disciplines;
- a willingness to exchange knowledge with others;
- using and testing theories;
- a willingness to reject 'commonsense' understanding if there are better explanations.

At university you are learning to acquire knowledge in this sort of way, mostly indirectly. Lectures and textbooks merely discuss some subject—aspects of the law, tourism, management. They do not comment on the intellectual principles and practices that underlie and make possible their subject matter as we do in this book. They take them for granted. Yet it is these underlying ways of generating and organising knowledge that really count in terms of education. It doesn't matter that much of the information will eventually be out of date. It doesn't matter that you may study tourism but end up working in some other field. In your university education you have been exposed again and again to models of good thinking, and you have had opportunities to do some of it yourself.

There are other kinds of knowledge—other ways of approaching problems—such as 'We've always done it this way', 'I just had a hunch. It felt right so I went ahead and did it', or 'It worked for me last time'. You don't need university education for this. And other kinds of knowledge have their value (the 'hunch' might have been a good one which earned someone $10 million, and will continue to be used), though reliance on intuition and rough-and-ready practicality is tending to make way for more organised knowledge as more expertise becomes available for solving problems.

It is not the specific facts you learn that matter so much as being able to think critically, analyse and solve problems, put an argument together, and reason. Employers value these skills: they need employees who are intellectually alert and flexible enough to take into account all the factors that might be relevant, who can 'rethink' the old customs.

There are occasional complaints from employer organisations that graduates could be better prepared for the workplace than they are (though generally they seem reasonably satisfied with the quality of graduates). Academics in many disciplines (engineering, information technology, welfare, journalism, public relations, social work) are trying to develop ways of integrating actual work experience with formal courses. Students do projects relating to what goes on in a business firm or other organisation, and get credits for them. Some courses involve alternating periods of study with blocs of time spent working in the relevant industry.

New employees usually get some training in the particular procedures of organisations they join. This kind of knowledge is best acquired in the workplace. In some fields, cadetships or internships provide a way for graduates to pick up the additional literacies they need. Certainly universities cannot provide education to cater for every job category. Nor would it make sense for universities to train university students in, say, all of the written genres encountered in the world of business (the business letter, the minutes of a meeting, and so on). Although they might then be better prepared to swing into action on their first day at work, students would not have done enough 'higher-order' learning. Learning to think, analyse, reason and research are going to be more valuable in the long term. Essays are a better genre for dealing with ideas, and that is what students have to become good at. After the difficult work done at university, the kinds of reading and writing you will have to do in the workforce, especially at first, will not be too demanding, even if there are some superficial differences to get used to.

Two final points about making the move from university to the workforce:

- Start researching employment opportunities well before you graduate. Use the library—put to work the research skills you are acquiring.
- Market yourself to employers. Learn to compile a curriculum vitae (résumé, or CV). It's probably not too early to begin noting down things that might be worth including (part-time jobs, involvement in student affairs, cultural activities). You might mention in your CV some of the literacies or generic skills that you feel are your particular strengths.

## CONCLUSION

University offers a lot—friendships, a great social life and the opportunity to prepare for a rewarding career. But even more than this, it offers you the chance to shape yourself as a person. It is fairly common for students to change their goals, attitudes and values to some extent during their university years. This is to be expected. You find out more about the world and more about yourself. New opportunities become evident and priorities change. What lies on the other side of university often turns out to be different from what you expected.

University study is a very real challenge—there are pressures, distractions, confusion and stress. Yet the challenge of a university course helps you prepare for the demands of your later career. It also allows you to prove that you have what it takes. We hope that this book has convinced you that education is not something to be passively endured, but a process in which you must be actively and thoughtfully engaged.

# Appendixes


## APPENDIX I   SAMPLE TEXT (American)

This appendix relates to pp. 98–9 and p. 166 of the text. It is extracted from Ian Robertson, 1989, *Society: A Brief Introduction*, Worth, New York, pp. 339–41.

### Interest groups

1. An important effect of the distinctive American party system is that it encourages people to try to influence the way individual legislators vote on specific issues. In other democracies, there is little doubt about the outcome of a vote in the legislature, because most legislators 'toe the party line' and are not subject to much external influence. Thus, if the Australian Labor Party has, say, a 20-seat majority in Parliament, it can rely on a 20-vote majority—minus any legislators who are unable to attend—on virtually any vote. In contrast, the loose nature of the American parties and their lack of internal discipline means that it is most unusual for all Republican or all Democratic legislators to vote the same way. Instead, a new and different coalition of congressional votes has to be assembled on every issue. This feature gives outsiders a genuine opportunity to affect the law-making process—and many of them seize that chance through an interest group. An **interest group** is a group or organisation that attempts to influence political decisions that might have an impact on its members or their goals. These groups may be large or small, temporary or permanent, secretive or open, but they all try to gain access to, and sway, those who have power.

2. Interest groups may use a variety of tactics. They may collect petitions, take court action, advertise in the media, organize floods of letters to legislators on particular issues, pledge their members' votes to certain candidates, donate money to election campaigns, or even resort to outright bribery. Frequently, they use **lobbying**, the tactic of directly persuading decision makers. Many large interest groups—including over 500 corporations—maintain highly paid, full-time professional staffs of lobbyists who meet regularly with legislators and government officials. Other groups hire the services of free-lance lobbying firms, which are often staffed by former members of Congress and government officials. The professional lobbyists usually charge handsomely for their services: it is not uncommon for an interest group to pay $7,000 for getting a Bill introduced, $10,000 for getting it through a committee, and $25,000 for its passage on the House or Senate floor. The total number of professional lobbyists is believed to be around 20,000, or more than 30 for each member of Congress.

   Evan Thomas, 1986, 'Peddling Influence', *Time*, 3 March, pp. 26–36.

3. Many interest groups make generous donations to help politicians get elected. It can be very costly to run for election to Congress: in recent elections, the winner of a House seat spent an average of over $325,000. Senate campaigns are even more costly: the average winner spends nearly $3 million . . . Who pays for all this? A large part of the money—about a third of the cost of House campaigns and about a fifth of those for the Senate—comes from political action committees (PACs), which are organizations established by interest groups for the purpose of raising and distributing campaign funds. We may well suspect that these interest groups expect and obtain some payoff in return for their generosity; one does not shower lawmakers with money, year after year, for no reason.

4. Some PACs act on behalf of broad constituencies, such as conservatives or environmentalists, but most represent very narrow interests, and some of them are established for the purpose of promoting or opposing a single piece of legislation. The number of these organizations is increasing rapidly, which suggests that interest groups consider them useful and effective. In 1974 there were about 600 PACs in operation, and they contributed about $12 million to candidates; by 1988 there were more than 4,000 PACs, and their

contributions had swelled to over $100 million. About two-thirds of the contributions go to incumbents; about one-sixth goes to challengers of incumbents; and about one-sixth goes to candidates in 'open' contests in which no incumbent is running. Incumbents are usually reelected; on average, about 90 percent of House members and a slightly lesser proportion of senators are returned to office.

Elizabeth Drew, 1983, *Politics and Money: The New Road to Corruption*, Macmillan, New York.

Larry J. Sabato, 1984, *PAC Power: Inside the World of Political Action Committees*, Norton, New York.

5. Political sociologists are divided over whether the activities of interest groups are beneficial or harmful to democracy. On the one hand, these groups, frequently operating in secrecy, are often able to win favours that might not be in the public interest. The ordinary voter's influence is thus reduced. Also, how can someone who is not rich and who refuses to accept PAC money run for Congress on an equal basis against those who accept such donations? On the other hand, the existence of a number of interest groups, many of them with conflicting goals, may prevent the development of a monopoly of power and influence. Furthermore, the interest group provides an effective means for otherwise powerless citizens to gain political influence. A mass of unorganized citizens concerned about shoreline pollution or child abuse, for example, has little means of exerting influence. If they form an interest group, they have potentially far greater access to the decision-making process.

6. American political culture thus encourages an informal, behind-the-scenes interaction among parties, elected officials, and private interest groups. An understanding of this process gives a much fuller picture of the political order than an analysis of formal processes alone. But where does power really lie? Who makes the decisions?

## APPENDIX 2   SAMPLE TEXT (American)

This appendix relates to p. 166 of the text. It is extracted from Dennis S. Ippolito, Thomas G. Walker & Kenneth L. Kolson, 1976, *Public Opinion and Responsible Democracy*, Prentice-Hall, Englewood Cliffs, p. 8.

## Interest groups

1. Interest groups bring together individuals with common policy interests and concerns. While there are extreme variations in the size, activities, and effectiveness of interest groups, the assumption is that the leaders of interest groups will convey the views and interests of their members to governmental officials. This can be done directly, by lobbying in Congress or exerting pressure on the executive branch for example, or indirectly through involvement with political parties. From this perspective, the public depends on its group ties.

2. The membership of interest groups (the organized segment of the public) controls its own leadership by the rewards and sanctions it can employ within the group. Continued membership, selection of group leaders, and willingness to act in support of group positions (by, for example, voting or petitioning) represent means by which the membership can insure that the group's leadership accurately represents its preferences.

3. Externally, the group's influence is based upon the rewards and sanctions it, and its members, can employ against the parties, candidates, or officeholders. For large groups, this might include votes and various forms of campaign assistance; for smaller groups, campaign funds or publicity.

4. There is no question that interest groups are a major element in the political process and that some interest groups have established effective connections with political parties and with government. The legitimacy of this activity is based upon First Amendment guarantees of free speech and the people's right 'to petition the Government for a redress of grievances.' But despite the extensive and legitimate involvement of interest groups in politics, this model has serious limitations. First, many important interests and many segments of the public are not organized. The interest group model can obviously work only for organized segments of society. Second, it appears that certain members of groups do not accurately represent the views or opinions of their members. Indeed, some groups are characterized by clear differences between leaders and the membership in terms of opinions about issues and political tactics and strategy. And third, it is important to recognize that group leaders may have the same difficulty in assessing and evaluating member preferences as governmental representatives have in dealing with the mass public.

# APPENDIX 3   SAMPLE TEXT (Australian)

This appendix relates to p. 167 of the text. It is extracted from Ian Ward, 1991, 'Federal Government', in *Institutions in Australian Society*, John Henningham (ed.), Dept of Journalism, University of Queensland, Brisbane, pp. 16–17.

## Pressure groups

1. The federal system is similarly reflected in the organisation of a great many pressure groups. Pressure groups, or organisations which seek to influence policy decision without attempting to capture government as parties do, are a ubiquitous feature of Australian politics. There are literally thousands ranging from large, established national lobbies—for example the National Farmers' Federation, the Australian Council of Social Services and the Australian Council of Trade Unions—to relatively small, loosely organised and often transient neighbourhood action groups. The imprint of federalism is most evident upon larger, established pressure groups. For example, most individual trade unions are federations of state-based organisations. Collectively unions form trades and labour councils at state level, and come together at the national level to form the ACTU peak association. Farmers' groups are similarly divided, forming separate state-based organisations which are united at the national level by the NFF. This federal organisational arrangement which is typical of many pressure groups is to be expected of associations which may have to defend their interests by dealing with state governments in some instances, and the Commonwealth in others.

2. There are many different kinds of pressure groups. Sectional groups such as the Australian Medical Association mostly defend the narrow interests of their members, while promotional groups such as Greenpeace or the Women's Electoral Lobby have broader objectives. Some are wholly political organisations, whereas others (for example the Royal Automobile Club of Queensland and its sister state automobile associations) are not. Some but not others are insider groups welcomed by and having regular contact with policy makers. Some (usually promotional) groups will be transient and disappear when their cause is won or lost, while other (usually sectional) groups are quite permanent organisations. And of course pressure groups vary widely in the financial, membership, media interest and other

resources which they can muster. Some wield considerable power. This is especially true of producer groups comprising professional associations and established business, union and primary industry groups whose strategic economic importance has enabled them to forge close links with government.

3. The influence which pressure groups—especially producer groups such as the Business Council of Australia, Australian Medical Association, Australian Mining Council or ACTU—can have over governments and particular areas of policy-making arguably weakens the chain of accountability. Mostly pressure groups pursue minority, sectional interests. Few are publicly accountable, and their influence over areas of public policy may not always be visible. Thus they can be seen as exerting undesirable pressure and distorting the processes of representative government. However pressure groups can also be seen to assist good government. Some may voice alternatives and scrutinise a government's actions, or educate and mobilise popular opinion and involvement in policy-making. Competition between groups to influence public policy can also encourage the representation and reconciliation of diverse interests. Further, pressure groups can be a source of valuable specialist knowledge about the policy areas and questions with which they are concerned, and this explains why groups will cluster around and, in some instances, forge ongoing links with particular public service departments.

## APPENDIX 4  SAMPLE TEXT (Australian)

This appendix relates to p. 167 of the text. It is extracted from Malcolm Waters & Rodney Crook, 1993, *Sociology One: Principles of Sociological Analysis for Australians*, 3rd edn, Longman Cheshire, Melbourne, p. 212.

Weber called the social groups that were differentiated on the basis of power, parties. In modern contexts the term *party* has come to mean a formally organized group of political activists which has the intention of maintaining or gaining control of the executive branch of government by either violent or nonviolent means. Society is not differentiated into parties within this meaning of the word. Most Australians are not members of a political party and for many of those that are, party membership is not an important influence on their social lives. Weber's use of the term 'party' is much closer to the modern usage of the term 'interest group'. An *interest group* is a group of people who have particular needs or desires which they wish to see realized through political processes. Examples of interest groups would include the Returned Servicemen's League, sections of which seek increases in defence spending and controls on immigration; the Wilderness Society; the Australian Institute of Mining and Metallurgy; the League of Women Voters; and the National Civic Council which urges resistance to Communism. Interest groups have a variety of ways of influencing political processes—including demonstrating, lobbying (i.e. earbashing politicians), advertising, organizing voters, and occasionally resorting to terrorism and assassination. None of the organizations mentioned uses this last tactic. On some occasions, an interest group can become so successful at attracting members and gathering support that it takes on the characteristics of a *social movement*, a mass organization which seeks to influence the political process by sheer weight of numbers. The Wilderness Society and various abortion law reform movements are examples of social movements.

## APPENDIX 5 CONCEPT MAP

This concept map was done from memory some time after reading the four sample texts on interest groups (Appendixes 1–4). Note that question marks indicate points that could not be remembered. Concept maps are a good way of differentiating between what you know and what needs further research or revision. The links between the facts and concepts are labelled ('operate by', 'examples' etc.)—this helps to establish *relationships*.

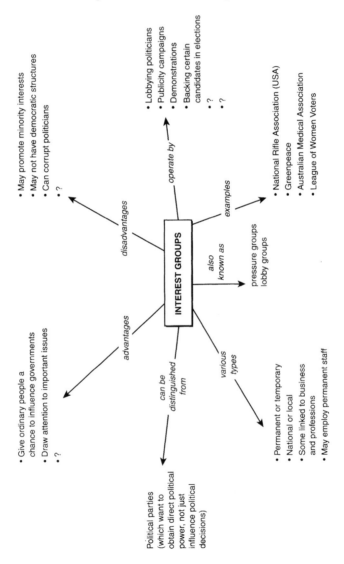

# APPENDIX 6   CONCEPT MAP

This concept map was drawn up, without consulting any sources, by a person with no special knowledge of tourism. Concept maps are *thinking tools*, ways to explore the different aspects of a topic. It doesn't matter that they are incomplete or a bit messy.

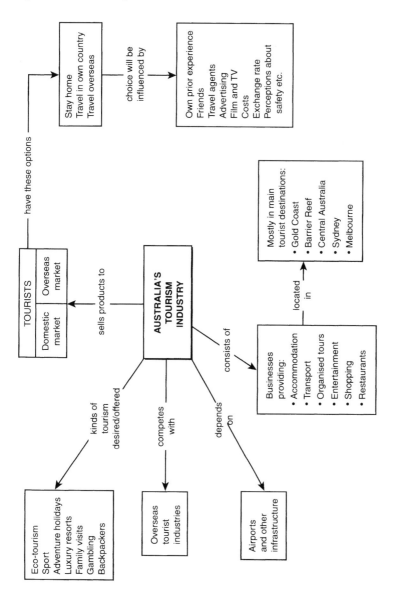

# Endnotes

## CHAPTER 4

1. Anne Thomson, 1996, *Critical Reasoning: A Practical Introduction*, Routledge, London, p. 12.

## CHAPTER 6

1. Richard L. Gregory (ed.), 1987, *The Oxford Companion to the Mind*, Oxford University Press, Oxford.
2. Barbara Tuchman, 1979, *A Distant Mirror: The Calamitous 14th Century*, Penguin, Harmondsworth, UK.
3. Elizabeth Marshall Thomas, 1997, review of *The Nature of Horses*, by S. Budiansky, in *The Australian Review of Books*, November.
4. Jerome Carcopino, 1956, *Daily Life in Ancient Rome*, Penguin, Harmondsworth, UK, p. 44.
5. J. Carcopino, *op. cit.*, p. 203.

## CHAPTER 7

1. Adapted from Irwin L. Joffe, 1984, *Opportunity for Skillful Reading*, 4th edn, Wadsworth, Belmont, CA, pp. 92–94.

## CHAPTER 8

1. Suggested by a list in Ricki Jeffery, 1996, *Team Building*, Workbook for CQU Action Workshop, June 1996, Centre for Continuing & Professional Education,

Central Queensland University, Rockhampton. This list was adapted from Robert B. Maddux, 1988, *Team Building: An Exercise in Leadership*, Crisp Publications, Los Altos, CA, p. 5.

2. See Larry L. Barker et al., 1991, *Groups in Process: An Introduction to Small Group Communication*, 4th edn, Prentice Hall, Englewood Cliffs, NJ, pp. 46–47 and Steven A. Beebe & John T. Masterson, 1986, *Communicating in Small Groups: Principles and Practices*, 2nd edn, Scott, Foresman, Glenview, Ill. & London, pp. 58–59.

3. See Beebe & Masterson, pp. 146–48 and Barker et al., op. cit., pp. 184–86.

## CHAPTER 14

1. This simplified terminology is used by R.F. Bailey in his 1984 book, *A Survival Kit for Writing English*, Longman Cheshire, Melbourne. Note that a support unit as defined by Bailey can be a single word: in '**Susan**, unfortunately, **laughed at Jack**', 'unfortunately', although it is an adverb like 'mockingly', relates to the whole control unit rather than only to one particular word in it.

# Recommended books

## CRITICAL THINKING AND ARGUMENT

Allen, Matthew 1997, *Smart Thinking: Skills for Critical Understanding and Writing*, Oxford University Press, Melbourne.

Barry, Vincent E. 1994, *Invitation to Critical Thinking*, 3rd edn, Harcourt Brace, Sydney.

Diestler, Sherry 1994, *Becoming a Critical Thinker: A User Friendly Manual*, Macmillan, New York.

Mayfield, Marlys 1994, *Thinking for Yourself: Developing Critical Thinking Skills through Reading and Writing*, 3rd edn, Wadsworth, Belmont, CA.

Thomson, Anne 1996, *Critical Reasoning: A Practical Introduction*, Routledge, London.

## READING

De Leeuw, Manya & Eric 1990, *Read Better, Read Faster: A New Approach to Efficient Reading*, Penguin, Melbourne.

## GROUP COLLABORATION

Schultz, Beatrice G. 1995, *Communicating in the Small Group: Theory and Practice*, HarperCollins, Sydney.

## GENERAL STUDY SKILLS

Burdess, Neil 1998, *Handbook of Student Skills*, 2nd edn, Prentice-Hall, Sydney.

Marshall, Lorraine A. & Rowland, Frances 1993, *A Guide to Learning Independently*, 2nd edn, Open University Press, UK.

Orr, Fred 1997, *How to Pass Exams*, 2nd edn, Allen & Unwin, Sydney.

# WRITING SKILLS

Bailey, R.F. 1987, *A Survival Kit for Writing English*, 2nd edn, Addison Wesley Longman, Melbourne.

Clanchy, John 1998, *How to Write Essays: A Practical Guide for Students*, 3rd edn, Addison Wesley Longman, UK.

Kane, Thomas S. 1984, *The Oxford Guide to Writing: A Rhetoric and Handbook for College Students,* Oxford University Press, Oxford.

Taylor, Gordon 1989, *The Student's Writing Guide for the Arts and Social Sciences,* Cambridge University Press, Cambridge.

# ORAL PRESENTATIONS

Macnamara, Jim & Venton, Brenda 1990, *How to Give Winning Presentations*, Archipelago Press, Sydney.

Mandel, Steve 1987, *Effective Presentation Skills*, Crisp, Los Altos.

Verderber, Rudolph 1991, *The Challenge of Effective Speaking*, 8th edn, Wadsworth, Belmont, CA.

# Index